EASIER FATHERLAND

STEVE CRAWSHAW

EASIER
FATHERLAND

GERMANY AND THE
TWENTY-FIRST CENTURY

continuum
LONDON • NEW YORK

Continuum
The Tower Building, 11 York Road, London SE1 7NX
15 East 26th Street, New York, NY 10010

www.continuumbooks.com

First published 2004

British Library Cataloguing-in-Publication Data
A catalogue record for this book is available from the British Library.

ISBN 0-8264-6320-7

Typeset by Kenneth Burnley in Wirral, Cheshire
Printed and bound in Great Britain by Cromwell Press Ltd, Trowbridge, Wilts

For Ewa and Ania

'Es gibt schwierige Vaterländer. Eins davon ist Deutschland.'
'There are difficult fatherlands. One of them is Germany.'

Gustav Heinemann,
President of the Federal Republic of Germany, 1969–74

CONTENTS

PREFACE

Germany in the twenty-first century is a country in flux – more now than at any time since 1945. Partly, that is the result of German unification in 1990. The fall of the Wall in 1989, German unity, and the end of Communism and the Cold War unleashed political earthquakes in Germany and across the continent. These upheavals paved the way for the more self-confident Germany that we see today – an important reason why many foreign politicians (and some Germans, too) were so frightened of the new Germany after the Wall came down. Unification removed the limits which the Allies had imposed on Germany and which Germany had imposed on itself after 1945.

Unity is, however, only one reason for the transformation of Germany that we see today. The generational change is crucial, too. Unification permitted the acceleration of a process already under way. *Easier Fatherland* tells the story of how German society has moved in the past 60 years, including dramatic changes in perceptions and memory – and how the country has gradually begun to become more comfortable with itself. The changes in attitude are greater than many non-Germans seem to believe, and perhaps greater than the Germans themselves acknowledge. We come to think of the beliefs of a democracy as more or less fixed; in reality, attitudes can change radically, and in a relatively short period of time.

The starting point for writing this book was a lecture that I was invited to give at the Goethe-Institut in London, on the occasion of the 50th anniversary of the Federal Republic in 1999. The lecture was part of a series under the umbrella title 'Germany, My Germany'. Each speaker in the series was, as the title implies, encouraged to give a personal view.

In focusing on that theme, it became clear to me just how different were the various Germanies which I wanted to describe. I have known and lived in different Germanies since 1968. My perception of the country is a composite of contrasting impressions at different times. Germany has changed radically – even while seeming not to do so. Those continuing changes formed part of the theme of *Germany Inside Out*, a series of five television programmes which I co-presented in 2001, and which provided the immediate spur towards writing this book.

Easier Fatherland is about the repression and unwrapping of memory, about denial and responsibility, and about a society in sickness and in health. This can be seen as a story of three generations. In the 1950s and 1960s, the Federal Republic of Germany was a country in almost complete denial – as an examination of the recommended schoolbooks from that time makes depressingly clear. Many who had lived in the Third Reich were eager not to confront the enormity of the crimes. That repression of truth led directly to the rebellion, a quarter-century after the war, of the 1968 generation – a rebellion more radical in West Germany than anywhere else in Europe or the United States. This radicalism, in turn, spilled into the murderous terrorism of the 1970s, culminating in an orgy of violence in autumn 1977 – all allegedly in search of a 'better' Germany. That, in turn, paved the way for an increasing revulsion against violence – and a new form of radicalism whose commitment to non-violence was a core element from the start. The Greens' impact on German society – before and after they became part of the German ruling coalition in 1998 – goes well beyond the party's limited electoral support.

The fall of the Wall in 1989, and German unification the following year, opened the way for a whole new set of problems, economic and social. The sense of wonder quickly gave way to bitter and endless recriminations. The two Germanies quickly fell out of love with each other once they were living together in a single home. It has taken 15 years, till the beginning of the twenty-first century, for that 'wall in the heads' to begin to be demolished.

Meanwhile, Germany's twentieth-century history begins to be seen in the round for the first time. In the 1950s and 1960s, children were taught about how much Germans had suffered; they were taught little about German crimes. In more recent decades, that pattern was reversed: the emphasis was on German crimes, while the terrible German suffering in and after 1945, when millions of civilians were killed, was passed over in near-silence in Germany, let alone abroad. Until a few years ago, the rebellious generation of 1968, by now the new establishment, were so focused on the crimes of their parents' generation that they were reluctant to permit any attention to be devoted to German suffering. They believed that they had heard too much of that from their parents.

Now, at the beginning of the twenty-first century, many who were once eager to focus only on German crimes have acknowledged that shutting one's eyes to the nightmares suffered by ordinary Germans – 15 million driven out of their homes, of whom 2 million died; rape on a mass scale; half a million civilians killed in Allied bombing raids – is equally one-sided. German crimes led directly to the German suffering. But that, it is now widely agreed, is no reason for German suffering to be passed over in silence.

A similar opening-up can be seen on a whole range of taboo topics – including the sending abroad of German troops, which seemed unthinkable less than a decade ago. A Green foreign minister, representing an almost pacifist party, argues successfully for German troops to be sent to Kosovo and even Afghanistan. When Germany drew the line offering support for the war in Iraq in 2003, that was not because it was deemed inappropriate for German soldiers to be sent to Baghdad – but, in another unprecedented departure, it was a public German defiance of the wishes of Washington.

This book draws on the Germanies that I have known at various times in my life: in north-west Germany as a schoolchild in 1968; in Berlin as a student in the early 1970s; visiting friends, while living in neighbouring Poland, in the late 1970s and early 1980s; and as a foreign correspondent in East Germany at the end of that decade, including the privilege of witnessing the extraordinary revolutions across the region, and the magical moment of history when the people of Leipzig forced the all-powerful regime to retreat, on 9 October 1989. Between 1992 and 1995, I was Germany correspondent for *The Independent*. In 2001, I was reporter and co-presenter on the *Germany Inside Out* programmes for the BBC. Finally, I returned to Germany in 2003 and 2004 while writing this book.

One thing that these Germanies have in common is that each grapples, in its own way, with identity and with the demons of the past. A book like Daniel Goldhagen's *Hitler's Willing Executioners* – which argues that Germans were eager to organize a Holocaust even before Hitler arrived on the scene – shoots to the top of the German bestseller lists and stays there for months, even though most serious historians believe its arguments to be flawed. And, at the same time, fears of the neo-Nazis remain strong. Meanwhile, the idea of a multicultural Germany (*multikulti* is a new German buzzword) remains just around the corner, with the introduction of new citizenship laws. Closer than it was a few years ago, but still elusive. Even as politicians scrabble frantically to reform the once-proud German economy, the new Germany continues to regain its political self-confidence – looking forward into the future and unflinchingly back into the past. One day (not yet, but one day) Germany may even become normal once more. This book tells the story of that confused journey towards normality.

There is no shortage of those who argue that a powerful Germany remains an intrinsically dangerous proposition, because of what happened there 60 and 70 years ago. One can also argue the opposite: that the lessons of the 1930s and 1940s have helped protect Germany against the spread of modern nationalism, even while far-right parties all across Europe have enjoyed remarkable success. In Germany, no far-right political party has succeeded in winning a single seat in the Bundestag. In terms of its stability and its commitment to democracy, today's Germany seems to be the best Germany we have ever had. That might all yet change. For the moment, however, for all the country's manifold flaws, that is, perhaps, a reason for cautious celebration for Germans and non-Germans alike.

London, February 2004

ACKNOWLEDGEMENTS

A word of explanation is appropriate about the judgements with which this book is littered. I started writing this book while still a journalist at *The Independent*, and completed it after going to work for Human Rights Watch. *Easier Fatherland* remains the book that I would have written – peppered with personal opinions – had I not taken up my post at HRW. I hope that my opinions are backed up with facts; they are not intended to reflect mindless prejudice. Nonetheless, these are my personal opinions, not those of Human Rights Watch.

Thanks to those with whom I have discussed the ideas in this book over the years, or who have found time to comment on earlier drafts – including Colleen Buzzard, Volker Hassemer, Theo Koll, Hucky Land, Kathy Lerman, Miriam Mahlow, Andrew Marshall, Sabine Sparwasser and Uschi Tiphine. Thanks also to executive producer David Wilson and producers Robert Cooke and Cosima Dannoritzer for my involvement in the *Germany Inside Out* programmes which helped kickstart *Easier Fatherland* – and to the BBC for permission to quote from interviews filmed for the series.

I am grateful to my colleagues, most especially to Carroll Bogert, Rory Mungoven and Kenneth Roth, for their generosity in giving me the time and space to complete the book.

1

Another Country

As a Jew, Rathenau was a German patriot; as a German patriot, he was a liberal citizen of the world.
(The German writer and historian Sebastian Haffner remembers the German foreign minister Walther Rathenau, assassinated in 1922)

It was, despite its failings, for us young Germans the best period of our lives . . . A new idealism beyond doubt and disappointment, a new liberalism broader, more comprehensive and more mature than the political liberalism of the nineteenth century.
(Haffner on the partial optimism of Weimar Germany)

Given everything that happened during twelve years in the first half of the last century, it is easy to forget that there was a before. A time when the words 'Germany' and 'mass murder' did not seem an obvious historical matching pair. A madman might dream up such a project, and even write about it, while in jail, in a book called *My Struggle*. But nobody (it seemed self-evident) would go along with such lunacy. Before 1933, the crimes of Adolf Hitler's Third Reich seemed inconceivable to Germans and non-Germans alike. After 1945, by contrast, those years have often been treated as if they were part of a natural German continuum – a lethal daisy chain stretching back into history, whose implications are still with us today.

Hitler has driven a wedge into our perceptions of everything from clothing to architecture and opera. The humble lederhosen as traditionally worn in the Bavarian mountains has come to seem associated with the Hitler Youth. A building which elsewhere would be described as modernist becomes, in a German context, 'Third Reich', as if the building were defined not by its shape and features but by the empty space above the doorway, where a swastika may have been chiselled away after 1945. Music that predates Nazism by many years is infected by the scale of Hitler's crimes. Thus, Richard Wagner was a favourite composer of many German Jews before 1939; his unpleasant views were perceived as irrelevant to aesthetic judgements. The Zionist Congress chose the *Tannhäuser* overture for its opening ceremony in 1898. Theodor Herzl, father of Zionism, was an enthusiast. Herzl said that, while he was working on *The Jewish State*, 'My sole recreation in the evening consisted in listening to Wagner's music, especially *Tannhäuser*, an opera which I went to hear as often as it was performed.' At the state funeral in 1922 of Germany's Jewish foreign minister, Walther Rathenau, the Siegfried funeral march from *Götterdämmerung* was performed. The orchestra which became the Israel Philharmonic performed Wagner at one of its inaugural concerts in 1936. Now, such choices all seem unthinkable. In the twenty-first century, a performance of Wagner's *Liebestod* (under Daniel Barenboim's provocative baton in Jerusalem in 2001) is still capable of triggering protests, because his music was beloved by Hitler. The Romantic painter Caspar David Friedrich, meanwhile, has been blamed for what Simon Schama describes in *Landscape and Memory* as 'the unacceptable historical consequences', a century after the painter's death, of the heroic and mythic tradition within which he worked. In the words of the waspish German author Florian Illies (exaggerating, but only a little): 'Anybody who still said that they liked Caspar David Friedrich stood accused for decades of not being sufficiently critical with regard to German history.'

It is sometimes difficult for us to look back at Germany before 1933 except through the murderous prism of Auschwitz, Sobibor and Treblinka – as if the extermination camps were the obvious culmination of everything that came before. When an extraneous piece of evidence is inappropriately blurted out in court, juries may seek in vain to obey the exhortation to 'put out of your minds what you have just heard'. Similarly, the rise and fall of the Third Reich so dominates our perceptions of modern Germany that it is difficult to remind ourselves that the pre-1933 past was another country; they did things differently there.

One bestselling work of recent years argues that the Holocaust was a natural extension of the murderous tendencies inherent in German society before 1933. Certainly, anti-Semitism was widespread in Germany long before Hitler came to power. In that, Germany was not alone. When Alfred Dreyfus was sentenced to life imprisonment on Devil's Island after a false conviction for treason, a German-Jewish student was so alarmed by the anti-Semitic climate – with crowds outside the Paris courtroom chanting 'Death to the Jews!' – that he wrote home to say that he would try to move back from the Sorbonne to 'a decent German university'. The German Jewish politician Eduard Lasker was shocked, when visiting the United States, to discover that Jews were banned from some hotels. He concluded that, in terms of integration, the United States lagged behind his own country. In Britain, anti-Semitism had supporters in high places; admirers of the British fascist leader, Sir Oswald Mosley ('The big Jew controls the parties, and the little Jew sweats you in the sweatshop'), included at least one leading newspaper tycoon. In Russia, the creation of the Pale of Settlement, prohibiting Jews from residing in the Russian heartland, forced Jews to live literally beyond the pale. In much of eastern Europe, anti-Semitic violence was routine. Russia and Ukraine gave the word *pogrom* – derived from the word for a clap of thunder – to the world, to describe the lethal attacks that became commonplace in the late nineteenth and early twentieth centuries. Poland introduced ghetto benches in universities in the 1930s and banned Jewish entry to the medical and legal professions.

In Germany, despite the eliminationism identified by Daniel Goldhagen in *Hitler's Willing Executioners*, things looked almost rosy by contrast. Because of the misery of tsarist rule, Jews in parts of eastern Europe treated advancing German troops in 1914 as if they were liberators. As Amos Elon points out in his portrait of Jews in Germany, *The Pity of It All*: 'In a sense, they were.' Boris Pasternak makes a similar point, through Yuri, the hero of *Doctor Zhivago*. Yuri contrasts the treatment of Jews in Russia during the First World War and their privileged situation in Germany, where Pasternak had studied philosophy before 1914. 'You can't imagine what the wretched Jewish population [in Russia] is going through in this war,' Pasternak's Zhivago tells a friend. 'Why should they be patriotic when the [German] enemy offers them equal rights and we do nothing but persecute them?'

More than in any other European country, Jews in early twentieth-century Germany were part of the national warp and weave. One of the country's best-loved poets, Heinrich Heine, was Jewish. (The Nazis would later be obliged to label his poems as 'author unknown', since it was difficult to keep his poems out of the anthologies completely.) The composer Felix Mendelssohn-Bartholdy was the grandson of Moses Mendelssohn, was 'the German Socrates'. In eighteenth- and nineteenth-century Germany, Jews faced huge restrictions; gradually, however, those restrictions were whittled down and civic equality was achieved.

Before 1933, Jews were prominent in Germany in arts, commerce, science and politics. The country's best-known theatre director, Max Reinhardt, was Jewish; so was the president of the Prussian art academy, Max Liebermann. So, too, was Germany's most distinguished scientist, Albert Einstein – a media star in his own right, who liked to stick his tongue out at what he called the *Lichtaffen* – 'flashbulb monkeys', the fledgling paparazzi who pursued him endlessly.

Goldhagen argues that the eliminationist mindset was a 'constant' in Germany before Hitler. German Jews at that time, despite their often-expressed concerns about widespread anti-Semitism, rarely saw things in such stark terms. Instead, they contrasted the relative tolerance of Germany with the dangers of anti-Semitism elsewhere. The journalist and novelist Joseph Roth, writing in 1920, describes the misery of Jews recently arrived in Berlin: 'Fear of pogroms has welded them together like a landslip of unhappiness and grime that, slowly gathering volume, has come rolling across Germany from the east.' For Roth and others, organized violence against Jews was something that happened to others; in Germany, it was (for the moment) unfamiliar.

Retrospective judgements make many things look different. A famous couplet about Germany, much quoted by Germans and non-Germans alike, comes from the Heine poem *Night Thoughts*, written in 1843:

Denk ich an Deutschland in der Nacht,
Dann bin ich um den Schlaf gebracht.

If I think of Germany at night,
Then I am no longer able to sleep.

A post-Auschwitz world has little difficulty in appreciating those sentiments, which even in the twenty-first century are sometimes treated as if they represent an eternal verity. Thus, during protests in 2001 against a government proposal to send troops to Afghanistan, Heine's doom-laden quotation was plastered on walls and lamp-posts all over Berlin, as if Heine were warning from the grave about the dangers of German militarism. The original context of the poem is different. *Night Thoughts* is a wistful poem of longing for Heine's German homeland, written from his Parisian political exile. Heine was the supreme ironist. He was serious, however, in insisting that his patriotism was more real than that of his reactionary critics could ever be. In his *Germany: a Winter's Tale*, Heine scorns his attackers, telling them: 'Calm yourselves: I love the fatherland as much as you do. Because of this love I have lived for 13 years in exile.' Heine was not alone in that view. The satirical writer Kurt Tucholsky ('a Jew without religion', in his own words) described himself in the 1920s in Heinian terms: 'We have a right to hate Germany, because we love it.'

At this time, Jewishness and Germanness did not seem implacable alternatives, but two sides of the same central European coin. The historian Sebastian Haffner, writing in 1939 about Walther Rathenau, argued that the foreign minister's Jewishness and German patriotism were complementary: 'As a Jew, Rathenau was a German patriot; as a German patriot, he was a liberal citizen of the world; as a liberal citizen of the world he was a strict servant of the law.' Rathenau's assassination by far-right extremists in 1922 was accompanied by abuse against 'the Jewish pig'. The most important focus of his murderers' indignation was, however, not his Jewishness (a useful additional target), but his role in signing the Treaty of Rapallo with the Soviet Union. (Matthias Erzberger, a Catholic politician who signed the November armistice, had been assassinated the previous year.) The response to Rathenau's death was overwhelming. Workers went on strike as a token of mourning and protest. The funeral was held in the parliamentary chamber of the Reichstag, which was transformed into a sea of flowers. A contemporary observer wrote: 'The effect was overwhelming. Many of those around me wept.'

Mistrust of Germany and of German power was widespread, long before Hitler. The poet Georg Herwegh wrote, in connection with Bismarck's unification of Germany in 1871 after the Franco-Prussian war: 'You have in fame-crowned murder become the leading nation in the world. Germany, I shudder at you.' The union of 25 states and kingdoms into a single country had potentially disturbing implications for the entire continent. Many Germans were themselves suspicious of Prussian militarism. In Bavaria, there was resentment of the Bismarckian order, with its Prussification and 'rule by sabre'. 'Prussian obedience' – a phrase which would take on a lethal, emblematic quality in the context of the Nazi era – was widely recognized as real. Carl Zuckmayer's comedy *The Captain of Köpenick* is based on the true story of how Wilhelm Voigt, a shoe-maker, who dressed up in an officer's uniform bought from a second-hand shop. Armed with nothing but a belief in Prussian obedience, he ordered soldiers to follow him to the town hall – where he arrested the mayor and took charge of the treasury. Awed by the power of the uniform, nobody felt able to disobey. Zuckmayer's play was hugely successful when it opened in 1931; unsurprisingly, it was closed down when Hitler came to power. In the words of the writer John Mortimer, the play's English translator: 'History, impatient with all gentle jokes, seized *The Captain of Köpenick* by the scruff of the neck and made it, in spite of itself, a dangerous satire.'

In short: anti-Semitism, yes; Prussian militarism and obedience, yes. It takes quite a leap, however, to get from there to the conclusion that the Nazi killing machine merely dotted the i's and crossed the t's of a peculiarly German tradition of murderous prejudice. It has often been said that Germany's historical *Sonderweg* – 'special path', which left Germany out of step with the rest of western Europe, in the process of state-building and the creation of national consciousness – helped pave the way for the Third Reich. Germany was 'a belated nation', in the words of a book first published in 1935. In retrospect, the *Sonderweg* may help us to understand how the nightmare developed. Before 1933, however, there was nothing self-evident about what was to come, even for the greatest pessimist. Until the nightmare was already under way, the extent of the crimes that Germans would willingly commit or avert their eyes from seemed literally unthinkable.

Despite the instability after the end of the First World War in 1918 and the Treaty of Versailles the following year, fascism hardly seemed preordained. On the contrary. Germany's Social Democrats had the largest membership of any political party in the world. The naval mutiny in the northern port of Kiel in 1918 triggered a string of further rebellions across the country, and quickly led to the abdication of the Kaiser and the collapse of imperial rule. It seemed briefly as though the Communist revolution that had swept Russia a year earlier might repeat itself in Germany, too. The new republican government seemed to bespeak a new Germany. Three regional prime ministers were Jewish. The old Reich collapsed with none of the bloody horror of the Bolshevik Revolution the previous year. Einstein was starry-eyed: 'None of us felt cold or hunger: was this not the dawn of a new era that had inscribed "Never Again War" on its banner? And had not this powerful, wonderful breakthrough started right here in Berlin?'

In Bavaria, a group of idealistic intellectuals seized power. Lenin's dictum that 'revolution could never grip Berlin – Germans would only storm a railway platform after first queuing for platform tickets' appeared partly disproved. In Berlin, the Spartacist rebels seized key public buildings before their uprising was crushed; two of the movement's leaders, Karl Liebknecht and Rosa Luxemburg, were murdered. All in all, it was a difficult birth for the new Weimar republic – so named because it was in the city of Goethe that Germany's first democratic constitution was drawn up in 1919. (Berlin was considered too unsafe.) The elected assembly convened in the cosy setting of the town's court theatre, with circumstance but little pomp. According to one contemporary observer, the atmosphere had 'not a trace of the greatness appropriate to this historic moment'.

The turbulence of the early months of the Weimar republic did not subside. There was widespread bitterness at the harsh terms of the Versailles treaty. Within the next few years came the legendary collapse of the currency – a catastrophe which ensures that, at the beginning of another century, the word 'Weimar' remains a familiar shorthand for describing an economic disaster zone and the political instability that accompanies hyperinflation. In 1921, there were 80 marks to the dollar; within two years, that had risen to 350,000 marks to the dollar. That was just the prelude. Through the summer and autumn of 1923, the currency plunged vertically – four million to the dollar in August, 99 million in September, 25 billion in October. Banknotes with a face value of millions of marks were less valuable than toilet paper. The mark finally reached its ultimate nadir, when it touched the meaningless exchange rate of four trillion to the dollar on 15 November 1923. Sebastian Haffner, writing from the perspective of 1939, emphasizes the unique quality of Germany's dangerous drama at this time:

That extraordinary year is probably what has marked today's Germans with those characteristics that are so strange and incomprehensible in the eyes of the world, and so different from what used to be thought of as the German character. In that year, an entire generation of Germans had a spiritual organ removed . . . All nations went through the Great War, and most of them have also experienced revolutions, social crises, strikes, redistribution of wealth and currency devaluation. None but Germany has undergone the fantastic, grotesque extreme of all these together; none has experienced the gigantic, carnival dance of death, the unending, bloody Saturnalia, in which not only money but all standards lost their value. The year 1923 prepared Germany, not specifically for Nazism, but for any fantastic adventure.

Thomas Mann, too, saw a connection between the insanity of Weimar inflation and the later insanity of the Third Reich:

Just as the Germans saw their monetary units swell to millions, billions, and trillions and then burst, they later saw their nation swell to the Reich of all Germans, to *Lebensraum*, to European order, to world dominion, and will also still see it burst. The market woman who in a dull tone asked a 'hundred billion' for an egg had at the time forgotten how to be amazed . . . Germans forgot to rely on themselves as individuals and learned to expect everything from 'politics', from the 'state', from 'destiny' . . . Robbed of everything, the Germans became a nation of robbers.

When currency reform – including the creation of a new currency in November 1923 – helped bring economic stability, many Germans saw it as a miracle. One Berliner, returning from abroad, summed up the change: 'People had their brass doorknobs out again – whereas in 1923 you couldn't find a brass doorknob in all Berlin: people would just steal it in the night.' The next few years were a time of almost-optimism. Haffner moves into lyrical vein, looking back on that time as a window of hope:

It was, despite its failings, for us young Germans the best period of our lives. All that we have experienced of the sweetness of life is associated with it . . . A new idealism beyond doubt and disappointment, a new liberalism broader, more comprehensive and more mature than the political liberalism of the nineteenth century.

In Weimar-era Berlin, the sense that 'anything goes' was strong. One foreign visitor complained: 'Berlin finds its outlet in the wildest dissipation imaginable. The German . . . enjoys obscenity in a form which even the Parisian would not tolerate.' Marlene Dietrich became famous as Lola Lola, the cabaret singer in Josef von Sternberg's *The Blue Angel*. In Paris, the film was banned; in Berlin, it raised hardly an eyebrow. 'Wild dissipation' or not, this was a period of enormous creativity, with films like Fritz Lang's *Metropolis*, the twelve-tone music of Arnold Schönberg, the dramas and musicals of Bertolt Brecht and Kurt Weill, the savagely satirical paintings of George Grosz. The Bauhaus movement, based in Weimar and then Dessau, opened up a revolutionary new world of architecture and design, led by a host of stars including Walter Gropius, Wassily Kandinsky and Paul Klee. In Germany, a hundred artistic flowers bloomed.

Then, in 1929, came the Great Crash. In the chaos that followed, those flowers were soon trampled underfoot. Even then, the long-term dangers were not immediately obvious. The Nazis' representation in the

Reichstag jumped ninefold in 1930; they became the second-largest party after the Social Democrats. Einstein was not alone in attributing the Nazis' success to a 'momentary economic slump'. In reality, everything was now about to change. In 1931, as the Weimar republic began to implode, one of the best-known Berlin cabaret writers, Friedrich Holländer, wrote *Münchhausen*, after the fantasizing baron of the same name. The angry and hauntingly sad *Münchhausen*, revived in recent years by the singer Ute Lemper, includes one verse after another of German impossibilities – a film where 'the audience clapped, although the heroes were mere civilians', where there are no nationalist flags, 'only black red and gold, no other flag is unrolled', and where the 'whatsits-name, the swastika' is nowhere to be seen. And then, after each verse, the wistful refrain: '*Lüge, Lüge, Lüge*. Lies, lies, lies . . . but wouldn't it be nice if it were just a little bit true?'

For some observers of German politics, the (admittedly dim) prospect of Hitler's accession to power spelt disaster that went beyond the limits of satire. Tucholsky explained in 1929 why he could not attack the Nazis directly. 'Satire has a limit at the top; Buddha is above it. It also has a limit at the bottom: the fascist forces in Germany. It doesn't pay – one can't shoot that low.' For others, even as the violence of the Nazis increased, it seemed impossible to take them quite seriously. Until too late in the day, many saw the Nazis as Haffner did, 'a ridiculous splinter party', deserving of mockery more than fear. The writer Arnold Zweig saw Hitler as 'Charlie Chaplin without the talent'.

Pre-Hitler Germany was a society in which Jews were highly integrated – to the Nazis' fury and dismay. In 1933, 40 per cent of Jewish marriages were to non-Jews. It was not anti-Semitism which gave the National Socialists their strength, but economic collapse – and the perception that the Nazis might turn this around. In the words of historian Ian Kershaw, Hitler found that 'anti-Marxism had a wider potential appeal than the mere repetition of anti-Jewish paroxysms of hate'. The diarist Victor Klemperer suggests in 1933, in an entry of terrifying perceptiveness:

The fate of the Hitler movement will undoubtedly be decided by this Jewish business. I do not understand why they have made this point of their programme so central. It will sink them. But we will probably go down with them.

By now, German society was already undergoing a dangerous transformation. The Nazis succeeded in making murder and war seem natural and inevitable. In his *Berlin Diary* of 1932–33, Christopher Isherwood describes a conversation overheard in a café:

> A young Nazi is sitting with his girl; they are discussing the future of the Party. The Nazi is drunk.
>
> 'Oh, I know we shall win, all right,' he exclaims impatiently, 'but that's not enough!' He thumps the table with his fist: 'Blood must flow!'
>
> The girl strokes his arm reassuringly. She is trying to get him to come home. 'But, of course, it's going to flow, darling,' she coos soothingly, 'the Leader's promised that in our programme.'

As Isherwood leaves Berlin in 1933, he himself seems bemused by the changes he has witnessed in such a relatively short time.

> The sun shines, and Hitler is master of this city. The sun shines, and dozens of my friends are in prison, possibly dead ... The trams are going up and down the Kleiststrasse, just as usual. They, and the people on the pavement, and the tea-cosy dome of the Nollendorfplatz station have an air of curious familiarity, of striking resemblance to something one remembers as normal and pleasant in the past – like a very good photograph.
>
> No. Even now I can't altogether believe that any of this has really happened.

If events seemed surreal for foreigners like Isherwood, they were stranger still for German democrats. Haffner notes that, before the Hitler takeover, few comprehended what the creation of the Third Reich might mean:

> There are few things as comic as the calm, superior indifference with which I and those like me watched the beginnings of the Nazi revolution in Germany, as if from a box at the theatre. It was, after all, a movement with the declared intention of doing away with us. Perhaps the only comparably comic thing is the way that now, years later [in 1939], Europe is permitting itself exactly the same indifferent attitude, as though it were a superior, amused onlooker, while the Nazis are already setting it alight at all four corners.

2

Twelve Years

It was Dante's Inferno. Dante come to life.
> (Franz Stangl describes the sight that greeted him when he first
> arrived to work at Treblinka. As commandant at Treblinka, Stangl was
> later responsible for the deaths of almost a million people)

One in a thousand.
> (Psychologists' prediction of the number who would agree
> to administer lethal electric shocks when asked to do so as part of a
> 'memory experiment' at Yale University)

It didn't bother me even to find that he was dead. I did a job.
> (A participant in the Yale experiment; he was one of the two-thirds
> majority who agreed to kill a perfect stranger)

Chameleons change their colour unconsciously – blending in for their
own protection, without even choosing to do so. Human beings sometimes do the same. Christopher Isherwood describes an early example of
adjustment to new circumstances. His landlady – who 'long ago, before
the [First World] War and the Inflation, used to be comparatively well
off' – reveals her new political sympathies, after Hitler comes to power in
1933:

This morning I even heard her talking reverently about 'Der
Führer' to the porter's wife. If I were to remind her that, at the
elections last November, she voted Communist, she would
probably deny it hotly – and in perfect good faith. She is merely

acclimatizing herself, in accordance with a natural law, like an animal which changes its coat for the winter. Thousands of people like Fräulein Schröder are acclimatizing themselves.

That acclimatization was often forceful. The Third Reich would in the next few years find it appropriate to murder dozens of elected MPs – in addition to the pressures on the rest of the establishment, from judges to bishops – in search of the perfectly Hitlerite Germany. The process of *Gleichschaltung* – 'moving into a single gear', a demand for Nazi uniformity – was brutal, sometimes lethal. As the Nazis tightened their hold, so, too, did popular anti-Semitism, though the effect was not immediate or universal. A Nazi boycott of Jewish businesses in April 1933 proved a fiasco. One remarkable account of life in the Third Reich is the diary kept by Victor Klemperer, a professor of Romance languages at Dresden University until he was forced out in 1935. Against all probability, Klemperer – son of a rabbi and cousin of the conductor Otto Klemperer – survived in Dresden throughout the Second World War. Like the historian and novelist Ricarda Huch, who believed the brutality of the Nazis to be 'un-German and unhealthy', Klemperer argued that he, not the Nazis, was the true German patriot. 'I am German forever, a German "nationalist" . . . The Nazis are un-German.' After his expulsion from the university he admitted that his principles were 'beginning to wobble like an old man's teeth'. As late as 1942, however, he clings like a shipwrecked mariner to his belief that this has all been a terrible aberration: '*I* am German and I'm waiting for the Germans to return; they have gone into hiding somewhere.' On the same day as insisting that he is the true German, Klemperer notes the strangeness of continuing as normal when all hope seems lost. 'To the very last moment, I want to live and to work, as if I were certain of surviving. *Je n'en ai qu'un très faible espoir.*'

Klemperer, with no special access to information from the outside world, knows what is happening there. In February 1942, he notes in passing that being sent to a concentration camp 'amounts to a death sentence'. An absolute fatalism overtakes him, even with respect to his own chronicling of the nightmare. In November 1942, a terse entry reads: 'Uncertainty, danger everywhere – a newspaper discovered is enough for Auschwitz.' Others were equally clear about what was happening. The Wannsee conference of January 1942, which organized the details of the Final Solution, was top secret; the effects of the conference were not. Thomas Mann noted in his diary a public comment by Goebbels, 'Whether Germany is defeated or victorious, the Jews will be eliminated.' Broadcasting to Germany in September 1942, Mann talks of the Nazis' 'maniacal decision for the complete annihilation of European Jewry', and tells his listeners that 700,000 Jews have already been murdered or tortured to death. 'Do you Germans know that? And what do you think about it?'

Most thought as little as possible, was the short answer. The details of this extraordinarily efficient programme of mass murder were concealed, with good reason; but the system relied on a general acceptance of the nightmare. It relied on a large number of willing participants, backed up by the compliance and complaisance of millions like Isherwood's Fräulein Schröder, cheering the Führer on from the sidelines. On the few occasions when German society showed itself ready to stand up against the crimes of the Third Reich, the Nazis partly backed down. Thus, the euthanasia programme which allowed the murder of tens of thousands of disabled and mentally handicapped ('worthless lives') caused disquiet, including a sermon delivered by the Bishop of Münster, Clemens August von Galen, in 1941. The sermon was reprinted and widely distributed. Within weeks, the euthanasia programme was (officially) cancelled. Such protests were, however, exceptional.

The post-1945 official West German description of Hitler's regime as a *Gewaltherrschaft* – 'rule by violence', usually translated as dictatorship – was simultaneously accurate and entirely misleading. Violence was indeed an essential part of the Nazi machine. As other dictatorships have shown, however, violence is not the only requirement needed to keep a brutal system in place. When Stalin died in 1953, many of the tears shed by millions of Russians were real. If Hitler had died in the late 1930s or early 1940s, he, too, would have been widely mourned. Those who attempted to resist suffered the full force of Nazi repression; but few were in any case inclined to try.

In the 1920s, optimism about Germany's future had still been possible. After a few years of Nazi rule, however (including Goebbels' tight control of newspapers and broadcasting), all that had radically changed. Sebastian Haffner partly foreshadows psychological experiments carried out in America many years later, when describing the changes he has witnessed:

We have here the systematic infection of a whole nation, Germany, with a germ that causes its people to treat their victims like wolves; or, to put it differently, the freeing and revitalization of precisely those sadistic instincts whose chaining and restraint has been the work of a thousand years of civilization.

When circumstances change for the worse, societies themselves change with bewildering rapidity. (The process of convalescence and recovery takes much longer – as would be vividly demonstrated in Germany and elsewhere in the years to come.) Sophie Scholl and her brother Hans, Catholic conspirators of the White Rose resistance movement, were beheaded in 1943 after distributing subversive pamphlets at Munich University. The Scholls were portrayed after 1945 as if they were representative heroes, achieving what millions of other Germans had been eager to do. Heroes they were. They were not representative, however – even if they hoped that they would be. On the morning of her execution, Sophie Scholl asked: 'What does our death matter, if thousands will be stirred and awakened by what we have done? The students are bound to revolt!' Her optimism was misguided. At a students' demonstration condemning the Scholls' actions, the crowds shouted and stamped their feet with excitement. It was, a witness said afterwards, 'one of the most terrible memories I have of those days'.

In July 1944 came the most famous attempt on Hitler's life. By this time, military defeat was looming. It was 18 months since the humiliation of German forces at Stalingrad. Soviet forces were preparing to chase Hitler's armies back on to German soil. In western Europe, the Allies had landed on the Normandy beaches six weeks earlier. That prospect of defeat helped strengthen support amongst generals for a plot against Hitler – including some who had been reluctant to act against him when he was still on his winning streak. Claus Schenk von Stauffenberg placed the bomb under a table during a staff briefing at Hitler's east Prussian headquarters, the Wolf's Lair (now a desolate museum-in-the-woods in northern Poland) on 20 July 1944. Only an aide's last-minute problem with map-reading saved Hitler's life. Heinz Brandt needed to lean across the table to look at the military map more closely. He moved the briefcase containing the bomb away from his and Hitler's feet, and placed it behind a massive oak table support. Hitler, protected from the full force of the explosion, escaped with a damaged eardrum.

Stauffenberg and all the conspirators in the July plot were rounded up and executed. After 1945, they were commemorated as heroes. They had indeed risked and lost their lives for what came to be known as 'the other Germany', *das andere Deutschland*. But not all participants in the July plot were staunch democrats from the start. On the contrary, there were some who, as Gordon Craig puts it, 'seemed to believe that the country would be better off if all the clocks were turned back to 1913'. Many Germans were in any case indignant at the aristocrats' plot against the Führer.

After 1945, there was much emphasis on 'German obedience' as a root cause of the Holocaust. That is partly because of the Nazi killers' insistence, at Nuremberg and later, that they were 'only obeying orders'. And yet, there is nothing uniquely German about the ability to turn a blind eye or participate in horrors that have been encouraged by a responsible higher authority. On the contrary, as demonstrated by the remarkable experiments conducted by Professor Stanley Milgram and his colleagues at the psychology department of Yale University between 1960 and 1963.

The experiment sought to answer the question: how ready are people to injure or kill others, when asked to do so? A local newspaper advertisement asked for volunteers, selected for a mixture of age and background, for 'a study of memory'. On arrival at the laboratory, volunteers were informed of the rules of the experiment, which (they were told) sought to test different ways of remembering word-pairs; could conditioning be helpful? The volunteers were divided, apparently at random, into 'teacher' and 'learner' (in reality, unknown to the guinea pig teachers, the learner was an actor). The teacher proceeded to read out a list of questions; after each incorrect answer, the teacher administered an electric shock. The shocks began with very mild, and increased steadily in response to incorrect answers. If the learner repeatedly gave the wrong answer, the shocks could thus increase to dangerous and life-threatening levels, as the control panel made clear. The markings ranged from 'slight shock' at 15 volts through 'moderate', up to 'Danger: severe shock' at 375 volts and finally a wordless 'XXX' at 450.

For the creators of the experiment, and for everybody else, it was clear that none but a dangerous lunatic would ever go that far. Milgram and his colleagues asked people the theoretical question: how far would *they* be willing to go? The results were – as common sense would suggest – unambiguous. Respondents insisted they would never cause pain or injury against a person's will. Thus, typically: 'I couldn't deliberately hurt a perfect stranger.' People are naturally liable to present themselves in a favourable light, so the question was tweaked. Ordinary people and professionals were asked to predict how *others* would perform, when faced with such a request. The predictions of both groups – again, following the dictates of common sense – were similar. All agreed that most people would curtail the experiment at the point when the learner asks for it to be ended, at 150 volts ('strong shock'). Psychologists reckoned that maybe one in 1000 would agree to administer shocks through to the deadly XXX level.

The reality, Milgram and his colleagues found, was very different. Some reacted in the way that everybody had predicted, with a logical, morally driven response. One participant declares: 'It's a hell of an experiment. The guy is suffering in there. No, I don't want to go on. This is crazy.' Another, told that he has no choice but to continue, retorts with blunt finality: 'I think we are here on our own free will.' We all hope and assume that our reactions would be so straightforward and humane, in similar circumstances. Against the professional predictions, however, such reactions came not from 999 out of 1000, nor even nine out of ten – but from a minority of those taking part. An astonishing two in three showed themselves ready, in practice, to kill a stranger.

Those who continue to the end of the scale are not enthusiastic executioners. They are not even especially willing. In the end, however, they carry the experiment through to its presumably deadly conclusion. A typical exchange, at 180 volts, runs as follows: 'I can't stand it. I'm not going to kill that man in there. You hear him hollering?' The experimenter explains: 'Whether the learner likes it or not, we must continue through all the word pairs.' After a few more protests ('who's going to take the responsibility if anything happens to that gentleman?'), the teacher increases the shock. The actor-learner screams to be let out, declaring: 'I absolutely refuse to answer any more.' And still the shocks continue up the scale, even after the subject refuses to participate further. (The technician prompts the teacher: 'If the learner doesn't answer in a reasonable time, consider the answer wrong.') At 360 volts, the learner fails even to grunt or groan in response to the shocks. The teacher is worried. 'What if he's dead in there?' 'We must continue. Go on, please,' says the man in the laboratory coat. And so the teacher does, to the bitter end.

Interestingly, those who at some point act according to a moral imperative and refuse to continue with the experiment seem more inclined, after the experiment is over, to feel guilt for what they have done than those who were ready to commit murder. One man who drops out before the end of the scale reproaches himself for his weakness in not stopping earlier:

> I should have stopped the first time he complained . . . I would put it on myself entirely . . . One of the things I think is very cowardly is to try to shove the responsibility on to somebody else. See, if I turned round and said, 'It's your fault, it's not mine,' – I would call that cowardly.

By contrast, those who have just executed the big, friendly man whose hand they shook an hour earlier (none of the participants questioned the veracity of the experiment; there was no hint that this was make-believe), appear to feel little connection with or responsibility for the death which they have just caused. Thus, one participant – a university-educated woman, who sees herself as 'unusual – I'm soft-hearted' – protests when asked to administer stronger shocks. 'Can't we stop? I'm shaking. I'm shaking. Do I have to go up there?' Whereupon she proceeds to murder the stranger in the next room, who earlier mentioned that he has a weak heart, with three 450-volt shocks in a row. When confronted at the end of the experiment with the man she has just killed, she is hugely relieved ('You're an actor, boy!'). She seems oblivious to her own moral abdication. Instead, she shares with the actor the extent of her own suffering while she was busy killing him. 'Oh my God, what he [the experimenter] did to me. I'm exhausted. I didn't want to go on with it. You don't know what I went through here.' Of guilt – apart from some *pro forma* apologies, and the declaration that 'My face is beet red. I wouldn't hurt a fly' – there is no sign.

The Milgram experiment was replicated in a number of countries around the world, with similar results. When the learner was being electrocuted in the next room – and when his screams for mercy or his banging on the wall could clearly be heard – 65 per cent of all volunteers carried the experiment through to its conclusion, by pulling the switch themselves. Many seem unbothered by what they have done. One man describes going through to the room where the actor-learner is lying dead on the floor. 'I faithfully believed the man was dead until we opened the door. When I saw him, I said, "Great, this is great." But it didn't bother me even to find that he was dead. I did a job.'

When seeking to understand the disturbing reality of the Third Reich, other findings are more remarkable still. If the teacher 'merely' asked questions, leaving a technician in the same room to do the hard work of pulling the switch, more than 90 per cent continued with the experiment to the end. Most remarkable of all was a pilot experiment, abandoned because its results were so unhelpfully uniform. In this version, the teacher could not hear the learner's protests; instead, he or she was expected to draw conclusions about the effect of depressing a switch with labels like 'Danger: severe shock'. In the absence of audible protests from the learner, virtually *every* subject went, in Milgram's words, 'blithely to the end of the board, seemingly indifferent to the verbal designations'.

In real life – as opposed to the laboratory conditions under which Milgram's experiment was carried out – responsibility can easily be shuffled off in different directions. Thus, Milgram notes of Adolf Eichmann, the man entrusted with deportations to the death camps:

Even Eichmann was sickened when he toured the concentration camps, but to participate in mass murder he only had to sit at a desk and shuffle papers. At the same time, the man in the camp who actually dropped Zyklon-B into the gas chambers was able to justify *his* behaviour on the grounds that he was only following orders from above.

In her account of the Eichmann trial in Jerusalem in 1961, Hannah Arendt famously talked of the 'banality of evil'. Milgram's experiments suggest that a permissive climate for killing is all that was needed for such evil to flourish. Arendt notes one of the peculiarities of the Third Reich:

> Evil in the Third Reich had lost the quality by which most people recognize it – the quality of temptation. Many Germans and many Nazis, probably an overwhelming majority of them, must have been tempted *not* to murder, *not* to rob, *not* to let their neighbours go off to their doom (for that the Jews were transported to their doom they knew, of course, even though many of them may not have known the gruesome details), and not to become accomplices in all these crimes by benefiting from them. But, God knows, they had learned how to resist temptation.

That shaping of a society was the key. Propaganda and social conditioning made the unthinkable seem normal. Here, too, there was nothing obviously or uniquely German about what happened, as another American experiment showed. The experiment conducted by Philip Zimbardo at Stanford University in 1971 divided student volunteers into 'prisoners' and 'guards' to test patterns of behaviour. The two-week experiment degenerated so appallingly into sadism that it had to be aborted after just six days. Zimbardo said it was 'dramatic and distressing' to see 'the ease with which sadistic behavior could be elicited in individuals who are not "sadistic types"'. Zimbardo suggested that the experiment showed how easy it is to create a climate where cruelty is accepted. 'These guys were all peaceniks,' he said afterwards of the student guards. 'They became like Nazis.'

It is easy for us to think of the most evil perpetrators of the Holocaust as intrinsically evil from the start. As Arendt indicated, the truth is perhaps more disturbing. In 1971, the journalist and historian Gitta Sereny interviewed Franz Stangl, commandant at the extermination camp of Treblinka and one of the worst war criminals ever known.

Under his command, 900,000 men, women and children were murdered. In conversation with Sereny in his prison cell, Stangl, a prime example of the banality of evil, talks of his reluctance when first approached by the Nazis to work on their euthanasia programme. In this conversation, Stangl sees himself as victim, not just as perpetrator. The former Austrian policeman hates the Germans 'for what they pulled me into – I should have killed myself in 1938'. He repeatedly talks as though he were at one remove from the killing machine for which he bore such a large measure of personal responsibility. He talks with horror of the scene – 'It was Dante's Inferno. Dante come to life' – when he first set eyes on the death camp which he would run so efficiently. He describes his first sight of Belzec camp, too, in horrified terms which would not be out of place in a survivor's memoir:

They had put too many corpses in the pit, and putrefaction had progressed so fast that the liquid underneath had pushed the bodies on top up and over, and the corpses had rolled down the hill. I saw some of them – oh God, it was awful.

He describes how he tried to extract himself from this nightmare:

When I got back to Sobibor, Michel and I talked and talked about it. We agreed that what they were doing was a crime. We considered deserting – we discussed it for a long time. But how? Where could we go? What about our families? All I could think of was that I wanted out. I planned and planned.

Sereny notes that none of this appeared to be retrospective self-justification on the part of Stangl, who accepted the life sentence he had just begun (he died of a heart attack shortly afterwards). Instead, she suggests:

Throughout the three days of this part of the story, he manifested an intense desire to seek and tell the truth. This need, strangely enough, was emphasized rather than belied by the extraordinary callousness of many of his explanations and anecdotes . . . He voluntarily but unwittingly told us more than the truth: he showed us the two men he had become in order to survive.

Evil is simpler to deal with when it is committed by obvious monsters – monstrous individuals, or (simpler still, for those who are not affected by the blanket accusation) a monstrous nation. Here, we are presented with a more disturbing picture. We see the potential monstrousness that can be released in the wrong circumstances and with the wrong leadership, when individuals are encouraged not to take responsibility for their own actions. This monstrousness is revealed by the Milgram and Zimbardo experiments in laboratory conditions in the United States; Zimbardo believed that his experiment showed 'how easy it is for good people to become perpetrators of evil'. It was revealed in the brutal reality of 1940s Germany, with the behaviour of men like Franz Stangl. Above all, it was revealed by the countless mini-Stangls all across the Third Reich – the equivalent of the friendly woman who killed a man by electrocution, then blamed the man standing next to her for the fact that she had just committed murder. Her understanding of her own responsibility was summed up in her insistence, after the experiment was over, that she 'wouldn't hurt a fly'.

With the creation of the Third Reich, a powerful poison found its way into the already sickly body politic of Weimar Germany. Respectable people committed criminal acts that they would previously have found unthinkable, as society adapted to the new leader and Goebbels, the propaganda master, wove his malign spells. In Milgram's and Zimbardo's experiments, brutality and murder become possible merely because of the polite requests of a man in a laboratory coat or the creation of a permissive climate. In Germany, the change took place with the full backing of the repressive mechanisms of the Third Reich. The American experiments and the reality of Hitler's Germany have one key point in common: participants fail to take any responsibility for the murderous project they are involved in – especially if the most murderous implications are kept at just one remove.

Even in real life, Germany is not, of course, the only place where such deadly abandonment of responsibility has been vividly demonstrated. A participant in the My Lai massacre – when US soldiers slaughtered hundreds of Vietnamese villagers, mostly women and children, on 16 March 1968 – explained how it happened. 'I felt like I was ordered to do it . . . at the time I felt like I was doing the right thing.' Asked how he felt able to shoot babies, the soldier seems confused by the question. 'I don't know. It's just one of those things.' Lieutenant William Calley, with on-the-ground responsibility for the killing spree, said later: 'I felt then – and I still do – that I acted as directed, I carried out my orders, and I did not feel wrong in doing so.' Army photographer Ron Haeberle, whose graphic photographs would later be published in *Life* magazine, was able to work unhampered during the shooting of the villagers, because few of the soldiers felt any sense of guilt; if the shooting of women and children was a crime, after all, somebody would stop them doing it. (Haeberle witnessed around 100 civilians being killed.) Ron Ridenhour, the US soldier who blew the whistle on My Lai, believed: 'My Lai didn't happen because Lieutenant Calley went berserk. There were similar acts of policy all over the country.' The commanders who circled the village in helicopters were never charged; nor was a senior officer who landed as the killings took place. More than 35 years later, details emerged of a separate series of killing sprees by the Tiger Force unit in the Vietnamese highlands where, in the words of one member of the unit: 'If they ran we shot them, and if they didn't run we shot them anyway.'

Taking personal responsibility to prevent crimes is sometimes perceived as a crime in itself. 'Haven't you got rid of them yet? I want them dead. Waste them,' soldiers at My Lai were told. A soldier in the Tiger Force unit who told his men to stop shooting civilians was rebuked by a commanding officer and told to see a psychiatrist. Eichmann emphasizes that he is proud of his *Kadavergehorsam* – his 'corpse-like obedience'. Bizarrely, Arendt describes how Eichmann the mass killer, eager to prove his innocence, feels 'somewhat uncomfortable' when admitting that he broke the rules on two occasions by helping a Jewish relative and Jewish acquaintances; he said that he 'confessed his sins' to his superiors.

Such amorality can baffle those who are used to different norms. Even as Hitler's crimes were beginning to reach a murderous climax, Klemperer was still puzzling in his diary over what had happened to the Germany that he knew, with reference to Alfred Rosenberg's *Myth of the Twentieth Century*.

> How does it come about that suddenly *one* of these ideas grips a whole generation and becomes dominant? – If I had read Rosenberg's *Myth* in 1930, when it appeared, I would certainly have judged it to be a tiny flame, the crazy product of an individual, of a small unbalanced group. I would never have believed that the little flame could set anything alight – set anything alight in Germany!

By 1945, the flame of hatred and murder had long since set Germany alight. Hitler had moulded the country to his own aims. Now, the country was itself destroyed by the conflagration he unleashed. On 30 April 1945, Hitler shot himself in the bunker; Eva Braun, his wife of one day, took the poison that had already been tested out on Blondi, Hitler's beloved alsatian, the previous day. The Führer's body was doused in petrol, as he had requested, and set alight. His physical elimination seemed absolute. His legacy would, however, poison the country for years to come.

In 1932, Kurt Schumacher – who spent years in Dachau concentration camp, before becoming leader of West Germany's Social Democrats after 1945 – had told Goebbels that Germans would need a decade to heal themselves from the Nazis' 'constant appeal to the inner beast in man'. His prediction might have sounded pessimistic at the time. In reality, his estimate proved over-optimistic. The recovery took not one decade, but several. Germany was exposed to the power of Hitler for a mere 12 years. The process of restoring normality to the country would take much longer.

3

Dishonest Democracy (or the World of 'hinzu kamen')

In addition, came the victims who were killed in the concentration camps, the labour camps, the death chambers etc.

> (A brief postscript in a 1950s German schoolbook, at the end of a detailed catalogue of losses – including, for example, the number of Germans who lost a limb – in the Second World War)

With the collapse of the Third Reich in spring 1945, denial was the rule. Denial of knowledge, of participation, and above all of responsibility. Victor Klemperer noted the change, even before the Nazi surrender, when swastikas were already hastily being hauled down in towns and villages all over the country, in time for the arrival of the victorious Allies: 'The Third Reich is already almost as good as forgotten, everyone was opposed to it, "always" opposed to it . . .' Once the surrender became official with VE-Day on 8 May, the turnaround was soon complete. Millions of Fräulein Schröders, who quickly forgot in 1933 that they had ever *not* supported the Führer, now forgot even more quickly that they had in the meantime become his devoted admirers. The war correspondent Martha Gellhorn describes her travels through this land of denial:

> No one is a Nazi. No one ever was. There may have been some Nazis in the next village, and as a matter of fact that town about 20 kilometres away was a veritable hotbed of Nazidom . . . Oh, the Jews? Well, there weren't really many Jews in this neighbourhood. Two maybe, maybe six. They were taken away . . . We have nothing against the Jews; we always got on well with them . . . Ah, how we have suffered. The bombs. We lived in the cellars for weeks.

Gellhorn's conclusion:

> It should, we feel, be set to music. Then the Germans could sing this refrain and that would make it even better. They all talk like this. One asks oneself how the detested Nazi government, to which no one paid allegiance, managed to carry on this war for five and a half years. Obviously not a man, woman or child in Germany ever approved of the war for a minute, according to them.

This sense of denial affected all levels of society. An Allied intelligence analysis, quoted by Antony Beevor in *Berlin: The Downfall*, talks of the 'perverted moral sense' that the interrogation of hundreds of German generals reveals – including a reluctance to acknowledge the depth of the nightmare that their country has sunk to in the past decade. The generals' mindset is summarized in stark terms:

> Success is right. What does not succeed is wrong . . . That it is morally wrong to exterminate a race or massacre prisoners hardly ever occurs to them. The only horror they feel for German crimes is that they themselves may, by some monstrous injustice, be considered by the Allies to be implicated.

In terms of the long search for a return to honesty, it was not a good start. Thomas Mann's narrator in *Doctor Faustus* sums up the psychological challenge of what became known as *Stunde Null* – 'zero hour':

> Let us call them the sinister possibilities of human nature in general that here come to light. German human beings, tens of thousands, hundreds of thousands of them it is, who have perpetrated what humanity shudders at; and all that is German now stands forth as an abomination and a warning. How will it be to belong to a land whose history witnesses this hideous default.

Physically and psychologically, Germany was a nation of damaged goods. The country was a landscape of ruins, not least because of the Allied strategy of seeking to break civilian morale by firebombing German cities into oblivion. George Orwell described what he found in Cologne in March 1945 – though he could have been describing almost any German city at that time:

The whole central part of the city . . . is simply a chaos of jagged walls, overturned trams, shattered statues and enormous piles of rubble out of which iron girders thrust themselves like sticks of rhubarb . . . The *Herrenvolk* [master race] are all around you, threading their way on their bicycles between the piles of rubble or rushing off with jugs and buckets to meet the water cart.

To walk through the ruined cities of Germany, Orwell wrote, 'is to feel an actual doubt about the continuity of civilisation'.

The Allies carved Germany up between them – Hamburg and the north went to Britain; Munich and the south to the Americans; Koblenz and the south-west to the French; Dresden, Leipzig and the east became the Soviet zone. Berlin was divided up between all four. Germany was drastically reduced from its pre-war size. What began in 1938 with a series of expansionist wars now ended with the loss of huge swathes of German territory in 1945.

The rebuilding of Germany was an enormous challenge. Women especially – the *Trümmerfrauen* – 'rubble women' – painstakingly cleared the ruins so that the country's apocalyptic moonscape could become a livable space once more. In many respects, the difficulties of physical rebuilding paled into insignificance, however, before the challenge of psychological reconstruction.

A kind of democracy was quickly achieved in the Western zones. The creation of regional parliaments allowed a fragile democratic framework to be created, even as Stalinist one-party rule was tightened in the East. The growing tensions between the two sides came to a head in June 1948, with the creation in the Western zone of a new currency, the Deutschmark, which replaced the now worthless Reichsmark (the cigarette had long since replaced the Reichsmark for any serious transactions); the creation of the separate Deutschmark confirmed that the Soviet and Western zones now had different political and economic systems – and were thus becoming two separate countries.

In response to Western attempts to introduce the Deutschmark into Berlin, the Russians barred Allied land access to the German capital, in the heart of the Soviet zone. The aim of the blockade was clear: to starve West Berlin into submission, thus allowing all Berlin to fall under Moscow's control. From Stalin's point of view, it must have seemed a reasonable calculation. On this occasion, the Western Allies refused to be outfaced. Instead, American and British planes – the *Rosinenbomber* – 'raisin bombers', as grateful West Berliners named them – provided a lifeline for the city in the months to come. Five months into the airlift, the Communists sought to create a city council which would have juris-diction over both West and East Berlin; the Allies retorted by creating a West Berlin city council, led by the Social Democrat Ernst Reuter. Eventually, after the extraordinary face-off had continued for almost a year, Moscow backed down. Stalin's bluff was called, for almost the only time in his life.

One result of the airlift was that the Western Allies came to be seen as protectors, not just as conquerors. The end of this extraordinary con-frontation, which secured the West's access to West Berlin, seemed to be a victory for democracy. Equally, however, the West–East split was now unbridgeable. The Cold War – foreshadowed by Churchill's 1946 speech in Fulton, Missouri, about 'an iron curtain descending across the conti-nent' – had by now begun in earnest. The *Bundesrepublik Deutschland* – the Federal Republic of Germany, was created in the Western zones. The founding *Grundgesetz* – 'Basic Law', which forms the cornerstone of German democracy to this day, had been hammered out at Herrenchiemsee in Bavaria in a fortnight in summer 1948. Within days of the end of the airlift in May 1949, the *Grundgesetz* was officially approved; national elections throughout the 'temporary' new country were held three months later. The split quickly became official on the other side, too. On 7 October 1949, the German Democratic Republic was officially born out of the Soviet zone.

From now on, it was a question of business as unusual. In the West, parliamentary democracy developed, even as the one-party regime became stronger in the East. There was one thing the two sides had in common: both, in their different ways, sought to draw lines under the past. In East Germany, former Nazis were sometimes severely punished. (German democrats were punished, too, for opposing totalitarianism of any hue; Social Democrats and others who had spent years in Hitler's concentration camps were among thousands interned and killed in the Nazi camp at Buchenwald which the Communists took over after 1945.) But the new Communist authorities washed their hands of a broader responsibility for what had happened between 1933 and 1945. According to the comforting official version, West Germans were, in effect, the per-petrators of Hitler's crimes, and East Germans the victims. There was thus no need for the citizens of the new GDR to confront their involve-ment in their recent history.

The West German government would in the years to come take finan-cial responsibility, by making compensation payments, in the way that East Germany did not. From the start it was clear, however, that most West Germans were eager to move swiftly on. They were unimpressed by the war crimes trials that opened in Nuremberg in November 1945. Martha Gellhorn, who reported on the trials, noted the widespread refusal to acknowledge what Germans and Germany had done. The citizens of Nuremberg, 'looking remarkably fit', kept telling her that the concentration camp photographs plastered over the town 'were Russian propaganda, probably pictures of German prisoners of war'.

A broader de-Nazification process got under way which would in theory ensure that Nazis could no longer run the country. In practice, it meant that old Nazis returned to their desks as if nothing had happened. It is impossible to change the nature of society overnight, especially without the forceful *Gleichschaltung* that Hitler had at his disposal to bend Germany to his own ends. Professional skills are needed to run a country. This softly-softly approach hardly ensured a healthy new start, however. (Memory of the failures of this period, combined with a perhaps distorted understanding of the lessons learned, would have crucial knock-on effects, and cause bitter arguments, after the collapse of another German one-party system, four decades later.) The *Persilschein* – 'Persil certificate' – a piece of paper that washed politically whiter – was popular. Tribunals for screening out those with a Nazi past were described as laundries: you could walk in wearing a brown shirt, and walk out clad in shining white.

Konrad Adenauer, mayor of Cologne before 1933 and now Chancellor of the new *Bundesrepublik*, was himself no friend of the Nazis. (While he was held by the Gestapo, executions of children took place in a nearby room. He later wrote: 'I could hear everything. Before that time, I never really believed that the devil actually exists, that evil truly has power.') Adenauer privately noted the failure by many of his compatriots to confront the reality of what Germans had done to others – and the extent of knowledge, for those who wished to know:

> Even if people did not know exactly what was happening in the camps, people knew that personal liberty and the rule of law was being trampled underfoot, that terrible cruelties were being perpetrated in them; that the Gestapo, our SS and part of our troops in Poland used unparalleled cruelty against the civilian population. The Jewish pogroms of 1933 and 1938 took place in public.

'Don't ask, don't tell' was, however, the standard line. Some, of course, were honest to themselves and their compatriots. Free speech was permitted and the Federal Republic enjoyed a democratic constitution which would come to be envied and admired – not least by other European countries emerging from one-party rule 40 years later. The creation in Hamburg of publications like *Der Spiegel* magazine showed that independent German thought was far from dead, even after the suffocating years of the Third Reich. (*Der Spiegel*, like the weekly *Die Zeit*, is a self-described 'child of the occupation'. Chief midwife was a young British major who believed that an independent press could play a key role in rebuilding German democracy from the ruins. He met up with a 22-year-old by the name of Rudolf Augstein, and was impressed with Augstein's conspicuous reluctance to flatter the occupiers – an unusual trait at that time. Augstein was invited to edit a newsletter, which later became too outspoken for the military censors, forcing Augstein to cut loose. The rest – including Augstein's unchallenged position as the titan of independent journalism in post-war Germany – is publishing history.)

Despite publications like *Der Spiegel*, outspokenness was, however, hardly widespread at this time. The contents of West German schoolbooks from this period is, in this context, revealing. Seen from a contemporary perspective, the contents of those textbooks is sometimes startling, at best. When I first began leafing through the piles of school history books at the Georg Eckert Insitute for Schoolbook Research in Braunschweig – where all schoolbooks used in the Federal Republic since 1945 are gathered under one roof – I knew not to expect a no-holds-barred account of the crimes of the Third Reich. Even so, the extent of the authors' eagerness to avoid confronting the truth was remarkable.

Nazi crimes are treated as almost invisible. There are descriptions of endless military campaigns – Asia, North Africa, the Atlantic, Italy, the Eastern Front, and so on – for all the world as though this had been a classical military war just like any other. There is scarcely a word devoted to the programme of mass murder that lay at the heart of the Third Reich. In much of the writing, it is easy to get the impression that the authors are still impressed by Hitler's achievements. In one typical book, the invasion of Poland is described in tones of breathless excitement. ('The valuable industrial region of Upper Silesia was seized so quickly that nothing there was destroyed. The Polish army was no match for the modern technology of the German forces.') The bombing of Warsaw was regrettable. It came, however, 'it must be said, after repeated calls for surrender'. In other words: if the Poles had been more sensible and accommodating, by surrendering when they were asked to, the destruction of their capital need never have taken place.

In the same book, published in 1956, two short paragraphs deal with 'the fate of the Polish Jews', on the one hand, and the Soviet murder in 1940 of thousands of Polish officers in the Katyn forest, on the other.

Three of the nine lines devoted to 'the fate of the Polish Jews' (other nationalities are not mentioned) are taken up with an emphasis on the innocence of the German army. The killings at Katyn, meanwhile (the author concludes, in tones of endless piety), 'also proved what inhuman acts were possible in this war'. The 'also' neatly removes any pressure from the country which launched and almost completed a programme of mass murder. Instead, we learn that war – all war – is a sad business.

The book quoted above is not the exception but the rule at this time. Parcelling out blame more or less equally between Germany and others is a recurrent theme. There are words of regret when Neville Chamberlain, chief architect of appeasement, resigns in 1940. The British prime minister had, after all, 'made such efforts to keep peace'. (Put differently: he consented to Hitler's dismemberment of Czechoslovakia because it involved 'a faraway country' and 'people of whom we know nothing'.) In this context, Winston Churchill is portrayed as the dangerous warmonger, with Hitler as the peacemaker. Hitler, we learn, 'offered peace in vain' – an offer rejected by the unyielding Churchill because 'he knew that England had time, and that the United States would help'.

We learn that, sadly, none of the countries involved in the Second World War behaved with honour. 'In this war of life and death, neutrality and non-aggression pacts were disregarded.' America (which 'occupied neutral Iceland') and Germany (which 'ignored previous assurances' when attacking Belgium and Holland) appear as equal transgressors. And so on, page after page, book after book. The Second World War, schoolchildren in the 1950s learnt, was distinguished from previous wars by sophisticated technology – by which was meant tanks and aeroplanes. 'In earlier wars, what mattered above all was the bravery of the soldiers; now, military technology was decisive.' A scrupulously planned genocide, carried out with unique thoroughness, is not considered worthy of note.

When Nazi crimes *are* mentioned at this time, it is in the context of the ignorance of ordinary Germans. 'Few Germans knew of these terrible things. Nobody could believe the rumours, although a considerable proportion of the German nation had privately turned away from Hitler.' The isolated attempts at German resistance, meanwhile, receive more space than the Holocaust. Indeed, crimes committed against others are treated as if they were irrelevant. The trial and execution of the plotters of 20 July 1944 – a fraudulent show trial that was shocking enough on its own terms – is described by a 1957 schoolbook as if it were uniquely unjust, in its treatment of opponents of the Third Reich.

Dishonest Democracy

'Never in German legal history,' pupils learn, 'have the accused been treated with such brutality, with such a fanatical lack of consideration as in this trial.' Never, that is, unless the accused were any of the hundreds of thousands of men, women and children in German-occupied eastern Europe whose 'trials' for alleged crimes consisted of being machine-gunned on the spot or burnt alive. (This was not just random killing, though there was plenty of that, too, nor part of the programme of extermination. It was codified justice. In parts of eastern Europe there was a standard tariff: 50 civilians executed for an injured German; 100 for a dead one.)

Mass murder is treated as an afterthought, at best. One book provides a detailed catalogue of the 'horrific' losses of the war – including, for example, how many Germans lost a limb. Then, towards the end of this lengthy account, we are diverted for a moment by a sentence which begins with the words 'Hinzu kamen . . .' – 'In addition came . . .' The full sentence reads, in all its casual inhumanity: 'In addition came the victims who were killed in the concentration camps, the labour camps, the death chambers etc.' After that brief digression, we bounce back on to safer ground – to hear more about Germans who suffered at the hands of others, and about how badly industry was damaged.

In many respects, this 'hinzu kamen' postscript sums up many of the problems that Germany faced through the 1950s and 1960s – on the one hand, the relegation of a unique set of crimes to a brief, passing refer-ence, which allows the theme to be safely ignored; on the other hand, the refusal to engage with the significance of those crimes, for Germany itself. These schoolbooks were not seen as *parti pris* or polemic. On the contrary: in common with school history books all over the world, they reflect a consensus view – in effect, a collective self-portrait. These books reflect the extent that Germany was prepared to tell lies – to itself, to others, and above all to the next generation. The lies would backfire – sometimes peacefully, sometimes violently – in the decades to come.

Very gradually – beginning in the 1960s – the tone of the textbooks changes. After the Eichmann trial in 1961 and the Auschwitz trial that began in 1963, the Holocaust starts to receive more than just a passing mention. Still, however, we find the same contradictory mantra: on the one hand, everybody was always against Nazi crimes; on the other hand, nobody knew. 'Most Germans were shocked by what happened', even though 'those who heard about [the crimes] could not believe it'. For a new German generation, meanwhile, something else would be shocking – the refusal of many of their teachers to confront uncomfortable truths. In future decades, the perception of moral failure between 1933 and

1945 would itself become the new consensus. In the 1950s and 1960s, however, such changes still lay far ahead.

Economically, Germany was by the 1960s back on its feet. Ludwig Erhard, Adenauer's economics minister, was chief architect of the *Wirtschaftswunder* – 'the economic miracle', which impressed Germans and non-Germans alike – and which served as a distraction from the horror that lay behind. In the words of Theodor Heuss, the first president of the new Federal Republic, 'We are the trustees of the most infamous and fraudulent bankruptcy in history. We have practically only one chance – and that is work.' The affluence gave a chance for Germans to bury themselves in the new prosperity, and thus move on. Silence and emotional suppression were the order of the day. In his novel *The Tin Drum*, published in 1959, Günter Grass describes the success of a fashionable restaurant which enjoys huge popularity, although it only serves onions. Grass suggests that the success of the onion cellar is intertwined with Germany's complexes, including its difficulties in addressing the past:

> Until Schmuh put on his golden-yellow onions, the conversation was subdued, forced, dispirited. These people wanted to talk, to unburden themselves, but they couldn't seem to get started; despite all their efforts, they left the essential unsaid, talked around it . . . One gathers that the gentleman over there with the massive head, the intelligent face and soft, almost delicate hands, is having trouble with his son, who is displeased about his father's past . . .

Grass elaborately describes the customers' preparation of this ceremonial meal:

> The ladies and gentlemen peeled the onions with the paring knives. They removed the first, third, blond, golden-yellow, rust-brown, or better still, onion-coloured skin, they peeled until the onion became glassy, green, whitish, damp, and water-sticky, until it smelled, smelled like an onion. Then they cut it as one cuts onions, deftly or clumsily, on the little chopping boards shaped like pigs or fish; they cut in one direction and another until the juice spurted, or turned to vapour . . .

And so it continues, for page after page, until the gastronomic and psychological climax:

What did the onion juice do? It did what the world and the sorrows of the world could not do: it brought forth a round, human tear. It made them cry. At last they were able to cry again. To cry again. To cry properly, without restraint, to cry like mad.

Grass concludes:

Our century, in spite of all the suffering and sorrow, will surely be known to posterity as the tearless century. It was this drought, this tearlessness that brought those who could afford it to Schmuh's onion cellar, where the host handed them a little chopping board, a paring knife for 80 pfennigs, and for 12 marks an ordinary field-, garden- and kitchen-variety onion.

In the fictional onion cellar, tears could flow, courtesy of Schmuh. Out on the real German streets, meanwhile, painful truths were not yet spoken. Countless Germans, like Grass's gentleman 'with the intelligent face and soft, almost delicate hands', did not yet tell their sons and daughters what they wanted to know. The confrontation, when it came, would prove both painful and cathartic. In the meantime, Nazi connections in the 1950s and 1960s were everywhere, as part of what came to be called 'the cold amnesty'. Ministers in Adenauer's government included a former company commander in the SS and a company commander in Hitler's stormtroopers, the SA. One of Adenauer's closest aides was Hans Globke, who was closely associated with the infamous Nuremberg Laws of 1935 which removed basic rights from Jews.

While Nazis were absorbed into the fabric of post-war Germany, those who opposed Nazism were often shunned. More than a decade after the Second World War, Marlene Dietrich – who refused to return to Germany after Hitler took power – was accused of being a traitor and was greeted by banners declaring 'Marlene Go Home!' when she returned to her native Berlin. (She declared flatly: 'The Germans and I no longer speak the same language.' Only many years later would she be honoured in her home city, too.) The businessman Oskar Schindler later became renowned, especially after the release of Steven Spielberg's *Schindler's List* in 1994. By that time, Schindler would be acknowledged as a hero in his native country for the risks he took to save his *Schindlerjuden* from Auschwitz. During his lifetime, however, things were different. When Israel honoured Schindler as a Righteous Gentile in 1961, his business partner refused to work with him, because he was 'a friend of Jews'. When a man called him a 'Jew-kisser', it was Schindler who ended up in court: the judge lectured Schindler and ordered him to pay damages for punching the anti-Semite. Schindler commented: 'I would have taken my own life, if it would not have given them so much satisfaction.'

This was a twilight era. Gradually, the coming of age of a new generation made it difficult to confine the crimes of the Nazis to a '*hinzu kamen*' postscript. The Eichmann and Auschwitz trials made it difficult to leave the embarrassing past behind. As so often, writers formed a kind of moral vanguard. In 1963, Rolf Hochhuth's *The Representative* – adapted by Costa-Gavras, almost 40 years later, as the film *Amen* – addressed the failure to speak out against the Holocaust. The play was critical of Pope Pius XII and the Vatican. There was, however, a broader message, too. The director Erwin Piscator summed up the play's message: 'It is on the basis of this freedom [of action], which everyone possesses, and which everyone possessed during the Nazi period, that we must proceed if we are to assimilate the past.'

Auschwitz itself now became a theme. Peter Weiss, author of *Marat/Sade*, turned the transcripts of the Auschwitz trial into an 'oratorio in eleven songs', *The Investigation*. Weiss emphasizes that his main interest is not in the individuals in the dock. Instead, he sees them as 'symbols of a system in which many others were guilty, and who never appeared in the dock before this court'. Weiss's play highlights the extent to which the Nazi establishment emerged unscathed from the apocalypse that it had unleashed. German businesses like IG Farben made huge profits out of Auschwitz; IG Farben was broken up after 1945, but its constituent companies grew to be more powerful than ever in the years to come. (In another symbolic example of the widespread culture of denial at this time, *Brockhaus*, a leading German encyclopedia, described Zyklon B in the 1960s as a product 'for the extermination of vermin, fruit tree pests and so on'; the reason why the product was notorious throughout the world was passed over in silence.) Many exchanges from the trial reveal the extent to which West Germany itself was still infected by the past. Thus, typically:

PROSECUTOR:
> You and the other directors
> of the big businesses
> achieved through unlimited expendability of human beings
> turnovers of several billion . . .
> Let us remember
> that the successors of these businesses today

have magnificent financial results
and that they are, as the phrase has it,
now in a new expansion phase

DEFENCE:
We demand that the court
take note
of these calumnies

Weiss's play concludes with a ringing appeal from one of the defendants. Like so many Germans at that time, the defendants are eager to present themselves as the real victims.

One should not forget
what happened after the war
and what is still
being done against us.
We all –
I would like to emphasize this once more –
have done nothing but our duty
even if it was sometimes difficult for us
and if we wanted to despair.

Above all, the defendants argue, Germany's economic success is an important reason for everybody to turn their backs on the past:

Today
when our nation has once again
worked itself up
to a leading position
we should deal with other things
than with reproaches
which should be seen
as long outdated.
(Loud agreement from the defendants' bench)

West German society in the 1960s hovered in an empty space between the past and the future. The past was buried in a shallow grave, as depicted in John le Carré's *A Small Town in Germany*, published in 1968. Swirling resentments are hidden under a polite facade, where a populist leader is easily able to rouse the angry crowds by describing how

Germany is always obliged to be wrong: 'Democracy is to visit your conscience on the Germans! Democracy is to know that whatever you do, you will never be as bad as the Germans.' Le Carré's novel is a work of fiction, a successful thriller. The backdrop, however – the unacknowledged instability in the Federal Republic; the growth and popularity of the ever-resentful nationalist right, echoed by the rise of the street violence of the left – was rooted in the German reality of the time (le Carré himself had served as a diplomat and intelligence officer in Germany).

In the 1960s, Germany was still raw because of the wounds which it had inflicted on others – and thus, not least because of its prolonged silence, on itself. Nationalists loathed the *Kollektivschuldlüge* – 'lie of collective guilt'. In practice, that stance was often a mere excuse for turning one's back on the crimes of the past. Within a few years after its founding conference in 1964, the far-right National Democratic Party gained seats in seven of West Germany's regional parliaments. In the ultimate admission of defeat, for a party which was so successful at the polls, there was talk of banning the NPD to prevent it from gaining seats in the federal parliament, the Bundestag.

The strength of the nationalists, in turn, was more than matched by the growing anger of the new generation. By the late 1960s, West Germany was only just beginning to move on. Willy Brandt, who later became Social Democratic chancellor and who played a key role in helping to create greater honesty, was dubbed a 'traitor' because he had supported the anti-Nazi resistance, and had spent the war in exile from Hitler's Germany. Kurt Georg Kiesinger, who became West German chancellor in 1966, had been a member of the Nazi Party from 1933. For 20 years, millions of Germans had been eager not to stare the difficult truth in the face. Now, the children of those serial deniers – not just of the active criminals, but, above all, of those who looked the other way – were themselves coming of age. This new generation wanted clear answers to questions about what had happened in their own country two decades earlier. Soon, the floodgates would open.

4

Fathers and Children

There is no capitalist who does not have a terrorist in his own intimate circle of friends and relations.

(The West German interior minister, Werner Maihofer, acknowledges that support for violence against the establishment is more than an isolated problem)

When I first lived in Germany as a schoolchild in 1968, I stayed on a family farm set amidst beechwoods and rolling countryside near Hamelin, town of the Pied Piper. Germany – though I had little sense of it at the time – was in a state of political upheaval. In a regional election the previous year, the far-right NPD achieved its best-ever result, with almost 10 per cent of the vote. Meanwhile, left-wing violence was exploding on streets of German towns and cities as never before. The news was not all bad: Willy Brandt, who would in due course be respected by Germans from all the main political parties, was now foreign minister. The following year he would replace Kiesinger, the ex-Nazi, as Chancellor. This was, however, a country which was only just beginning to be forced to think about the past, hence the instability.

As a 12-year-old in a foreign country for the first time, my memories from that time are mostly unpolitical. There was the unfamiliar taste of foods like salami, which I had never seen before, let alone eaten. Another startling novelty was central heating, which meant that my bedroom was comfortably warm even while fields outside were covered in snow. In 1960s Britain, wintry weather outside the window generally meant that the bedroom, too, was icy-cold; the warmth of a well-insulated home was a novelty. In addition, however, one set of conversations with my school exchange partner left a lasting impression. My host – intelligent and from a friendly family – explained that Hitler was not as bad as foreigners tried to suggest. I remember being baffled rather than shocked. I was aware that my knowledge of the Third Reich was limited, but it had never occurred to me to see Hitler as anything other than a criminal or a lunatic or both. We tussled back and forth on the issue, unsatisfactorily. Only much later did I understand the context of those views, informed by the confusion that millions of young Germans shared at that time. The weasel-words of the post-war textbooks – reinforced by the evasiveness of teachers, many of whom were former Nazis – meant that such ignorance was preordained unless outspoken parents or an unusual teacher were eager to talk about the past. In the years to come, this historical void would be filled. The change would be radical, but did not come easily. The process also spawned senseless violence of its own.

The year 1968 was a year of rebellion throughout Europe and the United States. In eastern Europe, Polish students protested against the Communist regime, and Czechoslovakia enjoyed its brief Prague Spring before the Soviet tanks came. In Britain and the United States, huge crowds demonstrated against the Vietnam war. In Paris, rioting students ripped up cobblestones as part of the revolution of May 1968, with slogans like 'Let us be realistic, let us demand the impossible!'

The *événements* of 1968 were an extraordinary upheaval in French politics, and rightly became internationally famous. Outside Germany, the 1968 rebellion that engulfed West Germany is less well-remembered. Its impact on Germany was, however, at least as dramatic as the *événements* in France. After 1968, things would never again be the same. Partly, the German protests were on similar themes to those that exercised students at the Sorbonne, Berkeley and elsewhere: Vietnam, capitalism, free love, the bourgeoisie. Beyond that standard mélange, however, the German protests had an additional, crucial impulse. Those who grew up in the 1950s and 1960s repeatedly failed to get clear answers from their parents about what had happened in Germany just 10 or 20 years earlier. The question 'What did you do in the war, father?' rarely received a satisfactory reply. Father – now middle-aged or approaching retirement – usually refused to speak of what he had seen, known or done, unless it was on the safe subject of the hardship of life on the Eastern front. For a new generation, this was no longer sufficient. They scratched at the sores of the past, and scratched and scratched. One friend remembers from this time: 'I asked the important questions, again and again. But I was not always sure that I wanted to hear the answers.'

It was the same story across the Federal Republic. Eventually, that sense of frustration exploded. The immediate trigger of the revolution came on 2 June 1967, during demonstrations against a visit to Berlin by the Shah of Iran. Benno Ohnesorg, a student protester, was shot dead by a policeman while the Shah sat inside the opera house as guest of honour at *The Magic Flute*. The Shah himself was unbothered, telling his hosts: 'These things happen every day in Iran.' Some protesters, meanwhile, decided that Ohnesorg's death was itself a justification for violence against the state. A student named Gudrun Ensslin explained to fellow-protesters on the night of the shooting: 'This is the Auschwitz generation. You can't argue with the people who made Auschwitz. They have weapons and we haven't. We must arm ourselves!'

In many respects, the German revolution seemed mere anarchy loosed upon the world. The demonstrations gathered pace through the autumn of 1967. Rudi Dutschke, the best-known student leader, was seriously wounded in a neo-Nazi assassination attempt just before Easter 1968. Through the spring and summer of that year, there were huge protests and sit-ins all across the country. For some at least, the path to violence was quickly crossed. Ensslin and her boyfriend Andreas Baader fire-bombed two Frankfurt department stores. Baader was arrested – and was then sprung from custody with the help of a well-known television journalist, Ulrike Meinhof. On that day in 1970, the name 'Baader-Meinhof gang' was born – a group whose violence would put its stamp upon the decade.

By now, West Germany was already in the throes of democratic change. Kiesinger, the ex-Nazi, became part of history in 1969. The German President, Heinrich Lübke, was forced to resign over allegations connecting him with the construction of a Nazi concentration camp – a move that would have been unthinkable in earlier years. Brandt, on succeeding Kiesinger, declared that Hitler had finally lost the war, and called for Germany to 'dare more democracy'. In Warsaw in 1970, Brandt made his historic *Kniefall*, dropping to his knees at the monument to the 1943 uprising of the Warsaw Ghetto. 'Under the burden of millions of victims of murder,' he said afterwards, 'I did what human beings do when speech fails them.'

Thus, a new, politically more open Germany began to emerge with respect to the past. Meanwhile, however, the radical violence triggered a clampdown on civil liberties in the present. In 1971, Baader, Meinhof and Ensslin formed the 'Red Army Faction', with a manifesto entitled *The Urban Guerrilla Concept*. The RAF took its name partly in tribute to the damage that the Red Army, on the one hand, and the Royal Air Force, on the other, had done to Nazi Germany. It staged a series of robberies and killings across Germany in the years to come – allegedly in search of a cleaner and more honest Germany. Sometimes, the very fate of the Federal Republic seemed to hang in the balance. Brandt insisted: 'I have seen one German republic come to grief. We will not repeat that experience.' In 1972, the West German government introduced an employment ban which sought to keep radicals out of the civil service – including jobs ranging from primary school teacher to postman. The federal criminal agency held a terrorist index which included almost five million names of suspects or sympathizers. Many in the student movement remained opposed to violence from the start. Nonetheless, the use of terror enjoyed remarkably widespread support. Mao's description of guerrillas as fish amongst the people ('you have to have a sea of people for the guerrillas to swim in') could be seen as applicable to much of West Germany at this time. For the Red Army Faction, the sea of support was broad and deep. In 1971, after the killing by police of hairdresser-turned-gunwoman Petra Schelm, one in four West Germans under the age of 30 said they felt 'a certain sympathy' for the RAF and its struggle. One in 20 said they would be ready to offer their homes to fighters on the run; in north Germany, where the police hunt for the Baader-Meinhof group was focused, the figure was an even more remarkable one in 10.

Put like that, it sounds as if West Germany was falling apart: terrorism and widespread support for street violence, on the one hand (including a long-haired revolutionary by the name of Joschka Fischer) and heavy-handed state repression on the other. As it gradually became clear, this was part of a difficult German journey, not a final destination. The journey had already led from Nazi dictatorship through dishonest democracy to terrorist-threatened democracy. In due course, it would lead to almost-normal democracy, but that still lay years ahead. In 1967, Gitta Sereny noted the German failure to achieve 'public recognition of the truth – a catharsis they have never had and desperately need. This then might indeed become for them an end and a beginning.' Within a few years, that catharsis was taking place. Through the 1970s, the campaign of violence continued. Meanwhile, in discreet parallel to the obvious cancer of terror, the country stumbled towards long-term political health.

When I went to live as a student in West Berlin in 1973, the healthy confrontation with the past had scarcely begun. For many, especially older Germans, it had not yet taken place. One spring evening, in a cinema just off Kurfürstendamm in West Berlin, I watched the newly released *Cabaret*, based on Christopher Isherwood's diaries and stories in *Goodbye to Berlin*. In one of the film's most famous scenes, the customers in the charming, traditional biergarten, young and old together, join in the uplifting 'Tomorrow Belongs to Me'. Only one old man – who has, perhaps, seen too many wars already – sits dolefully apart. The others raise their arms proudly in the Hitler salute. The scene was Hollywood in presentation, but its message was accurate. It reflected the undeniable truth: that millions of Germans felt proud of their Führer and of the Third Reich. For some, that simple truth was a reason for discomfort. I became aware that my neighbour in the cinema, a man in his fifties, was wriggling uncomfortably throughout the biergarten scene. In common with many of his compatriots, support for Hitler was not something of which he wished to be reminded. It was easier to think of the Third Reich as something that he and his countrymen had suffered against their will – or, alternatively, a subject to be put to one side.

Those who questioned the 'cold amnesty' still found themselves socially isolated at this time. When the writer Heinrich Böll defended the student radicals, he was roundly abused as a 'spiritual father of terrorism' for doing so. Böll (who gave a home to his friend and fellow Nobel-prize winner Alexander Solzhenitsyn when the Communists expelled the dissident novelist from Moscow) hit back. In *The Lost Honour of Katharina Blum*, published in 1974, Böll tells the story of an innocent girl caught up in a smear campaign beyond her control. She is viciously hounded by the right-wing tabloid press, which is intent on portraying her as the terrorists' friend and, as such, uninterested in the truth. This new McCarthyism is portrayed as especially distasteful in the context of the totalitarian history that the 'defenders of democracy' are so reluctant to discuss. Böll suggests in *Katharina Blum* that an obliquely critical remark about the Nazi regime, many years earlier, could be enough to tar somebody as a dangerous Communist.

On both sides of the divide, this seemed to be a polemic that could have no resolution – terrorists or friends of terror on the one side, and Nazis or buriers of the past on the other. Change was, however, on its way. Böll's story, which resembled a political pamphlet as much as a conventional work of fiction, was adapted into a successful film. The success of the book and the film can in retrospect be seen as a turning point. From now on, despite the continued violence of the terrorist killers, those who wished to end the old silence were no longer automatically perceived as dangers to society, merely because they spoke out.

One example of the backlash against those who wished to remain silent was a remarkable (and remarkably simple) book published in 1977. The 350-page book consists of comments from essays by thousands of teenagers on a single theme: *What I Have Heard About Adolf Hitler*. The answer, it turned out, was: not much. Hitler was said to be a professor; he was Swiss, Dutch, Italian; he lived in the seventeenth century, the nineteenth century, the 1950s; he was a First World War general, the founder of the East German Communist Party, a leader of German democracy. Naturally, one can always find such ignorance on historical themes. Nonetheless, this was different. Dieter Bossmann, the author-editor, who talks of the 'historic illiteracy on a staggering scale', gave his book, which triggered a national debate, the simple and accurate subtitle: *Consequences of a Taboo*. There are occasional comments of matter-of-fact perceptiveness, like this from 16-year-old Dagmar:

> One reads books – for example, I have read Judith Kerr's *When Hitler Stole Pink Rabbit* – which talk about the fact that the Jews were persecuted. But the exact reason is rarely there in the books. Generally, people just say 'Hitler did this and that', but if the Germans really didn't like what he was planning, why did they do it?

Dagmar's question was one that few of her parents' generation were eager to answer. In explaining the motive behind the publication of *What I Have Heard . . .*, Bossmann quotes the German president, Gustav Heinemann: 'The present is nothing other than a great heap of history under our feet.' Without a sane understanding of the past, in other words, it would be impossible for Germans to find a stable footing in the present or the future. Bossmann concludes his introduction by quoting the partly depressing, partly heartening comments by 17-year-old Udo:

> I know very little about Hitler. In fact, absolutely nothing. I know that Hitler took power in Germany in 1933. And I know that around six million Jews were killed, but why this happened, I don't know. Now comes the question: are mere facts enough, in order to understand these people and this time? Is that dealing with the past, if we are told what happened, but not why? Am I wrong in my conclusion?

Udo was right. More importantly, for Udo's younger brother or sister, things would look different. A new generation of schoolchildren was taught to ask questions, and taught to seek explanations of what had gone wrong. Given its timing, the dramatic impact of Bossmann's book makes historic sense. More than a decade earlier, such a book would have sunk without trace in a society which had no wish to contemplate the destructive effects of a taboo. Even ten years earlier, the theme would still have seemed controversial. By 1977, when *What I Have Heard About Adolf Hitler* was published, the old taboos were ripe for the crushing.

Those who did not wish a bright light to be shone on the unpleasant aspects of German history were still vocal. From now on, however, power would no longer be on the side of those who thought it better for the country that they remain silent. The experience of Hans Filbinger was instructive in this regard. Filbinger, prime minister of Baden-Württemberg, was talked of as a possible president. He was bitterly critical of what he saw as the government's failure to crack down on the subversive left. It was a playwright who forced his humiliation. Rolf Hochhuth's *The Lawyers*, written in 1978, was based on the case of Filbinger himself, who had signed a death sentence on a teenage sailor for desertion in the last days of the war. Filbinger initially denied the allegations, but was obliged to resign. For 30 years, nobody had found his involvement in Nazi justice a serious embarrassment; now, things looked very different.

Terrorist violence continued through much of the decade. Willy Brandt was forced out of office in 1974, after the revelation that Günter Guillaume, one of his closest aides, was an East German spy (a human and political drama that forms the subject of Michael Frayn's twenty-first-century play *Democracy*). Helmut Schmidt succeeded Brandt as chancellor – and the violence got worse. In 1974, a senior judge was murdered in Berlin. In 1975, two diplomats were killed in Stockholm. In January 1976, supporters of the Baader-Meinhof group joined 'Carlos', the world's best-known terrorist, in an attack on a summit in Vienna of the organization of oil-exporting countries, Opec; three people were killed. (One participant, Hans-Joachim Klein, would appear in court a quarter of a century later – an appearance which reverberated in the politics of twenty-first-century Germany.) In July of that year, Germans were involved in the hijack to Entebbe of an Air France jet en route from Tel Aviv to Paris; the hijackers demanded the release of 40 prisoners, including members of the RAF. In 1977, the cycle of violence reached a bloody climax. In April, the public prosecutor, Siegfried Buback, his driver and a bodyguard were assassinated. In July, the head of Dresdner Bank, Jürgen Ponto, was shot dead at home. He opened the security gate because Susanne Albrecht, who introduced the killers into his house, was a family friend; her sister was Ponto's goddaughter. In September, terrorists kidnapped the head of the employers' federation, Hanns-Martin Schleyer – and killed his driver and three bodyguards. Then, on 13 October, a Lufthansa jet was hijacked to the Somali capital, Mogadishu. The hijackers killed the pilot and demanded the release from the high-security prison at Stammheim of their RAF comrades, including Baader and Ensslin. On the night of 17–18 October, German special forces stormed the plane and freed the passengers. That night, Baader and Ensslin both committed suicide in Stammheim. (Many sympathizers remained convinced for years afterwards that it was murder. They were wrong. In his updated edition of *The Baader-Meinhof Group*, Stefan Aust notes that one of the surprises that emerged from newly available evidence in the 1990s was 'how precisely people inside the RAF knew about the suicide of the prisoners at Stammheim, and how systematically they had woven the legend of murder'.). The RAF, in turn, murdered Schleyer and dumped his body in the boot of a car, announcing that the end of his 'corrupt and miserable existence' was in revenge for the death of their comrades.

This came to be known as Germany's 'hot autumn'. It was understandable if, from the perspective of 1977, it seemed that the country was spiralling lethally out of all control. In retrospect, the terrible weeks and months of *der deutsche Herbst* – 'the German Autumn', can be seen as the beginning of the end in this terrible decade. With reference to the involvement of Susanne Albrecht in the murder of her sister's godfather and her parents' friend, interior minister Werner Maihofer declared: 'There is no capitalist who does not have a terrorist in his own intimate circle of friends and relations. There are no circles, however high, in our society which do not have people like Susanne Albrecht somewhere in their immediate or more distant vicinity.' Until now, that had been true to a remarkable degree. From now on, that was about to change.

The 1970s were marked by murderous violence, on the one hand, and stepped-up surveillance and repression of radicals on the other: the West German state seemed inclined to believe that the anti-terrorist end always justified the means. This, however, was also the beginning of a renewal, which Germany had needed for so long. The employment ban of 1972 was intended to prevent the 'long march through the institutions' which radicals called for in 1968. In some respects, the ban had the opposite effect. True, the men and women of violence did not succeed. The long march of the peaceful radicals through those same institutions was, however, successful beyond all their hopes and fears.

Even as the German Autumn reached its bloody climax, a new radical movement was born with historic implications. In explicit contrast to what came before, a founding tenet of the new environmental party was its opposition to violence of all kinds. *Gewaltfrei* – 'violence-free', was an important slogan from the start. Through 1977, the new not-quite party gained momentum. It soon came to seem an unstoppable force. Despite the concerns of many about becoming too involved in the political establishment, the Greens put up candidates in elections in 1978. In the European elections in 1979, more than a million Germans voted Green; the party broke through the five per cent hurdle to gain its first seats in a regional parliament in the same year. Then, in January 1980, two years after the murder of Schleyer and the suicides at Stammheim, the Greens organized an official founding party conference in Karlsruhe.

One can be reasonably confident in stating that none of the 1000 delegates attending that chaotic two-day meeting – under the slogan 'ecological, democratic, social, non-violent' – could have imagined for a moment the prospects for their new party in the years to come. Within just a few years, the Greens would gain seats in a string of regional parliaments, and then in the Bundestag in Bonn. By the end of the century, they would form part of a ruling government coalition in Berlin. A Green politician would be the foreign minister of a united Germany. For delegates in Karlsruhe that day, the prospect of such change would have seemed a bizarre (and, for many, disturbing) fantasy. It was just one indication of how far Germany was about to move.

5

Radicals Without Bombs

Those who had begun by turning away as anti-fascists from their parents' generation had ended with the same deeds and language as the Nazis.

(Joschka Fischer, the future foreign minister,
explains why he broke with the political violence of the 1970s)

The swirling patterns of history are sometimes surprising. If one were asked to list possible catalysts of social and political change, an imported TV mini-series would be unlikely to top the list. Student rebellion, a public act of contrition by a government leader, the creation of a new political party: each of these markers of change in West German society in the 1970s has identifiable parallels elsewhere. Few could have predicted, however, that an important milestone in the shaping of modern Germany would prove to be the broadcast of a television tearjerker. *Holocaust*, whose stars included Meryl Streep and Sam Wanamaker, was aired in West Germany on four nights in a single week in January 1979. Elsewhere, critics had derided the series as trite – 'genocide shrunken to the level of *Bonanza* with music appropriate to *Love Story*' was one assessment. Certainly, there was little surprising about the content of *Holocaust*. The sometimes clunking storyline portrays two sets of parallel lives: we meet the family of Josef Weiss, doctor and assimilated Jew, on the one hand, and the family of Erik Dorf, a careerist member of the SS (and patient of Josef Weiss), on the other. As an aide to Reinhard Heydrich, Dorf becomes intimately involved in the implementation of the Holocaust. By dint of some contrived twists of the plot, he witnesses (and thus shares with the audience) many key episodes in the history of the Third Reich.

Thus, we are introduced to the Nuremberg decrees in 1935 and the Wannsee conference which sealed the details of the Final Solution in 1942. We are shown deportations, the ghetto and the camps. As far as the facts go, none of this was very startling. Details of the concentration camps, so notably absent in the years after the war, were by the end of the 1970s standard fare in school textbooks. Nonetheless, *Holocaust* marked a watershed. Suddenly, viewers were confronted with the fact that this was about flesh-and-blood human beings. In truth, it never required a great leap of the imagination to realize that Hitler's millions of victims lived real lives, with which ordinary Germans might be able to identify. Nonetheless, it was a leap too few had made, until those extraordinary few days.

The series gave life to Grass's fictional onion cellar. At last, human tears began to be wept. Ordinary Germans made an emotional connection for the first time. The series was watched by 20 million Germans; tens of thousands telephoned with questions and comments – about knowledge and ignorance, about responsibility and washing one's hands. A typical commentary in *Stern* magazine was headlined: 'Yes, I was too cowardly'.

'Did you know?' is the question that our children and grand-children have been asking us, since *Holocaust* finished on Friday . . . We would have had to know, if we had only wanted to know. No soldier in the east could be unaware of the shootings of Jews, the mass graves, and, during the retreat, the disinterred and burnt piles of corpses . . . The Holocaust is everywhere. Even today, even after 40 years.

Following *Holocaust*, the real impact of Nazi crimes could no longer be consigned to the status of a 1950s-style '*hinzu kamen*' afterthought. Entire books were published, devoted to the social and political effects of the series. One of these books summed it up: 'A whole nation began – as the result of a television film – suddenly to discuss openly the darkest chapter of its history.' The *Holocaust* effect was not simply a one-week wonder. The television series paved the way for a vote in the Bundestag a few months later, which finally abolished for all time the statute of limitations on Nazi-era crimes. Year after year, Germans had been trying to draw a final line under history, arguing that enough was enough. A statute of limitations was originally due to come into force in 1960, 15 years after the war. That was reluctantly extended to 1965, which allowed the Auschwitz trial to take place. In 1964, after much wrangling, the Bundestag agreed to extend the cut-off date by another five years to

1970. That, in turn, was extended to 1980 after much argument. Now, it turned out that what was intended as a final full stop merely marked the beginning of a new chapter – a chapter defined by the acknowledgement that such crimes could never be treated as mere history. After *Holocaust*, it was agreed that there could be no statute of limitations. From now on, the attitude could be summarized as 'Enough is never enough' – an absolutism which would in due course bring complications of its own.

It was in the 1980s that the *Bundesrepublik* which we recognize today began to be born, a country where the new generation felt able to grasp historical nettles which had seemed too painful for their parents' generation to touch. Seen from a twenty-first-century perspective, it is easy to think of the greatest changes in modern Germany as having taken place in 1989 and 1990, with the unification of the country. In many obvious respects, that is accurate. In addition, however, the precondition for the Germany that we see today was the generational change that was by the 1980s already well under way.

In 1982, the Christian Democrat Helmut Kohl succeeded Schmidt as Federal German chancellor, after 13 years of Social Democrat rule. The bulky Kohl, who liked to boast of his ordinariness, was endlessly mocked and criticized by German liberals for talking of the *Gnade der späten Geburt* – the 'blessing of late birth'. His critics regarded this as an unforgivable washing of hands, implying that Germans of a later generation bear no responsibility for their history. In reality, Kohl's phrase – though perhaps inappropriate in the context of a visit to Israel; diplomatic timing was never Kohl's strong point – was apt. A generation too young to have known the pressures of the Nazi regime first-hand, and thus too young to have personal blood on their hands, was fortunate to have avoided that experience. They never had to confront the perhaps bitter knowledge of whether or not they would have acquiesced in evil. They did not know whether, seen in terms of the Milgram experiment, they would have killed or allowed others to kill (statistically, as Milgram's experiment made clear, these were the more likely options), or whether they would have been one of the principled minority who retained a moral perspective.

It is precisely this lack of knowledge and thus lack of personal guilt which made it easier for the late-born to speak out, through the 1970s and increasingly in subsequent decades. It is indeed a 'blessing of being born late' that younger German generations were never confronted with those choices. Equally, the new openness should not be seen as worthless, merely because it comes from those who did not experience the Third Reich themselves. Reproaches about *damals* – 'at that time' – as in 'you can never understand what it was like to live at that time' – are not, in the end, a sufficient answer. The new openness which began in the 1980s seeks to comprehend how a society – any society – can take a murderously wrong turn. That, in turn, helps provide a valuable form of political inoculation, with lessons that go well beyond Germany's own experience, allowing 'Never again!' to become more than just a pious phrase.

Even in the 1980s, many Germans still found it difficult to deal with the past. The teenager Anna Rosmus enraged local dignitaries in the picture-postcard Bavarian town of Passau when she wrote an essay in 1981 on 'My home town in the Third Reich'. Rosmus's research revealed the extent to which her town was still steeped in denial. The local bishop told Rosmus (in a phrase that Martha Gellhorn would have recognized from her travels through Germany in 1945): 'We had no Jews in the town, no. Passau was such a small town, we never saw Jews.' It was untrue. Rosmus traced a Jewish woman who sat next to the future bishop for years on the same school bench. There were eight concentration camps in the area – three in the town, five in the surrounding countryside. Hundreds of Jews were deported from the main railway station. In Rosmus's words, 'The mayor of Passau picked out several of them personally and brought them to the train station, and told them: "Now you have to leave forever."' Their property, much of it now a modern shopping mall, was confiscated and Aryanized. Modern Passauers did not wish to speak of such things. Germany was, however, on the cusp of change. It was a German director who a few years later made a film based on Rosmus's story, *The Nasty Girl*, documenting the hostile reaction to Rosmus's work. In future, the deniers of Passau, and those like them, would increasingly be on the defensive, not the offensive.

Honesty about the crimes of the past came to be prized, not feared. Photographs of German suffering in the early post-war textbooks – ruined cities, humiliated prisoners, frightened German children – had by the 1980s been replaced by photographs of German crimes, at home and abroad. The make-it-human techniques of *Holocaust* were imitated, too. German schoolchildren learned about ordinary, named Jewish families, to gain an understanding of what the Final Solution meant in human terms.

For many years after 1945, polite talk about democracy helped to conceal the fact that few of the underlying essentials had changed, with regard to understanding the country's history. In the 1980s, by contrast, changes came thick and fast. On the 40th anniversary of the end of the war, the German president, Richard von Weizsäcker – who served as a junior officer on the Eastern front, and whose father was a senior Nazi diplomat – addressed questions of ignorance and knowledge more openly than ever before. 'When the unspeakable truth of the Holocaust became known at the end of the war,' he declared, 'all too many of us claimed that we had not known anything about it or even suspected anything.' Controversially for many older Germans, von Weizsäcker insisted that 8 May 1945 should be seen not as a date of defeat but of liberation. A date, in short, when the new Germany could be born.

A partial retort to von Weizsäcker came in the form of a broadside from the historian Ernst Nolte the following year. An article in the *Frankfurter Allgemeine Zeitung* marked the launch in earnest of the *Historikerstreit* – 'quarrel of the historians'. The phrase sounds abstruse. In German terms, it was doomed to be anything but. The *Historikerstreit* can be seen as defining the battle for the soul of modern Germany. Nolte's article was entitled: 'The past which will not pass away: a speech that could be written but not spoken.' Nolte believed he had been 'uninvited' to deliver his planned speech in Frankfurt, because his thesis – in effect, that one could talk too much about the Holocaust – was considered unacceptable. All this talk of the Final Solution, he suggested, diverted attention from 'the presence of "genocide" in Vietnam yesterday and in [the Soviet occupation of] Afghanistan today'. Nolte portrays Auschwitz as a consequence of or a response to the horrors of the 'Asiatic' Stalinist regime and the camps across the Soviet Union in which millions died: 'Did the Gulag Archipelago not come before Auschwitz? Was the class murder of the Bolsheviks not the logical and factual precursor of the Nazis' racial murder?'

In the refined pages of a historical journal – or as an intellectual debate that could take place anywhere else in the world – a discussion along the lines of 'Who was the worse tyrant, Stalin or Hitler?' might not seem especially controversial. Martin Amis's *Koba the Dread* partly addresses the theme, noting the traditional reluctance of some on the left to condemn the killing of millions in the Soviet Union with the same vigour with which they condemn the crimes of the Third Reich. Anne Applebaum makes the same point in *Gulag*, her history of the Soviet camps.

In Germany, by contrast, comparisons between Nazi Germany and the Soviet Union could never seem historically neutral, however many years have passed. Many Germans understood Nolte's verbal hand grenade as an attempt to bury Germany's past, by relativizing Hitler's and Germany's own crimes. Such relativization – suggesting that Nazi crimes were regrettable, but not unique – had been an integral part of the self-justification of the 1950s, when crimes committed by both sides were balanced out, thus leading to the reassuringly generalized conclusion that 'inhuman acts were possible'. In the 1950s, that deliberately fuzzy line seemed uncontroversial. Now, by contrast, the uniqueness of the Holocaust was, for most Germans, a given. Nolte's arguments were a red rag to the liberal bulls. Most bullish of all was Jürgen Habermas, professor of philosophy at Frankfurt University, who 20 years earlier had warned of 'left fascism' but had also been an *éminence grise* for rebellious students there. Now, this elder spokesman of the left complained of what he saw as the danger inherent in Nolte's approach:

> He kills two flies with one blow. The Nazi crimes lose their singularity because they become at least understandable as a response to the (continuing) threats of destruction by the Bolsheviks. Auschwitz shrinks to the format of a technical innovation and is explained as the 'Asiatic' threat from an enemy who is still outside the gates.

The debate went back and forth in the months to come – not just between the academics, but spilling on to the front pages of the newspapers. The central question, sometimes implicit and sometimes explicit: can one draw a *Schlussstrich* – 'a final line', under German history? The historian Christian Meier laid out the case for memory, making an argument which would be widely accepted in Germany in the years to come. Meier notes: 'We live in a fairly stable democracy, and try to be a normal people. Should we not finally finish with all the reproaches?' The unambiguous answer, he concludes, is no.

> Just as collective guilt does not exist, so equally we are responsible for what was done by us and in our name, if German history is to belong to us. Because that is so, the younger ones among us must also keep the memory of the crimes alive. We owe that to the victims. If we try in any way to muddy the clearcut condemnation of what took place, by relativizing and by excuses, then any attempt to win a new relationship to our history is built on sand.

Arguments about alleged revisionism would occur again and again in the years to come. The main argument – 'It's time to move on', versus 'How dare anybody think of moving on?' – remained the backdrop to all German debate. By the time that the most bitter stage of the *Historikerstreit* was over, only three years before the fall of the Berlin

Wall, it seemed like a score-draw. In reality, those who wanted a final line to be drawn under history were fighting a battle which could never be fully won. To be exact: it could only be won by *not* fighting the battle. We must assume (and hope) that Germany in 500 years' time will no longer feel obsessed by the burden of the crimes of the Third Reich. But where might we draw a line? In 100 years' time? 50? 20? None of the above, one might argue, if some continue to insist that the debates must end, *right now*! Those who actively argue for those crimes to be put to one side are, by so doing, postponing the date when that can happen.

Practitioners of the Alexander technique – which aims to reduce stress-induced pain through the achievement of a healthy and relaxed posture – like to warn of the dangers of 'endgaining'. 'Endgaining' – thinking constantly about the desired goal – is perceived as destructive because the very act of thinking about how to relax makes it more difficult for a relaxed posture to be achieved. In political terms, Germany faces the same challenge. By focusing on the past, it becomes easier for Germany to move on from its history. If, however, the moving on becomes the goal, not the result – in other words, political endgaining – Germany's complexes are not buried but revived. Gradually, memory must be woven into the fabric of the country. This is a process that began before the *Historikerstreit* and has continued steadily – despite occasional apparent lurches in the other direction – ever since.

Of all the main political parties, questions of memory have been most important for the Greens, who in the years after their founding conference in Karlsruhe in 1980 became a national force to reckon with. The party's most obvious agenda was, as the name suggested, concerned with environmental and nuclear issues. Hundreds of thousands demonstrated against the construction of a nuclear reactor, against a reprocessing plant and against the proposed deployment of new US missiles in Germany. The distinctive red-and-yellow '*Atomkraft? Nein Danke!*' stickers – 'Nuclear power? No thanks!', soon became a booming export, seen in windows or on car bumpers (especially the chugging little Citroen 2CVs – not gas-guzzlers, naturally) all across western Europe.

Issues like acid rain, recycling and nuclear power provided themes around which huge numbers of (mostly young) Germans could gather. Environmental issues were not, however, the only reason for voting Green. A strong bent towards non-violence was important from the start. This was partly for self-interested reasons. Germany was likely to be on the front line of a European war between Nato and the Warsaw Pact, if things got that bad; and in the early 1980s, many believed that that they might do. Almost three million Germans signed an appeal against the deployment of US Cruise and Pershing missiles for use in the German theatre of war.

The Green identity was bound up with the party's abhorrence of the Nazi past. In that sense, the party could be seen as the natural heirs of the Sixty-eighters. But, because it was also dedicated to non-violence, it was also the opposite of the terrorism of the 1970s, the deadly outgrowth of radical German politics in the previous decade. The Greens, whose best-known leaders were the charismatic young Petra Kelly and her companion, Gert Bastian, a former general, were a broader church than the sectarian revolutionaries which preceded them. One of the party's founders was a former Christian Democrat. Daniel Cohn-Bendit – who first gained fame as the student leader Danny the Red in Paris in 1968 – became a leading Green, as did Otto Schily, former defence lawyer for members of the Baader-Meinhof group. The Greens rarely used the word *Deutschland* in their literature: the word smacked too much of unpleasant history even to be spoken aloud. Nonetheless, many Greens were indeed seeking *das andere Deutschland* – 'the other Germany'. This would soon prove to be more than just a fringe movement. It affected and reflected changes taking place in all the main political parties, as modern Germany sought a new and more comfortable identity.

From early on, there was a battle for the soul of the anti-authoritarian Greens, between the *Realos* – the 'realists', on the one hand, and the *Fundis* – the 'fundamentalists', on the other. The *Fundis* were constantly wary of their own party's success, believing that power (and dealings with power) were fundamentally corrupting. Meanwhile, however, the party's popularity continued to grow. In 1983, a *Realo* landmark was achieved when the Greens gained seats in the federal parliament. The 'long march through the institutions' that the radicals talked of in 1968 was beginning to become real. It was at this time that the 33-year-old troublemaker Joseph Fischer – known to all by the diminutive name Joschka – took his seat in the Bundestag. In the months to come, his stream of irreverent repartee made him a media star. Like a Shakespearean jester, the future foreign minister always had a one-liner ready with which to put the king himself in his place. His easy repartee embarrassed Helmut Kohl's ruling Christian Democrats, and Kohl himself, more successfully than the often half-hearted opposition of the Social Democrats.

Despite his ruffian image (on one occasion, he was excluded from the chamber for foul language), Fischer became a parliamentary insider, too. He would later express gratitude to Wolfgang Schäuble – then seen as Kohl's crown prince, later Fischer's opposition shadow and a candidate to be German president – for teaching him the tricks of the parliamentary trade. Still, though, the Greens remained the quintessential outsiders. Most of them preferred it that way. When they entered parliament, they carried flowers with them. The sunflowers or sprigs of yellow forsythia at every desk – a Green ritual, a kind of parliamentary uniform – served as a way of emphasizing how different they wanted to be from the dull men in suits. Their absence from executive power left them with the unchallenged moral high ground. Even that could not last. Soon, they were sharing power, too.

On 12 December 1985, the Greens – the eternal rebels – entered a government coalition with Social Democrats in the state of Hesse, which includes Frankfurt. Fischer, with the environmental portfolio, was sworn in as the first Green minister in the world. He marked the occasion by wearing a sports jacket, jeans and a new pair of trainers specially purchased for the occasion. 'My old ones are over the hill,' he confided to his diary. 'Shod in magnificent white, I shall take the oath in the state parliament in Wiesbaden, and then: never again trainers!' Those trainers are now in a museum, as a symbol of the new, not-quite-so-obedient German style. A small, Fischer-shaped chunk of history.

The Greens preached – at sometimes exhausting length, some might say – the importance of tolerance, and of what the murdered revolutionary Rosa Luxemburg had famously called the *Andersdenkende* – 'those who think differently'. That was a key difference with what had come before. Some of the Sixty-eighters were so driven by their righteous anger that they scarcely noticed when they or their comrades were as reluctant to accept dissent as the Nazis themselves had been. For the Greens, by contrast, dissent was in the blood. They were one of the most argumentative political parties the world has seen – not least over the issue of whether they wanted a share of power, or whether they regarded such a prospect as a dangerous soiling of principles.

Fischer, the old revolutionary, soon became a convinced Green *Realo* – a change of attitudes that many of his generation went through at this time. Fischer himself was no stranger to violence. As would be revealed three decades later, a helmeted Fischer was photographed beating an unprotected policeman to the ground in Frankfurt in 1973. Through the 1970s, Fischer was at just one degree of separation from men and women who espoused and practised terrorist violence. Many years later, in a different century, he would stand in a courtroom on behalf of one of those friends. For Fischer, a key moment which persuaded him to condemn his comrades' love of violence was the hijacking of the Air France plane in 1976, which ended with the Entebbe raid, when Israeli forces successfully stormed the plane. One episode during that hijacking became Fischer's personal Damascus. German terrorists helped to separate Jewish and non-Jewish passengers. The non-Jewish passengers were released; if the authorities did not meet the hijackers' demands, the Jewish passengers would be killed. The historical echoes of this selection process were impossible to ignore. Fischer knew two of the Entebbe hijackers, killed when the plane was stormed. Some of his Frankfurt friends were indignant at the deaths. He himself believed, however, that an uncrossable line had been crossed: 'If Germans again become associated with carrying out a selection of Jews and non-Jews, they deserve no less.' Fischer argued later that 'those who had begun by turning away as anti-Fascists from their parents' generation had ended with the same deeds and language as the Nazis.' The Auschwitz-style *Selektion* was, he suggested 'an abyss'.

A year later came the Mogadishu hijacking – the deaths of the hijackers, the deaths of Baader and others in Stammheim high-security jail, and the murder of Hanns Martin Schleyer. Schleyer had worked in Prague with Reinhard Heydrich, architect of the Final Solution. Now, it seemed as though those who claimed the right to kill, allegedly in order to purge Germany of its Nazi past, had learned nothing from their country's brutal history. ('Schleyer's death does not bear comparison with our pain and our anger at the massacre of Mogadishu and of Stammheim,' read the RAF communiqué announcing his murder.) They acted, as Fischer noted, 'as political killers, with a horribly good conscience and with the same methods'. Fischer turns the spotlight partly on his own views: 'What shocks me is that we did not see how quickly we came close to doing what we had rejected so strongly in our fathers' generation.'

Following this most sordid of confrontations, Fischer and many others of his generation became disillusioned with *all* politics, that of the establishment and of the powerfully violent anti-establishment alike. In an essay published in 1978 – headlined 'Why not, after all?' – he explored the possibilities of reconciling the apparently irreconcilable, signalling his gradual move away from the *Sponti* ('spontaneous') world of street clashes towards the emerging Greens. Fischer puts the choices in stark existential terms:

> Why did we not vote Brandt in 1969, nor in 1972? Why have we never voted . . . and are supposed to vote now? If it is not just a matter of voting, but because even the building-up of a parliamentary ecological party depends on the *Spontis*, that makes us think less of elections than of Hamlet's 'To be or not to be . . .'

In the 1980s, the worst of German terrorism was over. Liberals began to untangle their confused sympathies of previous years. Films like Rainer Werner Fassbinder's *The Third Generation* and Margarethe von Trotta's *The German Sisters*, released in 1979 and 1981 respectively, are deeply ambivalent. *The Third Generation* (Fassbinder: 'I don't throw bombs, I make films') treats terrorists almost as if they were participants in a surreal farce – Baader-Meinhof meets Dada. *The German Sisters* gives a barely fictionalized account of the life and death of RAF leader Gudrun Ensslin and her sister Christiane (to whom the film is dedicated); the Ensslin character is praised after her death as 'an extraordinary woman'. The film implies – wrongly, as it later turned out – that Ensslin's death was murder, not suicide. Such ambivalence was common among liberals at that time, even as they distanced themselves from the permissiveness of violence in previous years. (After Ulrike Meinhof's death, the theologian Helmut Gollwitzer had described her as a woman 'who made her life hard by allowing the misery of others to affect her so much'.)

Through the 1980s, the Federal Republic continued to mature and to discover real stability at last, replacing the artificial stability – based on living a lie – of previous decades. That, in turn, continued to weaken the support for the RAF. In the 1970s there had been widespread underlying support for violent solutions which would shake the establishment to its core. Many young Germans and the wealthy *schili* (the *schicke Linke* – 'chic left') had been ready to follow Rudyard Kipling's prescription for ignoring nefarious activities – 'Watch the wall, my darling, while the gentlemen go by' – for example by offering a bed for the night. Now, that was long gone. The RAF was not yet dead. But the Maoist sea for the guerrillas to swim in was almost dry. Instead, Germans on left and right alike felt a loyalty to the democratic achievements of the West German state as it approached its 40th birthday in 1989. Common-or-garden patriotism, such as other nations enjoyed, remained unthinkable. German history was too complicated for that. In the meantime, however, what Jürgen Habermas and others described as *Verfassungspatriotismus* – 'constitutional patriotism' – was strongly embedded. Habermas, who had opposed violence from the start, argued that the strength of Germany's new attachment to democratic values was partly 'because of Auschwitz' – in other words, the lessons learned. Warning against a revival of strictly national values, he argued that Germany must remain anchored in the West: 'The only patriotism which does not alienate us from the West is constitutional patriotism.'

By the end of the 1980s, the Federal Republic was affluent, stable, and – more than ever before – honest about its past. That did not yet make it a happy place. The subtitle of a respected book on modern Germany, published in 1989, describes Germans as 'rich, bothered and divided'. Within a few months, new editions would need a change of name. The permanent division of Germany proved to be not so permanent, after all. The revolution that was about to erupt would make Germany less bothered (we're united, hurrah!) and more bothered (we're united, God help us and the world!) in the years to come. These would be a tumultuous few years.

6

Falling Walls

The German Democratic Republic is only thinkable as a socialist state. What justification would a capitalist GDR have next to a Federal Republic? None, of course.

> (Otto Reinhold, leading East German ideologist, explains why
> East Germany did not wish to contemplate reform)

We are ready and willing to defend what we have achieved . . . If need be, with weapons in our hands.

> (Through a reader's letter in the *Leipziger Volkszeitung*, the
> Communist regime signals its readiness to use the Tiananmen Square
> option against demonstrators in Leipzig on 9 October 1989)

I felt as if I could fly. Now we knew that there was no going back. It was the most fantastic day I have ever known.

> (A demonstrator describes her feelings when she realized that the regime,
> faced with the scale of the Leipzig protest, backed down at the last moment
> from threats to use violence. A month later, the Berlin Wall was down)

By 1989, the two Germanies – the Federal Republic in the west, and the German Democratic Republic in the east – had reached an almost comfortable form of middle age. As both countries approached their 40th birthdays, there was a weary mutual tolerance, if not much affection. The 1987 edition of the *Random House Dictionary of English* merely acknowledged the obvious, when its editors relegated the concept of a single Germany to the dustbin of history, by defining the G-word as 'a former country in central Europe'. This past-tense view of the country's historical geography was widely shared by Germans in East and West alike. It had been implicit for many years. It became explicit in the 1970s, with Willy Brandt's policy of *Ostpolitik* – a cautious dialogue with and opening up to the East. *Ostpolitik* was by no means universally popular, not least because it implied acceptance of Germany's new eastern border, including the loss of German territory to Poland and the Soviet Union. There were, however, practical benefits – not least for separated families who could see each other more easily at last. The gradual normalization of relations between the two German states continued under Brandt's successor, Helmut Schmidt, and reached its high point under Helmut Kohl, 38 years after Germany was formally divided in two.

In September 1987, West Germany rolled out the red carpet for East Germany's 75-year-old leader, Erich Honecker, on a visit to Bonn. It was the first official visit by an East German leader – and, as it turned out, the last. The band played both East and West German anthems, and the two flags flew side by side: black, red and gold for West Germany; black, red and gold plus the socialist hammer-and-compass emblem for the honoured Communist from the East. In short: East Germany, everyone agreed, was here to stay. Politicians on left and right agreed that the idea of unification was a mere chimera, and mocked those who thought otherwise. Egon Bahr, one of the Social Democrats' leading thinkers, said talk of reunification was 'lying and hypocrisy'. Wolfgang Schäuble, one of Kohl's closest allies, argued: 'Reunification is completely beyond reality.'

Such acceptance had been a long time coming. After 1945, West German politicians repeatedly insisted the separateness of the two Germanies was a temporary aberration, and that the country would come together again, even as the division continued apace. Konrad Adenauer implausibly declared that the signing in May 1949 of the Basic Law, and the creation of a separate Federal Republic, was 'a major contribution to the reunification of the German people'. One reason why the Basic Law was not called by its proper name, a constitution, was to emphasize the allegedly temporary nature of the arrangement.

In the Soviet zone, acceptance of the new German Democratic Republic was, initially at least, by no means a given. There were many early acts of defiance – such as when, in 1950, a Dresden football crowd pelted the guest of honour, Communist Party leader Walter Ulbricht, with tomatoes. (Shortly afterwards, the entire team defected en masse to the West.) Most dramatic of all was the workers' uprising of 1953. It began on 15 June, with small strikes against raised norms on the huge construction site where an avenue named after the late Soviet dictator was being built – Stalinallee, the 'first socialist street in Berlin'. The following day, what began as small protest against the unrealistic new targets on Stalinallee quickly built up into a march of thousands. Within a few hours, the demands had changed. Slogans called not just for the scrapping of the raised norms. By the end of the day, there were calls for a general strike.

On the morning of 17 June, tens of thousands of protesters gathered in the centre of East Berlin. Hundreds of thousands were on strike all across the country. Demonstrators called for unity and free elections, and the Communist red flag was torn down from the Brandenburg Gate in the heart of Berlin, to the cheers of the crowds. This was the first major uprising against one-party rule in the Soviet bloc – and remained one of the largest that the region would see, along with later rebellions in Hungary and Poland, for the next four decades. For a few hours on 17 June, the very existence of the four-year-old East German state seemed in question. Communist Party and state security offices were ransacked in towns and cities all over East Germany, and propaganda posters were torn down. Meanwhile, violence was no object in suppressing the uprising. Hundreds of Soviet tanks moved on to the streets. Demonstrators were shot dead and a state of emergency declared. Around 100 people were killed (even now, the exact numbers remain unclear). As one striker later remembered:

When the police pointed their guns at us and shouted: 'Back, or we shoot!', the procession came slowly to a halt. I told the policeman that we were workers from Köpenick, but they said if we didn't go back they had orders to shoot. The crowd behind us moved slowly back. When we were a good 50 metres away, they shot anyway.

By the end of 17 June, the unbridled official violence meant that the protests were effectively crushed. In the weeks to come, many protesters received long prison sentences, others were sent to Siberian labour camps, and others again were executed. East Germany would take decades to recover from the wounds that were inflicted on the East Germans that day. Kurt Bartel ('KuBa'), head of the official writers' union, rebuked protesters for their insolence in daring to rebel against an unwanted regime. 'For you and for the peace of the world, the Soviet army and the comrades of the People's Police kept watch. Are you not ashamed, as I am?' Bartel, with the apparatchik's well-practised arrogance, argued that East German workers would 'have to build much and well and behave wisely in the future', before 'this shame of yours' could be forgotten. Bertolt Brecht had a ready retort in his poem *The Solution*.

If the people had forfeited the confidence of the government, he suggested:

> Would it not be easier
> In that case for the government
> To dissolve the people
> And elect another?

The dissolution and election of a new people was, in 1953, only marginally more implausible than the prospect of East Germans being allowed to choose their own rulers. The one-party state now ruled and would continue to do so, almost unchallenged, with an ever stronger grip. In the years to come, following the trauma of 17 June, the GDR gradually settled down into its own abnormal normality. One aspect of this abnormality was that, despite the oppressiveness of the East German regime, borders with West Berlin remained open. Throughout the 1950s, tens of thousands of East Berliners went to work in the West every day, returning home in time for dinner. Many more, of course, did not return. By 1961, two million had fled East Germany. The numbers leaving – especially the young and the highly qualified – continued to grow, as did the rumours about measures to stop people leaving.

At a press conference in June 1961, Ulbricht said it was nonsense to suggest that a barrier might be erected: 'No one has the intention of building a wall.' Translated, this meant: we intend to build a wall very soon. Less than two months after Ulbricht's categoric denial, in the early hours of 13 August 1961, a barbed-wire barrier was erected which sliced the city in two. Within a few days, the construction of a permanent wall began. In the chaos of the early months, there were many extraordinary escape stories. People abseiled down ropes from houses overlooking the border, or jumped into blankets held out by the West Berlin fire brigade. (In the weeks to come, the authorities evicted the inhabitants and bricked up windows and doorways.) Hundreds escaped through tunnels – sometimes 20 or 30 in a single breakout. Gradually, though, as the security precautions were strengthened, and as the Wall was reinforced with a second 'inner wall', such escapes became almost unthinkable. Separated relatives could no longer even wave to each other across the forlorn divide, as they had done in the early days after the barrier was erected. The Wall became the most vivid symbol of the brutal division of all Europe – the Iron Curtain made visibly real. Although it was officially an 'anti-fascist protective wall', everybody knew that the concrete barrier had one purpose above all: to make it impossible for Germans to choose which German state they wished to live in. Those who sought to exercise that choice were either jailed or killed. East Germans were obliged to adjust to a reality which was clearly never going to change. As the author Günter de Bruyn later noted, it was impossible for East Germans to live indefinitely in a what-if world:

> In spite of everything, we had to learn to live with the Wall. We couldn't keep calling ourselves indecisive blockheads because we didn't go over to the West in time, we couldn't keep eternally pining for the Kurfürstendamm or the Britz village pond . . .

In the West, too, the Wall came to be taken for granted. In 1983, Peter Schneider wrote in *The Wall Jumper*:

> Living here is no different from living in any other city. I really don't see the Wall any more . . . For Germans in the West, the Wall became a mirror that told them, day by day, who was the fairest one of all. Whether there was life beyond the death strip soon mattered only to pigeons and cats.

Coachloads of tourists gazed over the barrier from a specially erected viewing platform, and bought then-and-now postcards of the traffic-busy and deathstrip-empty Potsdamer Platz. For most Berliners on both sides of the divide, however, it was simpler not to think about the elephant in the room – looming large, but constantly ignored. It was a natural, self-protective instinct, which enabled everybody to get on with the business of daily life. In their different ways, it suited both sides to pretend. East German maps showed a city called 'Berlin, capital of the GDR', i.e. East Berlin. West Berlin was marked as a vast stretch of *terra incognita* – a white space with only a few main artery roads shown; the inaccessibility of this foreign land was clear.

Western maps took the opposite approach. East Berlin was clearly marked; the barrier between the two parts of the city, meanwhile, was treated as if it did not exist. Thus, West Berlin maps implied that it was possible to travel on the underground from West Berlin into East Berlin and then onwards north into the Western sector once more. That was true, as far as it went. But the maps, which marked West and East Berlin stations as though they were identical, gave no hint of the reality – the ghost stations that the West Berlin trains rattled through without stopping, where peeling posters served as an eerie reminder of the day the political clocks had stopped in 1961. Nor was there any acknowledgement of the fact that Potsdamer Platz station, marked as if it were an ordinary station, was in the middle of the death strip. Only by making a separate, complicated journey into East Berlin – for example, on foot via Allied Checkpoint C (C for Charlie) at Kochstrasse or by the S-Bahn overground railway to Friedrichstrasse (the *Tränenpalast* – 'Palace of Tears', so called because of countless sad farewells) could one continue one's journey on the self-contained East Berlin underground or S-Bahn network. For a Western map to have acknowledged those self-evident truths would somehow have seemed defeatist at that time.

Despite the cartographers' attempts to portray East Berlin as an integral part of Berlin (which merely happened to be hidden behind a wall), East Germany came to seem little more than a collective blur for most Westerners. They had little reason to think about East Germany except at Christmas, when food parcels were packed up and sent off to the relatives who had ended up, by a twist of fate, on the wrong side. Susanne Leinemann, author of *Wake Up and the Wall's Gone*, describes how East Germany was, for millions of West Germans, a distant, alien entity:

> In our ranking of near and far, it came in even below *Ausland* – 'Abroad'. As the first Inter-Rail generation, we could have breakfast in Lyon, then go to the cinema in Madrid the same evening. We knew *Ausland*. We visited it constantly. The GDR couldn't be *Ausland*, otherwise we would have encountered it on our travels. But it certainly wasn't *Inland* – 'Home'. It was so far away that it had vanished off our map of the world.

By the late 1980s, West Germany was happy to be self-contained. This was simply the *Bundesrepublik* – the 'Federal Republic'. Neither its westernness (reminding us that the *Bundesrepublik* was part of a larger nation) nor its Germanness (hush!) were usually referred to. Few countries can have been less prepared for the revolutions that were about to change Germany and Europe.

Elsewhere in the Soviet bloc, there had been signs of radical change for almost a decade. In 1980, strikes broke out in the Polish port of Gdansk and all across Poland, leading to previously unthinkable concessions – including the creation of a free trade union whose very existence called into question the authority of the one-party state. The legalization of Solidarity, while the inflexible Soviet leader Leonid Brezhnev was still alive, represented the first crack in the Berlin Wall. It was a sign that even impenetrable barriers can be broken. At the time, few East Germans saw it that way. Many believed that the Polish challenge to the regime just meant more trouble all round. Solidarity was seen as *polnische Wirtschaft* – 'Polish economy', a traditional German phrase for complete chaos. The introduction of martial law in 1981 seemed to put Solidarity back in a box; but things never moved back to the *status quo ante*. When the reformist Mikhail Gorbachev became Soviet leader in 1985 – tasked with injecting life into the moribund economy, with the buzzword 'We can't go on living like this' – Poland and Hungary used the window of opportunity provided by increased openness to carry out wide-ranging reforms. The East German government, by contrast, unsettled by Gorbachev's *glasnost* policy of greater openness, dug its heels in. The authorities even banned the distribution of *Sputnik*, a German-language Soviet propaganda magazine, because it was too honest for official East German taste.

This attempt by the East German regime to prove that they could be more Communist than the Kremlin was almost comically absurd. From the authorities' point of view, however, it was logical. East Germany, more than any other country in the Soviet bloc, suffered from the dilemma that a Czech Communist official described in October 1989. 'We don't want to jump into the river,' he told me, 'because we don't know how deep the water is.' (Three weeks later came the velvet revolution in Wenceslas Square; the Communist rulers drowned in the democratic deluge.) The East Germans faced the same problem, but more so. Kurt Hager, head of ideology, insisted that the East Germans did not need to reform merely because their comrades in Moscow were eager to do so. 'If your neighbour changed his wallpaper, would you feel obliged to redecorate your own apartment?' His colleague Otto Reinhold gave what was intended as a robust defence of the country's refusal to reform – but which could also be interpreted as an explanation of why his country would soon cease to exist. 'The GDR is only thinkable as a socialist state. What justification would a capitalist GDR have next to a Federal Republic? None, of course.' Reinhold was right. Unlike Hungary, Poland and even Russia itself, East Germany had no meaning without a separate ideology. If East Germany went all the way down the road of political and economic reform, it would eventually be no different from the already existing *Bundesrepublik*. The leaders of East Germany, noting this looming difficulty, found themselves caught between a political rock and a hard place.

In 1944, Stalin had scornfully declared that Communism fitted Germany 'as a saddle fits a cow'. In the following 40 years, however, the East German government had become eager saddle-wearers, and

Moscow's most loyal ally. In the words of Timothy Garton Ash, author of *In Europe's Name*: 'Napoleon said that all empires die of indigestion. The Poles gave the Soviet empire its biggest stomach-ache. By comparison, East Germany was positively eupeptic.' Now, it became clear that the government's desperate-to-please loyalty to the Kremlin would bring few benefits, as the authorities battened down the hatches, thus hoping to survive without reform.

By the beginning of 1989, the first seismic tremors of the earthquake yet to come were already making themselves felt all across the region. Under renewed pressure from Solidarity, the Polish authorities reluctantly agreed to re-legalize the opposition; Solidarity was allowed to field candidates in elections to be held in June. The Hungarians were already galloping towards radical reform. Hungary announced an event of incomparable symbolic importance – the reburial with honours of prime minister Imre Nagy, hanged by the Communists after the 1956 Hungarian uprising. Multi-party elections were promised within a year. In the Baltic republics, annexed by Stalin in 1940 under the terms of a secret deal with Hitler, pressure for restored independence was strong and growing; even the republics' Communist leaders were hinting at the need for a break with Moscow. In short, these were truly extraordinary times. 'Region where goalposts are on the move' was the main headline for a special two-page report on eastern Europe for *The Independent* in January 1989. In view of all the multiple simultaneous signs of change – multi-party elections on the horizon in Poland and Hungary, riots in Prague for the first time in 20 years, strong pressure for democracy and independence in the Baltic states, and a much-weakened Moscow with few cards left to play – I concluded: 'It is hardly surprising that, in predicting the future, all bets are off.' In Germany, meanwhile, these collapsing dominoes were scarcely noticed – even though dominoes were beginning to wobble in East Germany, too.

In East and West alike, most saw the prospects for change in East Germany not through the prism of East Germany's readiness or reluctance to rebel, nor in the context of Communist regimes imploding throughout the region, but above all with reference to the changing relationship between Bonn and East Berlin, on the one hand, and the policies of one man in the Kremlin, on the other. There was little interest in or awareness of the events in other countries which would have such a historic impact on Germany itself, in the months to come, whatever Mikhail Gorbachev decided to do. It was as though Germans still believed in their own *Sonderweg* – their own 'special path'. In reality, developments in East Germany were intimately linked to the multiple changes elsewhere.

It was Hungary which, for its own mischievous reasons – above all, to prove its own liberal credentials – paved the way for dramas yet to come. In what was designed as a photo-opportunity, Hungary snipped the barbed wire on the border between Hungary and Austria on 2 May. The wire-cutting ceremony confirmed an existing truth: Hungarian citizens could travel more or less freely to the West. For them, the Iron Curtain no longer existed. The Hungarian authorities, seeking a way out of their economic difficulties, wanted to prove to Western lenders that the bad old days were over. But the new gap in the wire had dramatic implications that, as quickly became clear, went well beyond the symbolic. By chance, the wire-cutting came just five days before local elections in East Germany, whose results were shamelessly manipulated even by Communist standards. The official tally was a 99.85 per cent yes-vote. More than 100 people were arrested when they tried to take a petition against the falsified elections to East Berlin – a small sign of the new restlessness that was yet to come.

That was only the beginning. Through the summer of 1989 the indignation grew, as did the regime's stubborn refusal to contemplate reform. Meanwhile, thousands of East Germans who visited Hungary on their summer holidays took advantage of Hungary's new liberal attitudes and slipped across the border. To the fury of the East German rulers, the Hungarians turned a blind eye. In September, the Budapest government, under a deal agreed with Bonn, announced that thousands of East Germans who had gathered in Hungary could now leave officially. East Berlin complained about the 'organized trade in humans' and talked of 'military-style provocation' by its supposed ally in the Soviet-led Warsaw Pact. But it was all to no avail. Even as East Berlin revoked visa-free travel to Hungary, that only stoked the pressure at home.

By now, the country was facing a double pressure. On the one hand, the country was haemorrhaging its lifeblood away, as mostly young East Germans streamed to the West in search of a better life. On the other hand – and this was about to prove even more dangerous for the regime – crowds of demonstrators gathered on the streets at home, chanting: '*Wir bleiben hier!*' – 'We're staying here!'. The deadly implication: we are staying, because we are determined that everything must change.

Through the summer and autumn of 1989, East Germany experienced a dramatic version of what the Polish writer Ryszard Kapuscinski has called, in describing the collapse of repressive regimes, the 'zigzag to the precipice': concessions (to ease explosive pressure) followed by clampdown (because the concessions seem to threaten the existence of the regime), followed by more concessions (because the clampdown has increased explosive pressure again) and then more attempted clamp-down . . . in an endless downward spiral. After the humiliation of the September exodus and the barring of the exit door via Hungary, the *Wir bleiben hier!* crowds continued to grow. Meanwhile, East Germans began to stream into neighbouring Czechoslovakia, hoping to leave from there. At the beginning of October, the international embarrassment of huge numbers of refugees gathered in the West German embassy in Prague persuaded the East German authorities to make their first concession – by allowing thousands out to the West in sealed trains. On their journey from Prague to West Germany, the packed trains passed through the East German city of Dresden; there were dramatic scenes when police clubbed crowds who tried to clamber aboard. Following that debacle (concession, followed by clampdown) the border to Czechoslovakia was also closed.

It was in this atmosphere that the 40th birthday celebrations of the German Democratic Republic took place. These were an extraordinary few days. The *Staatssicherheit* (or Stasi) – 'the state security apparatus', remained all-powerful. The Stasi had more than half a million employees, and kept files on five million East Germans – one in three of the population. On the face of it, the regime remained all-powerful, as it had always been. It was clear, however, that this was a very different East Germany from anything that anybody had seen before. The atmosphere of fear was strong – how could it not be, when police were ready and willing to arrest and beat those who resisted? But so, too, was the atmosphere of rebellion. Jens Reich, the soft-spoken biologist who played a leading role in the newly created opposition group New Forum, told me: 'We've been silent for too long. We've tolerated too much for too long.'

In the Gethsemane church in East Berlin, heartland of the new opposition, thousands gathered daily, happy simply to talk – and no longer intimidated by the likely presence of informers who might report rebellious words back to the Stasi. For a growing number, compliance was no longer on the agenda. The church, lit by thousands of candles for peace, was packed with those who insisted that East Germany had no choice but to reform. In one corner of the church, an elderly woman talked of her fears of the 'China solution' – a repetition of the Tiananmen massacre, just four months earlier. She concluded, however, with simple finality: 'The authorities just couldn't do it. Then, things would get even worse.'

Mikhail Gorbachev was guest of honour at the events to mark the 40th anniversary of the German Democratic Republic. The anniversary was intended to be a glorious set of celebrations, and was instead transformed by the East German winds of change into a funeral wake. When the Soviet leader arrived, he delivered the traditional comradely kiss to the frail Honecker, the man responsible for the construction of the Berlin Wall 28 years earlier. It was a killer of a kiss. Gorbachev's message to Honecker, made public by Gorbachev's spokesman, was unforgiving: 'Those who delay are punished by life itself.'

The punishment was not long coming. Even as Gorbachev prepared to return home to Moscow at the end of the official celebrations on the evening of Saturday 7 October, thousands spilled on to the streets of East Berlin – chanting Gorbachev's name and singing the *Internationale*. Protesters were beaten and plainclothes snatch squads regularly darted into the crowds, bundling people into marked and unmarked police vans. Beyond the fear, there was a strong sense of exhilaration. 'No violence!' the demonstrators chanted, even as windcheatered Stasi assistants violently dragged protesters away. People hung out of their windows, cheering the protesters on. 'Come on down!' the demonstrators shouted up to them – and some did. Old ladies leaned out of ground-floor windows, offering drinks to those on the street for all the world as if this were not a protest against the feared regime but a sporting marathon. To the protesters' delight, train drivers on the overhead S-Bahn railway tooted in solidarity. The demonstrators taunted the people's police, by chanting '*Wir sind das Volk!*' – 'We are the people!' The slogan harked back to a line from Ferdinand Freiligrath's poem *Trotz alledem* ('Despite All That'), written a century and a half earlier on the occasion of the European revolutions of 1848: 'We are the people, we are humanity . . . / You check us, but you cannot constrain us,/ The world is ours, despite all that.' As in Europe's earlier Springtime of Nations, defiance was everywhere. It trumped the fear. One old man who had been hauled off shouted down to me from inside the police truck, as I stood watching with my notebook. 'They've invited us to the birthday celebrations, don't you see!'

Even as I walked back to my hotel at the end of that extraordinary evening (a plainclothes policeman had tried to arrest me, but reluctantly conceded that my accreditation for the anniversary celebrations meant I was not committing an identifiable crime), it was clear that the events of that evening heralded unprecedented change. This was the biggest protest in the East German capital since the brutally repressed uprising of 1953. The border to Hungary – and thus, to the West – was now closed. But the 'we're staying here' pressures were more serious than ever. The authorities' options were few. Theoretically, tanks could move on to the streets to end the protests, as they had done to such lethal effect in

1953. In the short term, that could have succeeded. By now, however, tanks could only provide a very short-term solution to the authorities' problems. Things had already gone too far.

Even more remarkable than the Berlin demonstration were the events only two days later in the southern city of Leipzig. This was, in the words of a book devoted to the events of 9 October, *The Decisive Day*. It was the day when repression was defeated by lack of fear, with consequences for all Germany and Europe. For several years, Leipzig had played an important role for those who believed in the power of independent thought. The historic Nikolaikirche, where the *Christmas Oratorio* and other works by Bach had their first performance, was renowned for its Monday evening 'prayers for peace', which obliquely challenged the regime's authority. In the past year, arrests were increasingly frequent. Especially after the insultingly unreal local election results in May, the meetings – which now ended with a street protest – grew steadily in size and determination. The demands grew increasingly political, as thousands gathered inside and outside the church every Monday night.

The authorities wanted to put a stop to this. They were determined to ensure that, on and after 9 October, protesters would finally be terrified into staying at home for all time. Through the publication of a 'reader's letter' in the local newspaper, the regime publicly declared its readiness to carry out a reprise of the Tiananmen Square massacre four months earlier, when Chinese tanks killed hundreds of peacefully protesting students in the centre of Beijing. The letter to the *Leipziger Volkszeitung* insisted that 'hostility to the state must no longer be tolerated'. Signed by the leader of the 'Hans Geiffert armed militia unit', the letter concludes with a deadly flourish: 'We are ready and willing to defend what we have achieved effectively, in order finally and effectively to put an end to these counter-revolutionary actions. If need be, with weapons in our hands!'

Everybody understood, as they were supposed to, that this was not just an individual reader's letter. This was an official threat to kill. Nor was it mere bluff. As was later confirmed, the use of firearms was planned. Workers' militias were issued with guns, hospital wards were cleared, extra blood supplies were distributed to cope with the casualties. The city was cordoned off. Cars and trains arriving in Leipzig were checked, to keep protesters and foreigners out. (I was lucky to arrive a day early, before the main cordons had been set up, and luckier not to be picked up on arrival. Three colleagues who travelled with me were thrown out of the city within a few hours.)

Leipzigers knew what to expect. Before the service, in one sidestreet alone I counted 16 trucks filled with armed workers' militias. I found a passageway which looked as though it would be a safe place to cower when the shooting began. It was clear, however, that some Leipzigers would die in the next few hours, following the pattern set by the Chinese four months earlier – an action which East German leaders had publicly praised.

The East German authorities hoped that by advertising the planned bloodbath they would dissuade protesters from taking to the streets. As happened elsewhere in eastern Europe during that astonishing year, the opposite proved to be the case. Many who had previously not felt sufficiently indignant to go out on the streets now joined the protesters' ranks. As the bishop gave his sermon inside the packed church (to a congregation which included, it later turned out, large numbers of Stasi informers – much good did it do them), the chanting of the huge crowds gathering outside the windows could be heard. Despite and because of the threat of gunfire, more people had turned out for this protest than ever before, believing that a regime like this had to be confronted, whatever the cost. After the service ended, tens of thousands of protesters began to move off along the ring road – chanting '*Kei-ne Ge-walt!*' – 'No violence!', even as we waited for the shooting to begin.

What came next – and, more remarkably, what *didn't* come next – I remember as some of the most extraordinary minutes in my life. The non-event was the most important event of all. Two minutes passed quietly – not just without shooting but even, in contrast to previous demonstrations, without beatings or arrests. Five minutes passed, then 10, then 15. Gradually, it became clear that there would be no shooting. And, if not today, then never again. Finally, the regime had lost its nerve. With tender courage, a young woman tried to place a flower in the lapel of one of the armed militias standing beside his truck. The man recoiled in disgust but his colleague accepted the flower with thanks. Dialogues between the protesters and the militias broke out all along the street. In those glorious moments as the crowds streamed across Karl-Marx-Platz and on to the broad ring road that led past the Stasi headquarters, East Germany stumbled blinking into a different world, as it came to terms with the fact that the regime was more scared of the people than the people were scared of the regime. One Leipziger who took part in the protest later described the incomparable euphoria of that evening. 'I felt as if I could fly. It was the most fantastic day that I have ever known. Now, we knew that there was no going back. 3 October [the day of German unification a year later] was great but 9 October – that was the really special day.'

My detention and expulsion by the Stasi later that night (I had already filed my story from the post office before returning to the hotel, so was content to be expelled) did little to reduce the sense of privilege at having witnessed this astonishing retreat. Even the expulsion contained a reminder of the scale of the changes now under way. After the Stasi ordered me to pack my bags, the receptionist asked why I was checking out so suddenly in the early hours. I explained my crime – that I had witnessed the demonstration (and thus the humiliation of the regime) a few hours earlier. '*So eine Schweinerei!*' – 'What a pig's disgrace!', she loudly declared. I was grateful for the human solidarity. In addition, I was struck by the fact that she felt able to speak such words with impunity. A few weeks or even a few days earlier, such a contemptuous comment about the regime would have been a sure way for a hotel receptionist to lose her job or worse. Now the empire of fear was destroyed. Several years later, I met up with her again and she remembered how she had felt that day: 'We knew that we had won.'

From now on, the Leipzig demonstrations doubled in size every week. Even for the most obdurate hardliners, it was clear that the pressure cooker was exploding. Nine days after the Leipzig retreat came the next reform-friendly 'zig' (in the 'zigzag to the precipice'). Honecker was punished by life itself, replaced by his horse-faced lieutenant, Egon Krenz. The authorities, who until a few days earlier insisted that 'we should weep no tears' for those who had left suddenly reversed their line. Instead, in what sought to be a moment of touching humility, the government declared: 'We need every man and woman, and we are willing to find out and eradicate the reasons that have led to so many people turning their backs on us.' Then, in another official attempt to reduce the pressures caused by the 'We're staying here!' protesters, the restrictions on travel to Czechoslovakia were lifted on 1 November. Whereupon, unsurprisingly, the problems of the previous month began all over again.

Within 24 hours, the West German embassy in Prague was once more full to bursting – just as it had been a few weeks earlier, before the sealed trains, filled with refugees, were sent through Dresden to the West. Some tried their luck at the front door, others climbed over the back fence. Thousands camped in the diplomatic garden or squeezed into the embassy itself, the former home of an eighteenth-century prince. Ornately decorated salons bulged with triple-level bunks, packed so tightly that new arrivals could scarcely squeeze their way through. Broad staircases were submerged under sleeping bags. Hundreds of children played, cried and cuddled favourite toys. The number of arrivals increased by the hour; clearly the impasse could not last. The East German authorities now had two choices in order to reimpose some kind of control. On the one hand, they could clamp down again, by closing the border from East Germany to Czechoslovakia, thus stemming the flow of arrivals at the embassy in Prague. But they had already tried that a few weeks earlier, as the previous 'zig' towards the precipice – and look where it had led them. The *Wir bleiben hier!* East Germans had joined the biggest protest of all, in Leipzig on 9 October. Alternatively, the regime could try a last desperate move towards reform. They chose the second option – a surreal 'zag', even by East German standards.

On the evening of 3 November, it was announced that all East Germans in Czechoslovakia could leave, with no special paperwork. Put differently, all citizens could now leave East Germany for the West – as long as they planned their journey so that they travelled through a corner of Czechoslovak territory en route. The only requirement – not very onerous, in the circumstances – was that they must give up their East German identity cards at the border. A young woman who had just arrived at the embassy in Prague, accompanied by her husband and young daughter, could scarcely believe the news. 'I'm still afraid,' she told me, close to tears. 'But I'm so happy.'

If this condensed account of those dramatic weeks and months has been even partly coherent, the reader will perhaps have reached a similar conclusion to the one I outlined in my front-page story from Prague that night. Clearly, I wrote, the final precipice beckoned: 'It is difficult to see this latest retreat by the East German leadership as anything other than the beginning of the end for the East Berlin regime – and perhaps the beginning of the final act for East Germany itself.' This was not, as some have tried to suggest, a simple gift from Gorbachev. The reformist leader had little love of violence, but he had equally little desire to tear the Wall down. He merely wanted, as he made clear to the intransigent Honecker, to ensure that Communism was not punished by life itself. Nor – contrary to a version of events that later gained widespread currency – was the fall of the Wall an accident which, but for a mislaid piece of paper, might never have happened. On the contrary, the collapse of the existing barriers was by this time inevitable. In an article with the headline 'The redundant symbol of the Berlin Wall', published on 8 November, I pointed to the obvious consequences of events in the past few weeks and days:

> The implications of the decision last Friday night [3 November] to let all East Germans leave via Czechoslovakia can hardly be over-stated. It means that, to all intents and purposes, the Wall is already down . . . In a kind of political laundering operation, any East

German who sets foot on Czechoslovak soil can now leave that way, after showing only his identity card. If the East German authorities have already conceded that much, they might as well go all the way and knock a real hole in the wall. The half-liberalised travel laws announced this week satisfy nobody . . . The authorities' only other alternative is to batten down again, to close the borders entirely – a prospect which the continuing mass demonstrations make increasingly difficult to sustain . . . Popular aspirations for free elections can hardly be shut off again, like a tap – not, at least, short of Tiananmen-style violence which would provide no answers at all, for the rulers or the ruled . . .

Meanwhile, Nato strategists and Western politicians remain desperate not to confront the enormity of the changes. Free elections in the German Democratic Republic would, it is clear, imply some kind of reunified Germany in the longer term: the East German leadership has always been explicit that it is the separate political system which gives the GDR its reason for being there. Equally, the prospect of a single Germany presents problems for European stability, since it presupposes the final collapse of the existing blocs. But to seek to get rid of a problem by pretending that it does not exist is hardly a rational way forward. If Western politicians find it within themselves to deny that any nation has the right to free elections, then they ought perhaps to ask themselves just how selective that much-abused word 'freedom' is allowed to be.

It is an unfortunate breach of etiquette to quote at such length from one's own previously published work. It seems to me now, however – as it seemed at the time, and as I hope it may seem to the reader – that these conclusions were in any case mere common sense, given what had gone before. In view of the often-repeated 'nobody could have predicted . . .' line, it is perhaps worth making clear that hindsight is not needed for an understanding that the regime had by now reached endgame. Once the zigzags of 1989 had begun, nothing could stop them – any more than a single politician can halt the generational process of change in German society as a whole. The real surprise was that politicians in both Germanies and around the world often failed to grasp the significance of the changes that were taking place all around them at this time.

All that was required was an understanding that political change can come from within society, not just from political leaders – however important those politicians believe themselves to be. If one looked at East Germany's problems through that end of the telescope, it was clear that the question was no longer if the Wall would come down, but only when. *The Independent* began preparing a two-page 'obituary' for the Wall, which could be slipped into the paper at a moment's notice when the news broke. My editor asked me how long we could allow ourselves before the obituary, with a series of specially commissioned articles – reminiscence, analysis, and so on – had to be ready. I had no idea. 'Soon,' I said vaguely. 'Ten days? Two weeks?' At the time, the answer sounded foolishly radical. In reality, our preparations had barely got beyond drawing up a proposed list of contents when we received the answer – on the evening of 9 November 1989.

The immediate trigger for one of the most dramatic developments in European politics since 1945 was a slip by Günter Schabowski, a member of the ruling politburo, who was conducting a press conference in East Berlin. Schabowski read out a note that, he told journalists, 'will be interesting for you'.

Today, the decision was taken to make it possible for all citizens to leave the country through the official border crossing points. All citizens of the GDR can now be issued with visas for the purposes of travel or visiting relatives in the West. This order is to take effect at once.

The Schabowski announcement – the logical culmination of all the zigs and zags that had come in the past few weeks – was a bombshell. It was reported on West German television news, which could be seen in East Berlin. Huge crowds gathered at checkpoints throughout the evening. Initially, the guards reacted contemptuously to the suggestion that there had been a change in the rules. 'That one hasn't got all her cups in the cupboard,' one guard told *The Times'* Anne McElvoy when she suggested to the guards at Checkpoint Charlie that the border was now open. 'I suppose you think we're just standing here to be decorative,' retorted another. Gradually, however, the news of the Schabowski announcement, combined with the literal pressure of the crowds, meant that there was no alternative. It was necessary either to shoot to disperse the crowds (the option that had already been abandoned as impracticable at Leipzig a month earlier) or to give way. Harald Jäger, border officer at the Bornholmer Strasse checkpoint, on failing to get instructions from above, eventually called his Stasi superiors to announce: 'We can't hold up any more. I'm shutting down the controls and letting people out.'

The most impenetrable political barrier in Europe was about to fall. Guards moved aside the blocks of concrete that had lain across the road, which prevented the cars from passing more than one at a time. The astonished and astonishing crowds flocked through. The impossible became real, as if in a fairy tale. 'Going to West Berlin was as good as going to Australia for me,' one woman announced, as she crossed back into the east that night. 'It was just as far away. But now I've been there and back while my children were home in bed.' Another summed it up simply: 'I thought I was really in heaven.'

It later emerged that Schabowski's piece of paper contained an announcement originally planned for release the following day. This helped create the idea that things might have turned out differently if only Schabowski had not read the piece of paper by mistake. In the short term, that was true. Schabowski's slip hastened history by a few days, perhaps even a few weeks. But the regime was, by this stage, in free fall. As Schabowski himself noted, the intention was for this to be an orderly process:

> The fact that some were allowed to go and some weren't was silly and Kafkaesque. It demanded a solution . . . No one really thought about the result. We knew we had to take this step. As for its leading to the end of the GDR, none of us expected that at all.

There is no reason to disbelieve Schabowski when he says that neither he nor his comrades expected their actions to lead to the end of the GDR. But what else, in truth, *did* they expect? Powerful politicians often like to see themselves as 'pragmatists', whose understanding of the world is somehow more grounded than their unworldly critics. 'In the real world . . .' is a phrase that is often heard from those who hold great power. In reality, it is often those alleged 'pragmatists' who seem, in a historical perspective, to be naïve. Erich Mielke, head of the Stasi, had a revealing exchange with the chief of security for East Berlin, as unrest grew in summer 1989. The minutes tell the story:

> Comrade Minister Mielke: And how are things in the factories? What is the mood like there?
> Comrade Major General Hähnel: That is a very complicated question at the present moment, Comrade Minister.
> Comrade Minister Mielke: No. That is a very easy question. It is a question of power, nothing else.

Mielke's words betray the innocent ignorance of the complete cynic. Mielke's security service – 'the sword and shield of the Party' – kept files at its East Berlin headquarters which stretched for kilometres. This was a state which absolutely rejected the power of independent thought – and jailed those who thought differently. Mielke, in his insistence that power is everything, failed to understand that power can, in the right circumstances, be trumped by what the Czech dissident Vaclav Havel presciently called 'the power of the powerless'. Mielke's naïve cynicism explains why he was so famously baffled by the mocking laughter which greeted his resignation speech just after the Wall came down, when he told his audience – in a phrase which would enter the language, as a reminder of the regime's deceit and self-deception: 'But I love you all!'

Diehard communists were not the only ones who failed to understand the changes now irrevocably under way. Democratic politicians were equally startled. Helmut Kohl would, during the next few months, show visionary qualities in helping to ensure that the unification of Germany took place peacefully. He was, however, scarcely prepared for the initial explosion. On 9 November, Kohl was on an official visit to Poland. One of his aides, warning him to 'hold on to your seat', delivered the breaking news from Berlin. Despite all that had happened in the past few weeks, Kohl was quite unprepared for this sudden destruction of the certainties. His terse, disbelieving response: 'Ackermann, are you sure?'

7

Berlin Republic

A reunited Germany would represent a double danger for Europe. By its power and because it would create pressure for alliance between Britain, France and the Soviet Union. That would mean certain war in the twenty-first century.

> (President François Mitterrand, after the fall of the Wall in 1989)

I think they have a gene loose, though I don't know what the gene is.

> (Martha Gellhorn, explaining in 1992 why she will never return to Germany)

For me, the Berlin republic means that we have to combine the democratic traditions of the old Republic and the civic courage which has become visible in the revolutionary beginning. Then Berlin will play a new role like no other European city.

> (Gerhard Schröder, German chancellor, in 1998)

The end of Communism in East Germany meant that everything else was bound to change. Unity was inevitable. As the East German ideologists had already acknowledged ('The GDR is only thinkable as a socialist state'), a separate East Germany had no meaning once the threat of a multi-party system loomed. Helmut Kohl quickly seized the opportunities that were unexpectedly offered by history. Willy Brandt, forced into exile by one German dictatorship in 1933, rejoiced at the changes made possible by the end of another dictatorship more than half a century later: 'What belongs together is coming together.'

The mood amongst ordinary East Germans changed at dizzying speed during the final weeks of 1989. The protesters who risked life and liberty when they faced down truncheons and guns in September and October had chanted: 'We are the people!' Now, as the regime tumbled into the final abyss, those who had not joined the protests when they risked being arrested, beaten or shot felt safe to go on the streets without fear of punishment. They no longer wanted reform; they wanted regime change – which in practice meant country-change. No longer '*Wir sind das Volk!*', but '*Wir sind ein Volk!*' – 'We are one people.' When Kohl visited Dresden before Christmas, less than six weeks after the fall of the Wall, his words were drowned out by excited cries of 'Helmut, rescue us!' and '*Einheit!*' – 'Unity!'. By comparison with the protesters whose courage had paved the way for the collapse of the regime, the '*Wir sind ein Volk!*' sentiments might not seem especially uplifting or noble. The sentiments were, however, normal – a fact that some had difficulty in accepting. Many government leaders were reluctant to allow popular German aspirations to be met, merely because of an outbreak of democracy. Foreign politicians of different outlook and temperament were united in their opposition. The conservative Margaret Thatcher (who never hid her Germanophobia, nor her disdain for Kohl personally) said it was essential to 'check the German juggernaut', because the country was 'by its very nature a destabilizing rather than a stabilizing force in Europe'. The socialist François Mitterrand (who had always portrayed himself as Kohl's best friend in Europe) was even more categoric:

A reunited Germany would represent a double danger for Europe. By its power and because it would create pressure for alliance between Britain, France and the Soviet Union. That would mean certain war in the twenty-first century.

In Germany, some felt almost equally queasy. Kohl's left-wing challenger, Oskar Lafontaine, West German to the tips of his polished shoes, deeply mistrusted German unification. He did not put it in quite such bald terms, talking instead of social justice. Above all, however, he seemed worried that absorbing 16 million poor Germans into the comfortable and successful Federal Republic would change the equation; he feared (rightly) that German unity would drag the West German standard of living down. He later claimed to have been prescient in seeing that Kohl's predictions of 'blooming landscapes' in the East were foolishly optimistic – throughout 1990, he warned of the exorbitant costs of unity. In truth, the 'blooming landscapes' gaffe was merely grist to Lafontaine's mill. Like many of his (western) voters, he liked the Federal Republic as it was, and saw no reason why it should change.

The process of unification accelerated at breakneck speed through the months after the Wall came down. The German Democratic Republic (GDR) held its first free elections in March 1990 – elections which quickly resulted in the abolition of the country, when the GDR chose to become part of the *Bundesrepublik*. The new East German prime minister, Lothar de Maizière, a professional viola player before the Wall came down, pleaded for a marginal name change – German Federal Republic instead of the Federal Republic of Germany, which would at least hint at the idea of a merger rather than a takeover. He was rebuffed. East Germany was required to adjust; West Germany was not. On 1 July came economic union – the deutschmark for all, replacing the flaky East German currency in one fell swoop. The official abandonment of the East German state followed just three months later. Less than a year earlier, the East German authorities were arresting and beating those who dared just a little democracy. Now, on 3 October 1990, with fireworks and a million people gathered at the Brandenburg Gate, a united Germany was born.

A logical early consequence of German unification was the return of the government from Bonn to Berlin. West German politicians of all political parties had long agreed that this was the natural consequence of unification. That, however, was the theory. Now that the reality was within reach, it turned out that many were not so keen. This sleepy little town on the Rhine had long since come to seem the embodiment of the comfortable democracy of West Germany itself. It existed in a curious twilight zone, defining itself by everything in German history that Bonn was not. The Bonn republic was not-Nazi, not-totalitarian, not Weimar-unstable. In *A Small Town in Germany*, John le Carré describes the identity problems of this not quite real capital of a democratic Germany, which is 'permanently committed to the condition of impermanence':

One day, perhaps, they will move to Berlin; the contingency, even in Bonn, is occasionally spoken of. One day, perhaps, the whole grey mountain will slip down the autobahn and silently take its place in the wet car parks of the gutted Reichstag; until that happens, these concrete tents will remain, discreetly temporary in deference to the dream, discreetly permanent in deference to reality; they will remain, multiply and grow; for in Bonn, movement has replaced progress.

In 1949, when Bonn was chosen to be capital of the new Federal Republic, nobody had suggested that this could be a permanent capital. On the contrary. The very idea was, it was agreed, ridiculous. One reason why bustling Frankfurt lost out to little Bonn in the vote for the Federal Republic's new home was that Bonn suited the 73-year-old Konrad Adenauer better; the chancellor's home was in Rhöndorf, just across the Rhine. Above all, however, the choice of Frankfurt would have implied the acceptance of a permanent division. The idea that Bonn might permanently replace Berlin as the national capital was, by contrast, satisfyingly implausible. In case of misunderstandings, the new federal parliament announced at one of its earliest sessions that it would move to Berlin 'as soon as general, free, equal, secret and direct elections are held in all of Berlin and the Soviet occupation zone'.

Such clearcut aims were never officially abandoned. In the meantime, however, everything changed. Even after the bombed and burnt-out ruins of the Reichstag were rebuilt in the 1950s, the former parliament building remained a washed-up relic of history. It stood in an out-of-the-way corner of West Berlin, close to the Wall, in a political cul-de-sac. The building was occasionally used but had a haunted feel – like an imposing archaeological ruin, filled with mere memories of power. In Bonn, the insistence that the parliament would one day move back to Berlin meant that MPs met in a 'temporary' building for 40 years.

Finally, the discreet permanence dared to flaunt itself openly. Germany gave up on the dream and deferred to reality. Erich Honecker's red-carpet visit in 1987 forced West German politicians publicly to accept what they already privately regarded as a self-evident truth: that the two separate Germanies were here to stay. Waiting for unity was the political equivalent of waiting for Godot. A single Germany was indeed, as the lexicographers had pointed out, 'a former country in central Europe'. Work duly began in 1988 on a new parliament building, in final confirmation that Godot would never come. Whereupon, to general consternation, the unthinkable happened: Godot appeared. By the time that Germany was reunited in 1990, work on West Germany's first permanent parliament had barely got under way. (Günter Behnisch's elegantly redundant building was finally completed in 1993, three years after unity.)

For many supporters of the Bonn republic, the fact that a move to Berlin was now possible was perplexing. Politicians eagerly grasped for reasons why yesterday's emphatic theoretical 'yes' to Berlin could suddenly be replaced by today's equally emphatic practical 'no'. Partly, the arguments were about money. Moving the capital back to Berlin would be expensive. The taxpayers of west Germany, who quickly began pouring billions into the impoverished east, were feeling the pinch. 'If only there were enough money . . .', the argument ran, 'we would have no objection.' Or, in the words of a Berlinophobe sticker in Bonn: 'Yes to Berlin – in the year 3000.' Above all, however, the arguments were – as ever – about German history. Berlin's size was seen as a euphemism for power, which, in turn, was taken to be a synonym for Germany's dark history. Some were so hooked on the idea of the goodness of the *Bonner Republik* – a country full of sugar and spice and all things democratically nice, a few hours from Paris – that they were eager to regard Berlin as the opposite. Berlin was, the critics pointed out, 'the seat of Nazi power'. The Bonners' favourite syllogism ran something like this: Bonn is the birthplace and capital of the *Bundesrepublik* (true); the *Bundesrepublik* has become synonymous with German democracy (true); therefore (an interesting logical leap), German democracy can only exist in Bonn. Bonn portrayed itself and its attendant republic as the demure democratic maiden, by contrast with the lurking dangers of a *Berliner Republik* – almost as if the bracing Rhineland air was directly responsible for the development of German democracy. The crucial changes that had taken place throughout the society of the *Bundesrepublik* in the past 40 years – in which Bonn played a useful but symbolic role – were treated as if they were almost irrelevant. The pro-Bonn lobby genuinely seemed to believe that Bonn was the *cause* of late twentieth-century German democracy, not its manifestation. In effect: without Bonn, no democracy. It was a most peculiar logic. German democracy was perceived as safe, if its politicians remained in a university and spa town within easy driving distance of the French border – and endangered, if it moved to a city in the east where a German dictator had once ruled. The Nazis had enjoyed plenty of support in Bonn, not just in Berlin; but that detail was lost in the mix.

Parliament finally voted on the issue on 20 June 1991. The pro-Bonn faction was as confident of victory as the Berlin faction was resigned to defeat. An east German MP, Konrad Weiss, told the mostly west German MPs in the Bundestag chamber: 'Bonn belongs to the old Federal Republic. It is and remains strange to those of us from the east.' He knew he was in a minority, however. Only at the last moment, partly with the help of the passionately pro-European Helmut Kohl, did the argument swing the other way. Kohl argued:

> We want Czechoslovakia, Poland and Hungary to find their way to this Europe, too. Then Berlin will not be on the edge, but it will

have a geopolitically important and central function. That is the reason why I think that Berlin will be a good location in the year 2000 or 2005, when the face of the new Europe is visible – and that's why I'm voting for Berlin.

Seen from a twenty-first-century perspective, it may seem unremarkable that a clutch of former Soviet-bloc countries have joined the European Union, the politically and economically exclusive club of affluent democrats. At that time, however – 18 months after the fall of the Wall, and at a time when the Soviet Union still existed – it is difficult to over-emphasize how visionary (and how unreal) such a prospect sounded. Despite the apparent unreality, Kohl's words were persuasive in a remarkably close vote. If just nine votes had gone the other way, the *Berliner Republik* would never have come into being, and we might have been left with Bonn as the German capital for all eternity. And yet, as a friend who moved from Bonn to Berlin points out, the contrast between the two cities is clear. 'Berlin is like an open-air museum of German history in the nineteenth and twentieth century. In Bonn, it was easier not to confront our past. Here it is impossible to escape.'

The tussle between Bonn and Berlin represented an argument over what modern Germany stands for. On the one hand, the newly unified Germany yearned for the normality that the Berlin republic represented. On the other hand, millions shied away from such normality. The inhabitants of the *Bundesrepublik* had come to feel comfortable with the knowledge that they could grow rich without needing to think about international affairs. In the comfortable security of the Bonn republic, difficult questions about German identity did not have to be answered, not least because nobody wished to pose the question. Before 1989, the 'German question' was unanswerable and could therefore be left to one side. Now, by contrast, some kind of answer – what is Germany, and where is it heading? – was urgently needed.

In the early years of the Berlin republic, the answers often seemed bleak. The gloomiest pessimists could gloat: 'We told you so.' The evidence seemed to multiply that Germany was indeed reverting to (stereo)type, including an alleged inborn tendency to succumb to the lure of the far right. In east Germany especially, one neo-Nazi nightmare followed another. In September 1991, skinheads in Hoyerswerda, north of Dresden, stoned an asylum-seekers' hostel – with the approval of many locals. After six days of rioting, the authorities' solution to the response was not to crack down on the rioters, but to bus foreigners out. In the port of Rostock in August 1992, crowds cheered when rioters hurled stones and Molotov cocktails, which set ablaze a building full of Vietnamese; one hundred people were trapped in the flames but, remarkably, nobody was killed.

This and other acts of violence were bad enough. Hoyerswerda and Rostock were, however, just the prologue. On the night of 22 November 1992, neo-Nazis firebombed a Turkish family house in the quaint little town of Mölln, south of Lübeck, then telephoned police to announce: 'It's burning in the Mühlenstrasse. *Heil Hitler!*' Bahide Arslan died in the flames, together with her 15-year-old niece and her 10-year-old grand-daughter. The name of Mölln became shorthand for the monstrous dangers of a resurgent far right. Still, however, the threats continued. Turks received calls which began '*Heil Hitler!*' or 'You're next.' One man in Mölln told me: 'Whenever I hear a car stop in the street, late at night, I always get out of bed to see what it is. We live in fear.' The deaths of the Arslan family shocked Germany out of its apathy for the first time. Across Germany in the weeks and months to come, three million people took part in huge *Lichterketten* – candle-lit 'chains of light', sometimes with hundreds of thousands of marchers at a time.

Still, though, the country had not yet reached rock bottom. That point came almost six months after Mölln. The town of Solingen, in the indus-trial district of the Ruhr, is in most respects an unremarkable place. Until 29 May 1993, it was best-known for the quality of its kitchen knives. That Whitsun weekend would change that for ever. Solingen became a synonym for everything that many Germans feared most about them-selves, and that many non-Germans feared about the Germans. Young neo-Nazis set alight to a house in Untere Wernerstrasse, killing five girls and women from the Genc family. The youngest member of the family to die was aged four. A few hours later, a neighbour shook his head in disbelief as he gazed at the still-smoking shell. He asked me the same question that other Germans were asking, all across the country: 'How many children must die before the politicians do something?' His wife tried to speak calmly, but her voice cracked. 'You feel ashamed to be German.' In a nearby playground, the killers had swished a clearly visible swastika into the sand.

The Mölln and Solingen murders were a defining moment for the new republic. Some politicians in Germany were eager to downplay the importance of the murders. The foreign minister, Klaus Kinkel, spoke fatuously of 'a few ill-advised hooligans'. Others, however, gave a more thoughtful response. President Richard von Weizsäcker said: 'We owe it to the victims, as well as to ourselves, to be honest. The murders of Mölln and Solingen are not individual, unconnected acts. They come from a climate created by the far right.' Most Germans agreed; polls at this time suggested that 90 per cent took seriously the danger of an emerging far right. Nor were the problems just in the east. Solingen is in the heart of west Germany. In 1992, the far-right Republicans – led by Franz Schönhuber, a former member of Hitler's Waffen-SS – gained almost 11 per cent of the vote in the south-west German state of Baden-Württemberg.

Germans saw an obvious and worrying pattern to what was happening in their country. In the words of one typical commentary: 'The quintuple murder in Solingen shows that there can be another Mölln at any time – and probably will be.' If Germany was shocked by the resurgence of thuggish neo-Nazi violence – the 'brown plague' as it came to be known – the rest of the world seemed more shocked still. Admittedly, politicians like Jean-Marie Le Pen, leader of the French National Front, were already enjoying success elsewhere in Europe. Racism in Germany was assumed, however, to be part of a bigger and more dangerous pattern – something permanent, not conditioned by mere economic and social conditions or failure of political leadership at any given time.

Granta magazine, traditionally a forum for some of the most thoughtful writing in Britain today, published a special *Krauts*! issue which set out to find 'the uncomfortable answer to this simple question: what is the new Germany?' It noted that the vocabulary had changed in just a few years. '*Then* we used words like "a divided Germany". There was a "Berlin Wall", a "Cold War" . . . But what are our key words *now*? The new Germany. The extreme right. Neo-Nazi; asylum-seeker; hostel; foreigners out!' Even the way that *Granta*'s questions were framed seemed to take Germany's nastiness as a given. 'What is it about the German people that produces a nation so – what?' *Granta* asked. 'So ugly. So dangerous. So predictable.' Martha Gellhorn, who had accurately identified the problems of German denial in 1945 ('No one is a Nazi, no one ever was . . . It should be set to music'), believed she knew the answer: Germans are just born that way. In an essay subtitled 'Why I shall never return to Germany', she argued that thuggery and murder is in the German make-up. 'I think they have a gene loose, though I don't know what the gene is.'

For 12 years, many Germans turned a blind eye to or participated in terrible crimes – thus enacting, in real life, the disturbing conclusions of the Milgram and Zimbardo experiments at Yale and Stanford in later decades. That casual brutality had, in the meantime, come to be portrayed as if it were part of a distinctively German, self-perpetuating pattern of behaviour. If Gellhorn sought validation for her thesis about genetic killers, and if *Granta*'s editors wanted support for their thesis about ugly predictability, they did not have far to look. Some Germans seemed ready to share the view of a gene loose. Günter Grass wrote in 1992:

> Is there no end to German recidivism? Do Germans necessarily botch everything, even the unification that was handed to us on a plate? Are we condemned to relive our history? . . . It's time we Germans recognized the threat we pose once more, preferably before our neighbours do.

For Grass, the violence of Rostock and all that followed proved one thing above all: 'Now all the repugnant triumphalist din has stopped, and the past has tapped us on the shoulder.' Gellhorn, *Granta* and even Grass all seemed reluctant to contemplate the possibility that, to turn Gellhorn's phrase around, Germany might suffer not from a gene loose but an environment loose. Once poisoned, the society took many years before it began to become healthy. Johannes Rau, who later became German president, said with reference to the Solingen murders:

> The young people who commit xenophobic violence have not fallen out of the sky. They are children of our society. They are not acting in a vacuum. Their actions are, it seems to me, an extreme expression of a deep crisis of direction in our country.

Rau was right to place the violence in a social context, and thus, as a politician, take indirect responsibility for what had happened (in a way that other politicians still seemed reluctant to do). This taking responsibility is, however, quite different from the Gellhorn thesis which suggests that murderous German behaviour is in the blood, unaffected by mere social upheaval. Grass's own comments about recidivism may seem to provide German support for this generalization. But neither Gellhorn nor (more understandably) Grass, with his lacerating criticisms of his own country, seem interested in the 'deep crisis in direction' which Rau identified. The suggestion that violence does not take place in a vacuum in no way excuses such violence – especially if government leaders play down the problem with foolish and offensive talk of 'ill-advised hooligans'. It does at least, however, try to make sense of the senseless without resorting to talk of 'ugly predictability' or genetic explanations.

All eastern Europe went through a period of great instability in the 1990s after the totalitarian Communist bandages were removed. This was a time of economic crisis and political chaos, marked in almost every country of the former Soviet bloc by virulent nationalism of different kinds. Germany, especially eastern Germany, went through the same series of crises and more. East Germany suffered not just from a political and economic crisis, but from a severe identity crisis, too. Many east Germans, even as their lives were turned upside down, felt that they were treated – by the government in Bonn, by the west German media and by tens of millions of west Germans – as if their very existence were an unwelcome problem. They were part of the new *Bundesrepublik*; and, at the same time, they were not. Few other countries had such multiple confusions to contend with. The only other country which suffered from multiple identity problems of comparable severity was Russia – which, to quote Dean Acheson's phrase about post-colonial Britain, had lost an empire but not yet found a role. It was unsurprising that impoverished and diminished Russia also suffered from deep political instability at that time – including widespread support for the deranged nationalist Vladimir Zhirinovsky, described in Germany as the *Russen-Hitler*.

Crucially, too, East Germany had never confronted the Nazi past. It had thus never undergone the political inoculation against fascism which was by now taken for granted in West Germany. On the contrary. A socio-geographical alchemy had taken place. According to the official East German version of events, Germans in Düsseldorf, Munich or Frankfurt on Main were perpetrators and inheritors of the Third Reich. Germans in Dresden, Magdeburg or Frankfurt on the Oder, by contrast – within the morally pure zone of the Communist East – were deemed to have been unaffected by the Hitler virus. Buchenwald concentration camp outside Weimar was portrayed for decades as a place where good German Communists (in other words, East Germans) were locked up, tortured and killed. The official Communist-era exhibition at Buchenwald (which naturally passed in silence over the fact that it also became a Communist camp in the years after 1945) implied that the Nazi madness had nothing to do with the good working people of Weimar who suffered courageously at the hands of the Third Reich. After the collapse of Communism, a more honest exhibition was created, including a new section called 'In the Midst of the German People'. Exhibits included a telephone directory which showed the listed number of *Konzentrationslager Buchenwald* (telephone Weimar 6311) nestling between 'Konradi, Lina' and 'Kopf, Arno'. There was also a bus timetable (Weimar, main station, dep 1330; Camp, Buchenwald arr 1400). Buchenwald – 'beech forest' – was built in the middle of beautiful woods on the Ettersberg hill above Weimar; hidden away, however, it was not.

The East German avoidance of uncomfortable truths seemed useful for the creation of an artificial new stability after 1945, just as it had done for West Germany in those early years. The difference was that the GDR, in contrast to the Federal Republic, never changed until the very end. Only when the country's first and only democratic government was elected in 1990 did East Germany make a historic declaration of shared responsibility for the crimes of the Third Reich. The prolonged failure in past decades to deal with the crimes of the past was an additional reason for an underlying East German instability. Germany was forcibly reminded of a much broader truth: a society which is not built on truth is built on political quicksand.

After Solingen, the violence continued. In the east German town of Magdeburg in May 1994, neo-Nazis roamed through the streets in search of foreigners to beat up; the police failed to intervene until it was too late. People were 'hunted down as they were in the worst times of the SA', one government official noted with disgust. Economic crisis and soaring unemployment at the end of the decade helped create the fertile soil for a further upsurge of racist attacks in 2000. Between 1998 and 2002, the far-right German People's Union (DVU) held seats in the regional parliament in the east German state of Saxony-Anhalt. The Berlin republic no longer feels, however, like a system on the edge of collapse. Instead, a fragile stability has begun to take hold. Gerhard Schröder, when he became chancellor in 1998, had his own version of what the new order might mean:

> For me, the Berlin republic means: we have to combine the democratic traditions of the old republic and the civic courage which has become visible in the revolutionary beginning. Then Berlin will play a new role like no other European city.

In recent years, the *Bundesrepublik* has experienced extraordinary turbulence, as it seeks to bring two countries together into one, and as the perceptions of German identity and of the German role in the world have been turned upside down. Schröder's words may sound like pie-in-the-sky optimism. Whatever comes next, however, it is clear that the Berlin republic marks a new chapter for the twenty-first century. The rest of the story is only being written now.

8

West-Eastern Divan

'We are one people.' 'So are we.'
> (Popular summary of attitudes in east and west Germany in the years
> after German unity in 1990)

It felt strange. But I had to ask: who listens to us, who listens to
what we've been saying?
> (A former Stasi victim explains why she voted for the PDS,
> party of the ex-Communists)

Some hoped that the unification of Germany – a single nation that had
been divided for decades by barbed wire, minefields and a brutal regime
– would be a joyous experience. Briefly, it was. In the days and weeks that
followed the breaching of the Wall, bemused easterners streamed cheerfully through West Berlin, thronging their way into the shops and cafés
of Kurfürstendamm, walking along streets they had expected never to
see except as pensioners (East Germany liked to be rid of its pensioners,
because they cost money) or on West German TV. The westerners were
generous in rolling out the welcome mat for their almost-compatriots,
with official and unofficial gifts of cash, food, clothes and more. This
really was a period of sweetness and light.

That time of shared happiness was, however, short. Perhaps that
should not have been surprising. In 1983, when everybody accepted that
the Berlin Wall was here to stay, Peter Schneider indulged in a fantasy of
what might happen if the German–German world were one day to be
turned upside down:

What would happen if, say, both German governments took a year's vacation; if the journalists fell silent for a year; if the border police took a year to recuperate on the Adriatic and the Black Sea, and the people started their own East–West negotiations? After a brief embrace, they would discover that they resemble their governments much more closely than they care to admit. It would become evident that they have long since made their own crusade out of the biographical accident of growing up in different occupation zones – later, different social systems. As soon as someone asked which half offers a better life, the fight that both states carry on daily in the media would break out in the living room.

The embrace was indeed brief, and the fights in the living room broke out quickly. The East Germans freely chose unity. And yet, millions came to resent what many came to see as a form of annexation. The word *Anschluss*, harking back to Hitler's adventures in the 1930s, was heard with increasing frequency. Even as the real Berlin Wall was still being dismantled, it was replaced by what came to be known as the 'wall in the heads', much harder to dismantle than the concrete wall had been. The wall in the heads was – and partly remains, even today – an intricate pattern of mutual resentments, where both sides blame each other for everything that is wrong with their lot.

The east Germans resented what they saw as Wessi arrogance. The Wessis became the *Besserwessis* – 'better westerners', a pun on the word for 'know-it-alls'. Easterners resented the fact that they remained much poorer than their west German cousins, the BMW-driving fat cats of the country. East Germans suffered mass unemployment for the first time, as one factory after another was closed down in quick succession. Sell-offs under the hated Treuhand – literally 'faithful hand' or 'trustee', took place at startling – and, for many east Germans, horrifying – speed. The Treuhand crushed state businesses into a brutal new reality. The Dresden camera-maker Pentacon, which enjoyed a 10 per cent share of the world market in the Communist era, had 5000 employees in 1990; within a year, just 200 were left. At one stage, Treuhand was selling more than 100 companies a week. The perception of carpetbaggers was strong: notoriously, west German businessmen siphoned off Treuhand funds to prop up failing businesses in the west. With reference to the frenetic pace of Treuhand sell-offs, an east German joke asked: 'Do you have to ask an investor his name before you sign a contract with him?' Answer: 'You can if you like, but it slows down business a lot.'

The west Germans, in turn, resented the resentments – which they believed reflected ingratitude on the eastern side. *Jammerossis* – 'eastern whingers', became a standard phrase. From 1991 onwards, west Germans paid a special (and highly unpopular) solidarity tax for rebuilding the east – the 'Upswing East' that was proclaimed by huge roadside hoardings all across east Germany. Many westerners saw the complaining Ossis as feckless, work-shy or both. To admit that relations between east and west had quickly reached rock-bottom was, however, considered inappropriate in official discourse. Indeed, even to use the word 'east' was considered faintly impolite. In the years after German unity, the acceptable way to describe east Germany was as the *neue Bundesländer* – the 'new federal states', which conveniently omitted any reference to the east's core identity. The easterners were the new arrival in the federal household of the *Bundesrepublik*. They were expected to adjust to existing house rules. They were not expected to be involved in decisions about how the well-established household should be run. For politicians from the *Altbundesrepublik* – the 'old Federal Republic', that would have been a shocking thought.

Those who highlighted the mistrust were blamed for doing so. Shooting the messenger was a favourite pastime. A television sitcom which dared to expose the mutual dislike was roundly condemned for doing so when it was screened in 1993. Friedhelm Motzki, the slobbish, foul-mouthed main character, has no time for lazy and incompetent easterners (including his hard-working sister-in-law Edith in the now reunited family). Motzki declares: 'When they pulled down the shitty wall, that was a black day for our country, and an even blacker day for me.' The programme-makers expressed the hope that *Motzki* might be 'a cleansing storm'. But western viewers were indignant that their privately abusive thoughts were now revealed on TV. One woman complained: 'Now I can't look my relatives in the east in the eyes any more.' A string of senior west German politicians called for the series to be banned, allegedly worried at the offence that Motzki's words might cause to the citizens of the 'new federal states'. The president of the Bundestag, Rita Süssmuth, complained that the series was driving west and east apart. Heide-Ulrike Wendt, an east German columnist, spoke for many easterners when she retorted: 'Is she not getting cause and effect confused?' Wendt argued that a rude Motzki was better than an overdose of western quasi-politeness. 'Motzki curses his sister-in-law Edith as a "stupid eastern cow", but at least she knows where she is. The discreet charm of the bourgeoisie is much more difficult to take.'

West Germans felt that they had worked hard for their wealth. Why, they asked, should we suddenly be expected to share it all? A young

Düsseldorfer explained to me why the expectations of those living in the new federal states were so unreasonable. 'We have worked hard for many years to achieve what we have today. And now, they want everything instantly. It doesn't make sense.' In the narrow sense, he was right. It was impossible for East Germany to be transformed from a nation of Trabant and Wartburg drivers to a nation of BMW drivers overnight. And yet, the word 'we' was revealing. The young *Wessi's* own contribution to the affluence of the *Bundesrepublik* consisted, above all, in receiving an expensive, highly subsidized university education for many years (nobody does 'eternal student' better than the Germans). The random fact of his birth in Düsseldorf meant that he placed himself, however, in a different – more hardworking, more deserving and generally superior – category to an otherwise identical fellow-German who happened to have been born in Dresden.

Both sides found it hard to accept that the reasons for the differences were based, above all, on the chance circumstances of their separate fates during the past few decades. Peter Schneider was right: both sides became eager to make a crusade out of biographical accident. The east–west frictions cropped up even in the most trivial circumstances. In the east German town of Halle, I witnessed an altercation about who was rightfully first in a taxi queue. Two passengers had jumped into a cab which others in the queue believed was not theirs. The judgement of the rest of the queue was unanimous. '*Wessis!*' Bad behaviour, it seemed, could be best explained by the west–east divide.

By comparison with other countries in the former Soviet bloc, east Germany had a huge economic advantage and a huge psychological disadvantage. The economic advantage was that east Germany was now part of the wealthiest country in Europe, a country understandably proud of the democracy it had achieved. The psychological disadvantage was exactly the same: the affluence and stable democracy of the existing Federal Republic made it difficult for the new arrivals to feel at home. East Germany gained an instant sugar daddy, self-confident and with knowledge of the world, as the old West Germany swallowed the east and metamorphosed into the new united Germany – a change that took place, for west Germans, without so much as a name-change. Before and after, they lived in the *Bundesrepublik Deutschland*. The net effect of unification on west Germany was negligible (even if many westerners, obliged to tighten their belts a notch or two, did not perceive it that way). In the east, by contrast, life itself turned upside down.

At one level, Communism was quickly forgotten. With the billions of

Deutschmarks that sluiced in from the west, East Germany was richer than any of its eastern European neighbours. It made sense that Kohl's incautious promise of 'blooming landscapes' in the east was much mocked in the years to come. In purely objective terms, however, those landscapes *did* bloom, not least by comparison with the situation on the other side of Germany's eastern border – how could they not, when such vast sums were being ploughed in every year? Few east Germans were eager to recall the fact that they had ever shared an economic and political fate with their eastern neighbours, with whom they had shared uncomfortable adjoining bunks in the Communist barracks for more than 40 years. Still less did they wish to compare their current purchasing power with what the Poles, Czechs or Hungarians were able to buy.

In east Germany, wages were sometimes only two-thirds of wages in west Germany – a source of considerable bitterness. That was and is, however, several times higher than wages in any other former Communist country. An unemployed east German receives more in unemployment benefit than many Poles with a good full-time job. Through the 1990s, east Germany's crumbling cities were rebuilt and restored. A vast and sophisticated infrastructure was put in place – new roads, new telephone system, new everything. Purchasing power steadily increased. Every east German suffered at least once from the 'doorknob polishers' – door-to-door salesmen who arrived, contracts in hand, promising new furniture, new satellite TV, new lives. But that early naïvety – 'Sign here, and your dreams will come true' – was only a passing phase. In the east German town of Erfurt in the mid-1990s, a retired midwife was eager to tell me that all was not rosy. For example? 'There are big problems. There are so many building sites, traffic jams and diversions everywhere. It's *very* exhausting.' In any other country in the region at that time, it would have seemed unthinkable that a retired midwife might see too many cars (i.e., new purchasing power) and too much construction (i.e., new investment) as the main problem. Throughout the rest of eastern Europe, pensioners were understandably worried that they could barely afford to buy a few ounces of ham. In east Germany, by contrast, a basic standard of living quickly came to be taken for granted. Opinion polls confirmed that the overwhelming majority of east Germans believed that things were, in purely economic terms, getting better.

Meanwhile, other eastern Europeans knew that, however impoverished they might remain, any small improvement in their lot was down to their own hard work; progress was *their* achievement. Economic comparisons were made with the past, not the West. Even to be allowed into the outer waiting room of the European Union represented a moment of pride – from Communist mess to EU applicant, in just a few years. East Germans, by contrast, who in 1990 gained instant membership of what was still called the European Community, resented the humiliation of receiving constant vast handouts from the rich western cousins, on the one hand, and the poverty within which they remained trapped, relative to west German standards of living, on the other. These psychological problems were unique to Germany not because of the German absolutism or a grumbling gene, but because of simple geopolitics and history. If after 1945 there had been, say, not just a People's Republic of Poland (Communist one-party state) but also a separate West Poland (successful market economy and liberal democracy), West and East Poles would no doubt have been equally divided after the collapse of Communism and the abolition of their own internal border. As it was, the resentments were unique to Germany.

The irritability over economic issues – 'Why should we be so much poorer than the westerners are?' versus 'Why do the easterners always want more, despite the billions we give them every year?' – were only part of the story. In terms of coping with the political legacy of Communism, east Germany found itself in an equally unenviable position. Other central and eastern European countries made their own decisions about how to adjust to the new era, and how to deal with the past. For them at least, the 'Sinatra doctrine', announced by Gorbachev's phrase-making spokesman after the Wall came down, was now real: for better or worse, most eastern Europeans did it 'Their Way'.

There were endless arguments, of course. Each country made its own decisions – some tough, some soft – about whether (or when) Communist headteachers should remain headteachers in the post-Communist era, and whether a Communist police chief or precinct captain could remain in his post in a democracy, too. Morality and pragmatism tussled constantly; the themes of accountability and turning a blind eye were endlessly and openly discussed. Millions who had lived under a totalitarian regime knew all too well that apparently black-and-white issues often merge into shades of grey, when more closely examined. Some who co-operated with the regime were cynics or worse; some were cowards; some co-operated because they wished to achieve career fulfilment (how else could they gain that coveted academic post without joining the Party?), or because they did not wish others – a child, for example, hoping for a university place – to be denied opportunities because of a parent's obstinately independent spirit. Few east Germans expected that they would outlive the regime. (The very idea was, as one put it later, 'ridiculous'.) They thus made their own accommodations, for better and for worse, with the regime under which they were condemned to live and die.

Elsewhere in the region, countries stumbled towards their own version of democracy at varying speeds after 1989, and with much argument over how much digging into the past there should be. In some Balkan countries, where representatives of the old Communist regime remained strong, it was logical that there was little desire to examine the past. (This problem existed in Latin America, too: the murderous General Pinochet, for example, was able to guarantee his own immunity from prosecution, even after his regime of torturers and killers gave way to an elected government in Chile. It took many years for the laws that protected him and his associates to be unravelled.) Even in countries where multi-party democracy quickly took hold, however, the issue of 'lustration' – holding personal histories up to the light – was much argued over. In the Czech republic, there was controversy over *Red Cow*, a publication which resembled a three-volume telephone directory and which listed 150,000 secret-police informers. Some of the country's best-known former dissidents, including Vaclav Havel and Jiri Dienstbier (now president and foreign minister respectively), expressed their dismay. The list gave no context – no sense of whether people had co-operated a lot or a little, under pressure or of their own free will. The flotsam and jetsam who had for sad or selfish reasons co-operated with the regime were held up for public obloquy, while others who had perhaps committed more serious crimes went free. 'Can you imagine,' one former dissident asked me with reference to the publication of *Red Cow*, 'how those people who *really* represented the regime and secret police are laughing now?'

Throughout formerly Communist eastern Europe, all the main parties found that they had their own fair share of informers, which made political point-scoring complicated. Even Lech Walesa (Nobel-prize-winning jailed opposition leader, and later president of a democratic Poland) was alleged to have collaborated with the secret police under the codename Bolek. The debate generated much heat but very little light; every country eventually found its own way of muddling through. In Germany, by contrast, muddling through was not an option. There was to be no room for ambiguity or confusion. Many west Germans were acutely aware that lack of honesty about the past had damaged Germany's ability to heal itself after the defeat of Hitler in 1945. In what sometimes seemed to be a transference of delayed guilt, west German politicians and media now demanded political purity from the east. After the collapse of a second German totalitarian regime, west Germans did not wish the mistakes of the past, when Nazis remained in high places for many years, to be repeated.

This theoretically admirable attitude failed to acknowledge important differences between the German Democratic Republic and the Third Reich. Most obviously, there was a difference of scale: the many crimes of the East German regime did not, for example, include the careful planning and execution of genocide. There was a perhaps even more important distinction. In the Third Reich, the great majority of the worst German crimes were committed not against fellow-Germans, but against those – Jews, gypsies, Slavs – who the killers themselves defined as non-German. In that respect, a hand-washing exercise after 1945 was not merely inappropriate but an act of moral abdication. In the GDR, by contrast, it was East Germans who suffered the crimes and injustices committed by their compatriots. In those circumstances, it was clearly appropriate that ordinary East Germans should have a decisive say in how the prickly legacy should be dealt with.

As with Germany after 1945, honesty was needed for the former GDR to gain stability. But the fact that victims and perpetrators were Germans together – living side by side, in the same society – meant it was not always simple to distinguish the good and the bad from the just plain messy. Many east Germans, conscious of those complications, were wary of rushing to judgement – and, above all, suspicious of west Germans who sought to do so. Some easterners, including the courageous dissident Bärbel Bohley, believed a complete cleansing of the stables was required. The equally determined heads of the authority set up to deal with the legacy of the Stasi – the pastor Joachim Gauck, who was succeeded in that post by the human rights activist Marianne Birthler – were and are important East German voices. Beyond the Stasi authority, however, there was much resentment that the broader discussion about the Stasi past was driven by west German concerns – even though west-erners had never had to tussle with their consciences on the question which every East German had faced: to compromise, or not to compromise?

Those who had been informers (*informelle Mitarbeiter* (IM), – 'un-official collaborators', to use the acronym which became familiar to all Germáns after 1989) were no pillars of moral rectitude. Few people are. Timothy Garton Ash's *The File* is an account – based on an examination of the historian's own Stasi file – of those who spied on him when he was studying in East Berlin in the 1980s. He describes a series of face-to-face encounters with his betrayers, who respond to the embarrassing revelations with varying degrees of shamelessness and guilt. Garton Ash sums up his journey of discovery and the emptiness that he found:

> What you find is less malice than human weakness, a vast anthology of human weakness . . . If only I had met, on this search, a single clearly evil person. But they were all just weak, shaped by circumstances, self-deceiving; human, all too human.

For many west German commentators, the most agonising moral political dilemma that they had ever had to face was the question familiar from 1968: was it OK to throw stones at the police, or should one just yell slogans? Still, those who had never lived under a totalitarian regime seemed confident of their moral superiority, and were happy to sit in judgement on those who had – for sad, banal or sordid reasons – co-operated with the Stasi. Thus, the east German writer Christa Wolf, a respected and partly independent literary voice in the old East Germany, was pilloried in the west German press when it emerged that she had served as an unimpressive informer for three years between 1959 and 1962. Wolf was for many years herself the victim of informers; her own Stasi victim file was thick. But that counted for little in the climate of the 1990s. Finger-pointing was the sport of the day.

Sometimes, this absolutist approach was both appropriate and necessary. Clearly, those who had committed terrible crimes against their fellow-citizens should be brought to account. It is difficult not to feel moral queasiness with regard to those who have agreed to become informers. Some of the stories, like the experiences of those who found that they were spied on by their closest family, are horrifying. It sometimes seemed, however, as though West Germans were determined not to acknowledge what East Germans took for granted: that life in the GDR included difficult choices, too.

Those who had lived their lives with the brutal Stasi were often unimpressed by the IM feeding frenzy of the early 1990s. East Germans rallied not just to writers like Christa Wolf, but also to those who appeared to have more to feel ashamed of than she did. Manfred Stolpe, a Protestant pastor active in the opposition before 1989, was elected prime minister of the east German state of Brandenburg – and was then revealed as an informer, codename IM Secretary. Stolpe was reported to have received a steady stream of expensive gifts from his Stasi minders, including, bizarrely, a sixteenth-century bible. Stolpe's response to the accusations was embarrassment and defiance in more or less equal measures. The voters of Brandenburg, meanwhile, voted for him as though nothing had happened. Or rather, the accusations appeared to *boost* his popularity: Stolpe gained a more comfortable election victory after the Stasi revelations than he did before.

On both sides of the old iron curtain, the sense of mutual misunderstanding and resentment remained strong for years after unity. East German joke-books carried titles like *Five Years Are Enough!* ('Two pieces of news, one good, one bad. First the good news: the Russians have gone. And now the bad news: the westerners are still here.') Westerners and easterners liked to read different books, too. In the east, there was an endless selection of titles like *Employer West – Employee East* and *West-Eastern Divan* (after the work by Goethe of the same name), which asked if there were 'two kinds of Germans, the know-it-alls and the submissive'. *Verliebt, verlobt, verheiratet* – 'in love, engaged, married'), a collection of true stories of love across the divide, was widely available in east German bookshops, except in shops where it was already sold out. When I asked about it in west German bookshops, I was met with blank looks.

One character in *Verliebt, verlobt, verheiratet* is an east German music critic, grateful that her west German lover teaches her 'how to use a fax machine and how to deal with Western editors'. She finds that he, too, however, does not always regard east Germans as entirely real. 'Once, we were at a premiere in Antwerp. He looked round and said: "I'm the only German critic here." He didn't notice that I was standing next to him. After all, east Germans aren't Germans.'

For most east Germans, it was a given that westerners made little attempt to understand the circumstances in which they had lived. When Margarethe von Trotta showed her film *The Promise* to an audience in Dresden when the film was released in 1995, I was struck by the audience's surprise that a western director had tried to see things from an east German point of view. The story begins as the Berlin Wall goes up in 1961, and ends with the breaking open of the Wall 28 years later. The main storyline is about the dilemmas that its characters face – the conflicting demands of love and career and the whispered devilry of the Stasi ('a signature for a son', as the Stasi man sums up a Faustian deal). Some argued that even this film was too Wessi black-and-white. The leading east German actress Corinne Harfouch, one of the film's main stars, complained: 'I do not recognise my own country . . . We didn't just have autumn and winter, we had spring and summer, too. There were days on which we didn't have problems with the Stasi.' Most in the packed Schauburg cinema in Dresden that evening were, however, more generous. In a discussion with von Trotta after the film, many focused on what they saw as her un-Western readiness to suggest that moral issues in East Germany were sometimes complex. 'You didn't have personal experience, you didn't know from your guts what East German life was like, as we did. So how did you manage?' one woman asked.

The divisions between west and east had dramatic consequences for party politics, too. The New Forum movement played a key role in helping to force change in autumn 1989. After *die Wende* – 'the turn', as the collapse of the regime soon came to be known – New Forum was soon sidelined. This, too, was another pattern echoed all across eastern Europe, where political parties led by courageous former dissidents quickly became electorally irrelevant. Meanwhile, the reformed Communists – now renamed as the Party of Democratic Socialism – benefited handsomely from their compatriots' resentments. Many who voted PDS were old-time supporters of the Communist regime, irritable at the loss of the one-party state that they had been loyal to for so many years. Others, however, were not. The PDS became the party of lost identity – a party which insisted that not *everything* in the old East Germany should automatically go on to the historical scrapheap.

A few years after reunification, I taalked to Lothar Bisky, leader of the PDS, at a PDS weekend . . . for rest and recreation. Bisky, an amiable former film school rector (and another politician who would later be accused of collaborating with East German intelligence), scarcely mentioned economic deprivation, when explaining his party's appeal. On the contrary, he acknowledged, it was clear that east Germans were now better off. 'We can't make a policy of nostalgia,' Bisky believed. 'But we profit from the fact that we are from the east.'

Even those who might logically have most reason to loathe the Communists have sometimes ended up voting PDS – *Revenge of the East Germans*, as it was summed up by a book published in 2002. In a village set amidst the strange and beautiful rock formations of Saxon Switzerland, south-east of Dresden, I met Volker, a local doctor, and his wife Hannelore. Both had suffered at the hands of the Communists. Volker was jailed for three years for distributing leaflets criticizing the regime. After his release, he had difficulty finding work. Eventually, the couple were allowed to move into a dilapidated house in a little town which had been without a doctor for six years; they opened a surgery there. Local officials wanted them to buy the house so that they would take responsibility for much-needed repairs; the couple agreed. Despite their 'Category 4.3' status as enemies of the state, permission to buy was granted in 1988, and the deal was completed the following year. All in all, it seemed, a happy ending. The collapse of the hated old regime at the end of 1989 was the celebratory icing on the cake. The regime which had persecuted them for so long collapsed in humiliation, and the couple were happy in their home. Then, however, everything began to unravel. Writs arrived from the man who had previously lived in their house. He had left for the West in 1975, leaving his loan on the house unpaid. Now that the Wall was down, he wanted the house back – and the courts ruled in his favour. A judge said that Volker and Hannelore could keep their house only if they produced a (non-existent) certificate of proof of right to purchase.

One could hear variations of this story – a sense that the new western justice took too little account of natural justice – again and again, throughout the east. Volker argued: 'Many people are in our situation. All we want is not to have to beg. Our rights are nil.' On the shelves behind him and Hannelore as we spoke were lines of files, with thousands of pages of Stasi reports on the couple – grim testimony to their lives in the Big Brother state. In the circumstances, it was unsettling to discover how Hannelore had decided, five years after the Wall, to vote for the PDS – the preferred option for the stalwarts of the old regime, derided by its opponents as the *Partei des Stacheldraht* – the 'party of barbed wire'. Hannelore admitted that 'it felt strange' to vote PDS. 'But I had to ask: who listens to us, who listens to what we've been saying?'

For many east Germans, this was somebody else's democracy, not theirs. West German politicians repeatedly argued through the 1990s that the strength of the PDS meant the Communist nightmare might begin all over again. Helmut Kohl's Christian Democrats in Bonn launched a 'red socks' campaign ahead of elections in 1994 ('Off into the future, but not with red socks!') as a way of attacking coalition deals done between the Social Democrats and the PDS in eastern states, and the alleged threat to democracy that such coalitions posed. The east Germans themselves, meanwhile (the supposed victims of the red-sock conspiracy), seemed less bothered. One evening in the east German city of Halle, just ahead of the 1994 elections, I met Christoph Bergner, a former opposition activist unseated as regional prime minister because of a coalition deal between the Social Democrats and the PDS. The deal had shocked west German voters and led directly to the red-socks campaign. I asked Bergner if he regarded the demonization of the PDS by his party friends in Bonn as electorally helpful. 'Absolutely not,' was his unhesitating reply – even though the alleged purpose of the CDU campaign was to strengthen Bergner's own position. In reality, the campaign impressed west German voters (four-fifths of the electorate) but east German voters hardly at all. Nor were the Christian Democrats the only ones to see things through western eyes. The Social Democrats, the SPD, tried equally hard to snuff out regional deals with the PDS, again not because of the intrinsic risk to democracy but because such deals looked bad to the SPD's western voters. The Social Democrats' chief strategist, Günter Verheugen (who later became European Commissioner for enlargement), cheerfully conceded that the pressure from Bonn to prevent east German Social Democrats from doing deals with the PDS had nothing to do with democracy (though that was the official reason), and everything to do with western attitudes. 'For [the eastern state of] Mecklenburg it would be quite normal,' Verheugen told me. 'If one could isolate the problem in Mecklenburg, that would be quite different. But one can't. In the western SPD, feelings are very strong. Clearly, this is a west German matter.' Such honesty was, perhaps, only possible in conversation with a foreigner. In German discourse, the fiction was maintained that the exclusion of the PDS was not about keeping west German voters happy, but about keeping totalitarianism from the door.

One effect of the red-socks campaign – even for those who were deeply mistrustful of the cynical and incompetent PDS – was to confirm that Bonn had little interest in east German realities. Polls suggested that two-thirds of east Germans believed the PDS was unfairly treated by the west – in other words, including many who would never dream of voting for the ex-Communists, but who could see the dishonesty of the western position. Gregor Gysi, smart-guy lawyer and the PDS's most high-profile figure, led his *bunte Truppe* – 'motley crew', to one victory after another through the 1990s. Apart from a ready supply of clever one-liners, it was difficult to know what made him tick: perhaps a mixture of cussedness and vanity. He had been a lawyer for dissidents in the old East Germany; he, too, was accused of having been a Stasi informer. Above all, he knew how to play on popular resentments to good effect. Even a decade after German unity, the PDS remained strong. In 1998, the PDS achieved its largest share of the vote – more than one in five east Germans voted for the former party of oppression. In east Berlin, most remarkably of all, one in two voted PDS.

Through the 1990s, east Germans of all political persuasions became increasingly loyal to the east German products they had recently spurned. After the fall of the Wall, easterners were eager to identify with the West. 'Test the West', a popular advertising slogan, applied not just to a choice of cigarette but to all aspects of ordinary life. East German products were rejected because they were eastern; *Westprodukte* were *cool*. Within a few years, however, the pattern was reversed. Nostalgia for everything east German – '*Ostalgie*' as it was inevitably called – was everywhere. *Ostalgie* evenings were organized, where everyone dressed up in the uniforms of the FDJ, East Germany's blue-shirted Communist youth movement, and danced to cheesy East German hits. The *Ostalgie* evenings were sprinkled with irony. But shopping habits grew seriously *ostalgisch*, too – as reflected not least in the changing patterns of consumption of sparkling wine. While East Germany still existed, *Rotkäppchen* ('Little Red Riding Hood' – named after the glossy red foil that covered the wired corks) was hugely popular. When the Wall fell, so did Rotkäppchen. It came to be seen as the chugging Trabant of the drinks world, which east Germans were ashamed to be seen with. Sales collapsed, from 15 million bottles to three million bottles in just two years. Within just a few years, however, the trend was in the other direction. Soon, more bottles were sold than before the fall of the Wall. Little Red Riding Hood, once a source of shame, had again become a source of pride. Eventually, *Rotkäppchen* bought out the floundering west German firm of Mumm. In the words of a proud inhabitant of Freyburg, where *Rotkäppchen* is produced: 'We discovered that the western stuff isn't any better – and that's nice.' The same pattern was repeated with a range of products, from gherkins to face cream. Increasingly, east came to be seen as a badge of pride, not shame.

The shopping grew increasingly *ostalgisch*, partly as an act of defiance in response to the perception that the west scorned *everything* from the east. West Germans sought to dismiss every element of east German life – not just the hated Wall and the one-party state, but every detail of the way that east Germans had run their lives. Oddly, the most high-profile east–west clash of all came over an issue that neither side, on the face of it, had much reason to care about. The surprising and unexciting battleground was the preferred design for pedestrian-crossing lights. The story of the *Ampelmännchen* – 'the little traffic-light men', came to symbolize all the other divisions that nobody liked to speak of. East German pedestrians had for many years been confronted with a flat-hatted little red man (arms akimbo) or a little green man (striding ahead, hat perched at a jaunty angle), when they wanted to cross the road. Even if the East German state was inhuman, its *Ampelmännchen* were not. On the contrary, they made the upright little western figures seem dull by comparison. In ordinary circumstances, this should have been a matter of supreme indifference to all except those with an obsessive interest in municipal design. These were not, however, ordinary times. In the late 1990s, the east German *Ampelmännchen* came to be seen as the last surviving scrap of east German identity. The battle to preserve the eastern traffic-light men took on an emblematic quality, as East Germany's last stand.

The initial response to the east German *Ampelmännchen* campaign was impatience at yet another Ossi whinge. One West German official noted irritably: 'We cannot take any notice of *Ampelmännchen*. Unity means united traffic lights, too.' Meanwhile, however – for all the world as though this were some kind of reprise of Leipzig in October 1989 – east German resistance to the Wessi-imposed change became almost equally categoric, with slogans like 'Whoever kills our *Ampelmännchen* kills us, too.' The friendly *Ampelmännchen* began to multiply: on stickers, T-shirts and coffee mugs, and draped across the Volksbühne, one of the main theatres in east Berlin. The battle of the *Ampelmännchen* was yet another reminder of the gulf that has opened up between East Germany and other countries that survived Communism. Throughout the region, nobody thought it necessary to change roadsigns in order to prove that Communism was now over. Old traffic signs were 'Communist-era'; but the typeface and design were not seen as tarnished because of their association with a totalitarian regime; there would be plenty of time to modernize signs in due course, once money became available. In Germany, however, there were now two visual styles – east German (designed by Communist sign-makers, and therefore a hangover from a dictatorship) and west German (designed for the *Bundesrepublik*, and therefore compulsory for the new democratic era). Eventually, and remarkably, the west Germans backed down. The east German *Ampelmännchen* was permitted, after all. At the beginning of the twenty-first century, brand-new traffic lights with eastern *Ampelmännchen* can be seen all over east Berlin and eastern Germany. It was not exactly a huge victory, in terms of taking the wishes of east Germans more seriously. Perhaps it was, however, at least a start.

More than a decade after unification, the west–east frictions were still alive. On a wet afternoon in Hamburg in 2001, I was standing with a German television crew when a group of tourists moved in front of our camera just as we were about to start filming; nor did they seem inclined to move away. After waiting for a while, the cameraman asked if they could possibly move a few metres, so that filming could continue. One man reacted indignantly to the perceived impudence of the request. So far, so normal: television crews often irritate people by their very existence, let alone by their requests. In the visitor's mind, however, this was not just any old TV arrogance. As he turned on his heel, he spat out the single, angry phrase: 'West TV!' As it happens, the cameraman and sound recordist were both East German-born. Such details would, however, have made little difference to the Mr Angry's analysis. More than a decade after the fall of the Wall, he, in common with many of his compatriots, was still convinced that 'the West' was to blame for everything in his world that was not how he wished it to be.

On the one hand, it is depressing that the west–east divisions have remained so sharp for so long. Even at the beginning of the twenty-first century, Mars-and-Venus-style books continue to be published with titles like *You Just Can't Understand Us – Why West and East Germans Talk Past Each Other* or *The Book of Differences – Why Unity Isn't Unity*. This, too, however – like so much else in Germany in recent decades – may prove to be partly a question of generations. In Hamburg, the twentysomething soundman suggested that such instinctively Wessi-loathing reaction was already 'unthinkable' from an east German of his own age. That crucial generational change – a softening of the west–east divide at last – would become explicit and acknowledged within just a few years.

9

Kanak Attack

A state secretary said to me: 'Herr Özdemir, you should tell your compatriots . . .' And I told him: 'Herr Lintner, *you* are my compatriot'.

> (German-born MP Cem Özdemir finds, after his election in 1994, that
> the concept of integration is less developed in Germany
> than he might have hoped)

First we take your jobs, then your women, and now the prizes, too.

> (Kaya Yanar, one of Germany's most successful comedians,
> on receiving the German Television Prize in 2001)

The racist violence that exploded in the 1990s – Hoyerswerda, Rostock, Mölln, Solingen and more – represented a murderous streak that Germans hoped was long since confined to history. Many west Germans tried to suggest that this was purely an east German problem. Much of the worst violence was and is indeed in the east. In addition, however, all Germany was forced to confront the fact that the country's attitudes to foreigners and foreignness were complex-ridden and confused, in east and west alike. The German mindset is influenced by revulsion at the Nazi legacy, on the one hand, and by a lingering attachment to legislation left over from the imperial era and the Third Reich, on the other. Put together, those two apparently contradictory themes made for a deadly mix.

The revulsion is clear, and easily explained. For decades after 1945, West German asylum laws were more liberal than anywhere else in Europe, not least because of a German desire to emphasize, to itself and others, the gulf separating the new Germany from what came before. In the past, a tyrannical Germany had driven millions into exile and death. After 1945, West Germany was eager to give shelter to those seeking refuge and protection from death at the hands of tyrants elsewhere. Until 1989, Germany's uniquely permissive asylum laws were made easier to enact because of two factors, above all. While the Berlin Wall still existed, the promise of a German welcome for those fleeing oppression at home could be fulfilled with relative ease. The generosity of the West German state had limits which were conveniently set by the repressive regimes elsewhere. 'Come, you huddled masses – as long as you succeed in escaping past the mines and the guards and the watchtowers' was not an invitation that millions could easily take up. With the disintegration of the Iron Curtain, everything suddenly changed. 'Come, walk across the newly open borders, and we will offer you an indefinite supply of milk and honey' was, Bonn quickly discovered, a more difficult offer to sustain. In just a few years the number of asylum-seekers leapt sevenfold, to almost half a million. Germany took in far more asylum-seekers than any other country in Europe did – in 1992 it received four times more than those arriving in all the other countries of the European Union put together. In the same year, Hamburg alone took in more asylum-seekers than the entire United Kingdom did. Some countries which were quick to criticize German xenophobic violence also adamantly refused to provide sanctuary for those fleeing violence in the Balkans and elsewhere. In 1993, there was much excitement in Britain about the arrival in London of a single, telegenic 5-year-old, evacuated for medical treatment from the Bosnian war. In the same year, Germany took in 350,000 refugees from former Yugoslavia.

The generosity was linked back directly to the Nazi nightmare. If that generosity had been combined with a policy for integrating refugees into society, the policy would have been entirely laudable. Such integration – even attempted integration – was, however, not on the agenda at this time. Instead, German laws and German society treated non-Germans throughout the 1990s as fundamentally and irreparably 'other'. The concept of 'Germanness' was strictly ethnic – with all the complications it implies. Even those with the best intentions talked of the need for greater tolerance of the *ausländische Mitbürger* – 'foreign fellow-citizens', a phrase that sounds as other-worldly in German as it does in translation. The constant talk of *ausländische Mitbürger* emphasized the gulf between 'them', the foreign fellow-citizens, and 'us', the Germans. 'Germans bad, Turks good' came to seem almost as unhelpful as the more obviously brutal skinhead credo, 'Germans good, Turks bad'.

Above all, Germany has been hobbled by its citizenship laws, based on the *ius sanguinis* – 'law of blood'. Anybody who could demonstrate German ethnicity, into the *n*th generation, was guaranteed instant citizenship. Millions of ethnic Germans in Russia and eastern Europe were guaranteed instant citizenship of the Federal Republic, even if they spoke no German and had never set foot in Germany. Hundreds of thousands of such 'out-settlers' arrived in Germany in 1990 alone. The law dated originally from 1913; but its interpretation was heavily infected by the Nazi mindset, emphasizing the necessary 'Germanity' of upbringing.

Naturalization was long and laborious. The *ius soli* – the 'law of the soil', a key element of citizenship laws in most countries – how long have you lived here? where were you born? where were your parents born? – was treated as almost irrelevant. Even if one's family had lived in Germany for generations, there was still no automatic right to German citizenship. Put together, these strange anomalies – limitless generosity in letting foreigners in and then making it difficult or impossible for them to become integrated – were a recipe for instability or disaster.

On the one hand, there were those who (as in countries around the world) felt hostile to the foreign spongers, stealing jobs and dragging down living standards of the country. Others, meanwhile, were sympathetic to the plight of the poor foreign *Mitbürger*, and constantly apologetic. The two sides had one thing in common. They found it difficult to imagine that somebody with a non-German name or a dark skin could be fully German. That privilege (or burden) was reserved for those with names like Braun, Müller or Schmidt.

The huge new influx of asylum-seekers, on the one hand, and the dramatic rise in xenophobic violence, on the other, exploded old liberal certainties. Integration was still scarcely discussed in the early 1990s. But politicians on all sides agreed that a way out of the impasse was needed. In 1993, after much agonized debate, the Bundestag voted for a change in the German constitution, restricting the number of asylum-seekers who could arrive in Germany for the first time. The uniquely generous terms of Article 16 of the Basic Law were replaced with something closer to the laws elsewhere in Europe. Kohl's CDU-led government and the Social Democratic opposition agreed on the need for the change, thus making it possible to gain the necessary two-thirds majority. There was widespread disquiet at what was perceived as a betrayal of all the liberal values that the modern *Bundesrepublik* should stand for. Günter Grass resigned from the Social Democrats, condemning the party's failure to defend 'the jewel of our constitution'. Others were equally indignant. Some on the left, however, argued that change was essential. Freimut Duve, a leading Social Democrat intellectual, argued (with a sideswipe that was perhaps partly aimed at Grass) that the defence of Article 16 was pure hypocrisy:

> The world utopia of Article 16 stood for 40 years in the shadow of the Wall. I feel sick when I see how comfortably many of my friends crouch behind a moral hedge in order not to be dirtied by the mud of our time.

Crouching behind moral hedges was, in the 1990s, a popular position for German liberals. They knew what sort of Germany they did not want; that part was easy. They were not always so sure of what sort of Germany they *did* want. Such questions were now more difficult to avoid. A united Germany could no longer simply duck difficult questions, as the politicians of the old Federal Republic always liked to do. The change in the constitution was intended to curb the growing xenophobia. Its first effect seemed to be merely to encourage yet more violence. Just a few days after the parliamentary vote came the murders in Solingen – part of a much wider pattern of racist violence and intolerance at that time. A few weeks after the Solingen killings, I visited the uninspiring steel town of Hagen. (An album depicting the town's attractions included photographs of a McDonald's and a bus stop.) The mayor was in defiant mood when I visited him. A Social Democrat and former trade union official, he insisted that enough was enough. There would be no more asylum-seekers in Hagen. 'Whether that is legally acceptable or not,' he told me, 'I don't care.' He insisted that he was not giving succour to the far-right Republicans – though they had praised the mayor's 'exemplary behaviour'.

The rejection of foreigners – 'the boat is full', in the popular phrase – was by now an increasingly common response all across Europe. Lurid headlines about being 'swamped' by refugees helped stoke anti-foreign sentiment to a remarkable degree. In Germany, support for the far-right parties – the Republicans, the German People's Union and the NPD – remained low, by comparison with elsewhere. Sheer thuggery, continued, however, especially in the east – against Vietnamese, Africans and anybody who looked different or had the wrong-coloured skin. To walk among the concrete high-rise blocks in places like the east Berlin district of Marzahn was to visit Planet Skinhead, with its aimlessly circling groups of surly, close-cropped youths. For them, *somebody* had to be blamed.

The resentments most often expressed are especially against asylum-seekers and new arrivals – who are accused of taking people's jobs and of living well at the expense of the locals. However, some of the most lethal incidents have been against settled Turks, of whom there are more than two million in Germany today. Turks first arrived in large numbers in West Germany soon after (and as a direct result of) the construction of the Berlin Wall. When the flow of East German refugees to the West suddenly dried up, another source of labour was urgently needed, in the economically booming Federal Republic. In October 1961, just two months after the Wall went up, an agreement for the recruitment of Turkish workers was signed, thus launching the era of the *Gastarbeiter* – 'guest worker'. For many years, the guest workers were treated as just that – temporary visitors who would one day return home. In due course, the authorities made plain to the foreign guests that they had now outstayed their welcome. In 1983, a new law – not perceived as racist, by those who drafted it – encouraged Turks to return home. Turks received incentives to leave Germany; they had no right to a pension, including employers' contributions, even if they had worked in Germany for the past 20 years.

Those who stayed were not guests – they had been in Germany too long for that. Nor, however, were they allowed to become full members of German society. Most were not German citizens and could not vote. Few seemed to think in terms of a dual identity, where a single person could feel both German and Turkish at the same time. In effect, most Germans on left and right remained wedded to the categories set out in 1990 in the United Kingdom by Margaret Thatcher's inflexible home secretary, Norman Tebbit. Tebbit invented the 'cricket' test – 'Which side do they cheer for?' Tebbit asked – which implicitly contrasted the 'true British' with the 'not wholly British'. Tebbit's words can, in that sense, be seen as a partial updating of Enoch Powell's notorious 'rivers of blood' speech in 1968, in which he warned of the dangers of immigration for the stability of the United Kingdom. Tebbit's cricket test had no room for the concept of overlapping identities which lies at the heart of modern European societies. People may be devoted to the country where they have chosen to live or where their parents or grandparents came to live – and at the same time remain loyal to their ethnic roots.

In Britain, Tebbit has long since been left behind by all except a hardcore minority. Germany, however, has until now seemed reluctant to grasp the concept of integration. Instead, we are left with the legacy of the *ius sanguinis* – meaning that only if you have German grandparents and great-grandparents are you a true German. Phrases like 'black British' or 'Asian-American' have no commonly used German equivalents. Until recently, a person was either German or foreign; it was impossible to be both.

Kanak Attack

The beginning of an understanding that this was not, perhaps, a sensible basis for the development of a 'normal' Germany is an important change that began in the last years of the twentieth century and continues in the twenty-first. Cem Özdemir, the first German MP of Turkish origin (who later resigned in a low-octane corruption scandal involving unauthorized use of frequent-flyer miles), speaks of the strangeness of growing up in a democracy and yet not being allowed to vote. Such a situation would, he points out, be unthinkable elsewhere:

> Xenophobia and exclusion exist both here and there. But no Frenchman, Dutchman or American would think of describing children born in their country as a foreigner . . . No democratic society can afford to exclude a growing portion of its population from political participation in the long term.

When Özdemir was elected to the Bundestag in 1994, he found that the existence of an MP of Turkish origin was not to everybody's taste – especially since, as assistant speaker, he was seated conspicuously behind Helmut Kohl during the inaugural session, which was televised live. Nor was it only uneducated racists who regarded the idea of a Turkish-German politician as a contradiction. Özdemir was born in a small town in the Swabian hills of southern Germany. And yet, Özdemir describes how some MPs still regarded him as fundamentally un-German, even after his election to the Bundestag. 'After running out of other arguments, a state secretary said to me: "Herr Özdemir, you should tell your compatriots . . . " And I told him: "Herr Lintner, *you* are my compatriot".'

Herr Lintner apparently found the concept difficult to grasp. According to Özdemir, 'he looked confused'. German expectations of foreigners have frequently been low. Feridun Zaimoglu was told by his teacher that he was foolish to dream of being an artist or a writer: 'To become a car mechanic,' the future author was told, 'is quite skilled enough for a Turk.' Zaimoglu is part of a generation which has helped to turn the old prejudices on their heads. He has helped to reclaim the word *Kanak* – an abusive word for Turk – and fling it back in the abusers' faces, with his bestselling *Kanak Sprak* ('Kanak Talk'). In an essay entitled 'Kanak Attack', Zaimoglu talks of how 'people in this country treat Turks in the same way that TÜV, the Technical Control Board, treats foreign products. Again and again the hypocritical question is asked as to whether the Turk meets "our" safety standards.'

Gradually, the dawning of the twenty-first century has allowed a partial change of gear. Zaimoglu himself concludes his 'Kanak Attack', published in 2001, on a note of partial optimism – a soothing balm to accompany the rhetorical sting:

> As a chronicler, one must write of these things, for later, people will say: the story of the immigrants, of their children and their children's children, is the story of Germans of foreign origin who stayed – despite insults and humiliation, despite politicians' populism and xenophobia. They stayed, because it was worth staying in this land.

In the past few years, it has finally come to be accepted that the old legislation – giving preference to blood over soil, every time – is inappropriate for twenty-first century Germany, as the country seeks to turn normal. Even now, the country's attitudes to citizenship can hardly be described as modern. They are, however, very different from those of just a few years ago. Helmut Kohl liked to declare that Germany was 'not a land of immigration'. (It was merely a country which in the previous two decades happened to have taken in seven million foreigners, nine per cent of the population). After Kohl was gone, his party's line was adjusted somewhat: Germany became 'not a classic land of immigration' – a deliberately ambiguous phrase which meant something or nothing, according to taste.

In practice, all mainstream politicians now accept that German society is in the midst of change – however hesitantly that change seems to take place. This is, in the words of a Turkish-German politician, 'a revolution in homeopathic doses'. Stubborn political resistance scuppered proposals in 1999 to create dual citizenship. Any German-born Turk who takes a German passport is still forced to renounce his Turkish citizenship at the same time. Meanwhile, however, naturalization is much easier than before. On 1 January 2000, foreigners gained the right to a German passport if one parent has lived in Germany for eight years; children under the age of 10 are entitled to German nationality if they were born in Germany. With the introduction of the new rules, the number of non-ethnic Germans taking German passports jumped fivefold. Then came the introduction of a new green-card system, setting aside work permits for qualified foreign workers. Christian Democrats in the west German state of North-Rhine Westphalia, inspired by their success in resisting the proposals for dual citizenship, conducted an unashamedly racist election campaign, based on the slogan 'Kinder statt Inder' ('children, not Indians'), a reference to the fact that Indian IT specialists were expected to take advantage of the green-card offer. (The

Kanak Attack

green-card proposal was triggered, above all, by the urgent need to reboot a dangerously uncompetitive German industry before it finally crashed.) Unsurprisingly, the *Kinder statt Inder* campaign garnered horrified headlines around the world. Interestingly, however, this naked attempt to fuel xenophobia – a traditional votewinner worldwide – did the CDU little good. On the contrary, it contributed to a disastrous defeat. From then on, the subject was left alone.

In March 2002, a new and more liberal bill on immigration was (more or less) passed. Some extraordinary to-ing and fro-ing meant that the bill found itself in suspended animation. The Bundestag voted in favour (the government coalition enjoyed the support of the opposition Christian Democrats). But the second parliamentary chamber – the *Bundesrat* – 'federal council', made up of representatives of the 16 regional parliaments – was so confusingly split down the middle that nobody could decide whether this was legally a 'yes' or a 'no' vote. As ever, the politicians referred the difficult decisions to the constitutional court to find out whether the *Bundesrat* really had decided what it thought it had decided. The constitutional court in Karlsruhe, accustomed to ruling on such niceties, came up with the Solomonic judgement that the alleged 'yes' vote was not (yet) valid. Already, however, the direction of change is clear. It now seems implausible that a government of any political colour could return to the old blood-obsessed attitudes to citizenship. The less ethnically driven *ius soli* is at last beginning to rule.

The changes to the citizenship and immigration laws will be essential for Germany's political health in two important respects. On the one hand, the changes allow greater integration of German society for the first time, by breaking down the previously rigid divide between ethnic Germans and The Rest. That is in itself valuable, for Solingen reasons. In addition, the changes may help to diffuse the problems of Germany's self-image and perceptions of Germany abroad. One in six marriages in Germany is between a German and a non-German, and the proportion is increasing. Even the most insistent proponent of the thesis that 'Germans never change' may find it more difficult to accuse Germans of being Nazis at one remove, to talk of their 'ugly predictability' or to insist that they have a gene loose, if many of those Germans have black or brown skin, and if modern politicians and writers have names like Özdemir and Zaimoglu.

Some of the changes are, above all, symbolic. Germans celebrated the presence of the Ghanaian-born footballer Gerald Asamoah in the World Cup final against Brazil in 2002. The number of ethnically Turkish players in the German Bundesliga has steadily increased. Even now, the movement towards a *multikulti* society – to use the increasingly fashionable German phrase – is confused. Thus, a well-meaning official brochure published in 2002 makes a startling discovery: 'Many Turkish young people, in common with Germans of the same age, enjoy visiting discotheques.' (In short: people who live and have grown up in the same country sometimes have similar interests. Who would have thought it! They're almost like us!!)

There have been endless arguments in recent years about the proclaimed need for a German *Leitkultur* – a 'dominant culture'. Germany still seems deeply confused about who does or does not 'fit in'. Meanwhile, however, any Turk who has grown up or lived in Germany in the past 20 years notes the changes that have taken place. In Berlin, I met Canan, stylist in a fashionable hairdressing salon. For her, there was an obvious difference between then and now. 'My parents and others were here just as *gastarbeiter*, doing the hard jobs. Now, Turks and foreigners have become employers, too. One can show the Germans that it *is* possible to be integrated into German society.'

For the first time, Turkish-German comedians enjoy success among Turks and Germans alike – not least by confronting the fact that Turkish Germany and German Germany exist side by side. Kaya Yanar, more at home in his native German dialect than in Turkish, is one of the biggest TV successes of the new century. As *Der Spiegel* noted: 'The time was ripe: a child of the third immigrant generation in Germany, who documents a society's confused internal dialogues.' His trademark phrase – '*Was guckst du?*' – 'Whaddaya looking at?' – has become a national catchphrase. Even now, with his unparalleled success, he still mocks the old prejudices. His comment, when he received the German Television Prize, in 2001 was: 'First we take your jobs, then your women, and now the prizes, too.' Yanar says he fears that he will one day find it was all a misunderstanding – and that he will be told to 'go back home where you came from'. In reality, that no longer looks a likely option. The *Kanaken* are in Germany to stay.

10

German Soldiers Wanted

Because of the German past.
>(Social Democrat opposition leader Rudolf Scharping explains why
>he is opposed to German involvement in policing a no-fly
>zone over Bosnia in 1995)

No more Auschwitz, no more genocide, no more fascism. All that
goes together for me.
>(Green foreign minister Joschka Fischer explains why German ground
>troops should be sent to confront Serb forces in Kosovo in 1999;
>Rudolf Scharping, defence minister, was involved in this and
>other decisions to send German troops to the Balkans)

Few national debates have been more angry and agonized over recent
years than the question of sending German soldiers abroad. For almost
50 years, the question barely even came up – and if it did, it was instantly
dismissed. Now, in just a few years, all previous certainties have been
overturned.

After 1945, the Allies argued whether Germans should be allowed to
carry guns at all; even the use of uniforms was restricted. In 1949, the
new Federal Republic declared its determination 'by all means in its
power to prevent the creation of armed forces of any kind'. But all that
soon changed. The outbreak of war in Korea in 1950 created fears of a
Communist attack not just in Asia but in Europe, too. In those circumstances, West Germany was required to play its part. The Federal
Republic was authorized to raise a military force of half a million to help
protect western Europe in a possible war with the Soviet Union.

Even now, there was disquiet – not least because of the lack of commitment to democracy that the German military had shown. General Ludwig Beck had warned in 1938 of the need for a senior officer to 'take note of his overriding responsibility to his whole people', not just to obey military orders. Beck (later executed by the Nazis) was isolated at that time, a moral voice in the wilderness. Now, by contrast, the importance of 'inner leadership' was constantly emphasized. The new message was: obedience, yes; but only up to a point. The newly created Bundeswehr was, perhaps, the most civilian army in history. The first officers arriving at Nato headquarters in 1955 were dressed, one observer noted, 'like diplomats who had forgotten their umbrellas'.

In armies all over the world, continuity with the past is a key theme. In the post-war Federal Republic, such continuity was unthinkable. Instead, the clean break with the past was what counted, above all. Even so, West Germans remained wary. The numbers of those seeking exemption from conscription was much higher in West Germany than anywhere else in Europe. In 1980, a ceremony marking the 25th anniversary of the creation of the Bundeswehr was still capable of provoking protests and riots. Only gradually did the Bundeswehr come to be seen as the embodiment of German democracy – helped, as ever, by generational change. When the Bundeswehr was created, many of its most senior commanders had, inevitably, fought for Hitler. As Adenauer tartly noted, 'I don't think that Nato will be keen to receive 18-year-old generals from me.' In the 1980s, by contrast, the new intake of officers were, in generational terms, part of the rebellious 1968 generation. The Bundeswehr increasingly defined itself, implicitly and explicitly, by contrast with Hitler's Wehrmacht. This was an army which sought to achieve good, not an army which allowed itself to commit evil. Its officers were educated to think constantly about historical responsibility and truth.

Such feelings meant a permanent sense of hesitancy, when the words 'German combat troops' were mentioned. As early as 1965, US President Lyndon Johnson asked for German medical orderlies and a battalion of 1000 men to be sent to Vietnam. The German government regretted that it was unable to help – because of 'the effects of the Second World War', a phrase which let Bonn off the diplomatic hook. Even after the end of the Cold War and with German unification, the picture did not immediately change. When Iraq invaded Kuwait in 1990, shortly before unification, German headline-writers saw events through the prism of Germany's own history. 'Saddam invades Kuwait, as Hitler once invaded Poland', the tabloid *Bild* proclaimed. The US-led military action against

Saddam Hussein in 1991 took place with United Nations approval and the backing of a broad international coalition. But few inside or outside Germany suggested that Germany should play a military role. Opinion polls showed that more than eight out of 10 voters believed that the Bundeswehr should stay clear of international conflict, just as it had always done. Chancellor Helmut Kohl was able to buy himself a 'Get Out of Iraq' free card, by making a hefty eighteen-billion Deutschmark contribution towards the war.

Within the next few years, however, dramatic changes began. In 1992, when Germany sent medical orderlies to Cambodia, some saw even that as a warlike step too far. With a logic that some might find difficult to follow, they calculated that there was an unacceptable connection between crimes committed by Germans in Europe between 1939 and 1945, on the one hand, and the sending of medical staff to help a troubled country in south-east Asia in 1992, on the other. Cambodia marked only the beginning of a cascading series of changes involving Germans in war zones. When I flew into a besieged Sarajevo in July 1992, I found myself hitching a lift with the Luftwaffe. Because of the Serb gunners surrounding the city, we were required to wear flak jackets for the last few minutes of the flight into the Bosnian capital. In short, though this was not yet military action abroad, it was hardly a peacetime exercise.

In the next few months and years, as the layers of resistance were peeled away at startling speed, proponents and opponents of German involvement in military action alike harked back to the Hitlerian past. In most countries, political and military decisions are made on the basis of what politicians believe to be right, what society believes to be right, or what is useful for the national interest. (Sometimes, though by no means always, all three may coincide.) In Germany, by contrast, both sides argued the case not on the basis of facts, morality or power, but according to their respective interpretations of what the rest of the world might think. The Social Democrats argued it would be irresponsible for Germany to send soldiers abroad, and for war 'to go out from German soil' – otherwise, what would the world think? Kohl's Christian Democrats argued that it was Germany's duty to send soldiers abroad when needed – otherwise, what would the world think?

During the early years of the Balkan wars in the 1990s, German politicians openly advocated tougher action against the Serb leader Slobodan Milosevic and his Bosnian Serb allies, especially after the discovery of concentration camps in Bosnia. In the words of the defence minister, Volker Rühe: 'Concentration camps in Germany were stopped by soldiers, not by demonstrations in another country.' On the other hand, the government insisted that Germany itself could not possibly send troops – 'because of the Second World War'. The British government – eager at that time to find reasons for blocking outside pressure on Milosevic – gleefully accused Bonn of rank hypocrisy.

Even indirect German involvement in military action necessitated intricate manoeuvres. Thus, when the government coalition wanted German air crews to fly on board Awacs surveillance planes over Bosnia in 1993, the foreign minister, Klaus Kinkel (who was also leader of the Free Democrats, the junior coalition partner), added a surreal touch to proceedings by going to the constitutional court to challenge the decision which he himself had helped to take. The judges of the constitutional court eventually ruled in favour – by reference to political considerations, not legal paragraphs. (The Nato secretary-general and former German defence minister, Manfred Wörner, told the court that the participation of German air crews was 'decisive'; without them, 'things would go badly'.) Unsurprisingly, German commentators talked of 'madhouse Bonn'.

The constitutional court was again asked to rule, on whether politicians could send troops to Somalia. On this occasion, the judges lost patience with the politicians' serial failure to make up their minds on important issues, and sent the issue back for parliament to make up its own mind; parliament duly voted in favour. As German soldiers prepared to take part in a United Nations mission to Somalia in 1993, *Die Woche* argued: 'Perhaps it is now, not when the Wall came down, that the post-war era has ended. A new, uncertain era has begun, into which we are stumbling – naïve, lost and unprepared.'

That last sentence certainly seemed accurate. Attitudes were confused and contradictory. Even as the opposition Social Democrats dug their heels in, the ground continued to shift under their feet. In 1994, the German government upped the ante by agreeing in principle to a request from Nato for the use not just of German air crews but also of the sophisticated technology of German Tornado planes, for enforcing the Bosnian no-fly zone – for example, by detecting and knocking out hostile radar. The Tornado issue came to a head the following year, when Germany stood, as one commentary put it, 'before the abyss of history'. During a heated debate on 30 June 1995, Rudolf Scharping, leader of the Social Democrats, insisted that sending Tornados to the Balkans would be inappropriate 'because of the German past' (a view echoed by the Bosnian Serb leader Radovan Karadzic, who warned in an interview with German TV of 'unimaginable consequences' if German soldiers were to be seen in the Balkans). Scharping and the other opponents of German involvement were defeated. The Bundestag agreed – 386 votes in favour, 258 against – that Germans could once more fire shots in anger for the first time since 1945.

Opponents complained of the government's salami tactics, and in many respects they were right. The slices of change came thicker and thicker in the weeks and months to come. A few days after the historic Tornado vote, Serbs massacred thousands of civilians at the Bosnian town of Srebrenica, while UN peacekeepers in the town stood by. The mixture of horror and political humiliation forced the West to take a tougher stance for the first time. In September, Nato planes bombed Serb positions – with the assistance of the German Tornados. Just three months later, after the Dayton peace agreement that ended the Bosnian war, the German parliament voted overwhelmingly – 543 votes in favour, 107 against – for German troops to become part of the international military force that would now be sent to Bosnia. Two years earlier, such action would have seemed unthinkable. Now, it had begun to seem almost normal.

These changes in attitude, regarding what German soldiers should and should not be allowed to do in the late twentieth century, were dramatic. (Though not as dramatic as what was yet to come.) Meanwhile, there were equally dramatic changes in attitude towards what German soldiers had or had not done between 1939 and 1945. Schoolbooks after 1945 were eager – in addition, as previously described, to downplaying the knowledge and extent of Nazi crimes – to emphasize the unblemished reputation of German soldiers. At one level, this was understandable. Millions died on the Eastern Front; hundreds of thousands of captured POWs never returned from Stalin's camps; many of those who did return were scarred for the rest of their lives. Some who died at the front or in captivity were dedicated anti-Nazis, appalled by the crimes that their compatriots were committing all around them – like Wilm Hosenfeld, the real-life German captain who later became famous through Roman Polanski's film *The Pianist*. Hosenfeld rescued not just the pianist Wladyslaw Szpilman, as described in Polanski's film, but also a number of other Poles and Jews. Hosenfeld – an ordinary soldier, with no privileged access to secret information – wrote in his diary in 1942:

There is outright terror and fear everywhere, the use of force, arrests. People are taken away and shot daily . . . There is an action going on here to exterminate the Jews. That has been the aim of the

German civilian administration ever since the occupation of the eastern regions, with the assistance of the police and the Gestapo, but apparently it is to be applied on a huge, radical scale now.

Many other Germans, though they did not necessarily play such a courageous role as Hosenfeld, felt uneasy about the war in which Hitler had sent them to fight and die. For the schoolbooks of the 1950s, it was not enough to make that obvious point. The authors and teachers of that period wanted a clean bill of health, a *Persilschein* that would wash the entire Wehrmacht whiter. Only Hitler and his immediate associates were to blame for what had happened. Thus, typically:

> Undoubtedly hundreds of thousands, especially young people, followed Hitler's disastrous call with a clear conscience and in good faith. Millions went to war – not to serve Hitler's plans of conquest but to defend the fatherland. At that time, they could not see the whole truth, which today has been laid bare.

'Clear conscience', 'good faith', 'defending the fatherland'. These are comforting phrases, which do not sit easily with a 1942 entry in Hosenfeld's diary, where he talks of 'the dreadful cruelties, the animal brutality' in Warsaw. Hosenfeld foreshadowed the Stanford experiment on brutality when he noted that 'otherwise harmless countrymen' (what Zimbardo would later call his 'peaceniks') quickly began to commit atrocities. Like the minority who in Milgram's experiments doggedly refused to depress the lethal switch, Hosenfeld did not see himself as unusual. He merely retained a sense of morality and personal responsibility amidst the surrounding nightmare.

The textbooks of the 1950s, eager to devote as little space as possible to Nazi crimes against humanity, always find room to mention the fact that German soldiers were uninvolved. After all, 'Hitler knew he could not ask the German army or its officer corps' to do such things. (Hosenfeld: 'If what they are saying in the city is true, then it is no honour to be a German officer, and no one could go along with what is happening.') This insistence on the ordinary soldier's innocence remained a mantra even when schoolbooks of the 1970s and 1980s began to talk more openly and at length about Nazi crimes. Not until five years after German unity was this unbreachable Maginot line of German innocence finally broken.

In spring 1995, an extraordinary exhibition opened, which shattered previous taboos. 'I fought on the Eastern Front' had, with the help of the textbooks, come to serve as an old man's shorthand for 'I suffered terribly and my hands are clean'. The new exhibition, organized by the Hamburg Institute for Social Research, would change all that for ever. Its main premise:

> In 1995, 50 years after the war, it is time finally to jettison this lie and to accept the reality of a gigantic crime. Between 1941 and 1944, the Wehrmacht did not conduct a 'normal war' in the Balkans and the Soviet Union, but a war of annihilation against Jews, prisoners of war and the civilian population, millions of whom died.

The exhibition relentlessly catalogued German crimes throughout the occupied east. 'The Wehrmacht actively participated in the mass murder.' 'The Wehrmacht, together with the SS and the police, shot and burnt to death women and children, the sick and the old and transformed the land around the German bases into a dead zone.' And so on, in crushing detail. Letters home, on display in the exhibition, contained the comments of ordinary soldiers at the time. One letter-writer sounds a triumphal note: 'Yesterday, we and the SS were generous. Every Jew we caught was shot. Today, it's different. They are beaten to death with cudgels and spades.' Another tells his loved ones: 'These guys are as impudent as if it were still peacetime. More of these abortions of humanity should be put up against the wall than has happened so far.'

As ever, reactions to the exhibition divided partly along generational lines. A teenager visiting the exhibition with her school class told me: 'It still shocks me that something like this could happen. It's really important that it's shown.' An 80-year-old retired architect standing nearby was contemptuous. 'One can always find such things. We acted according to the Geneva Convention.' For obvious reasons, it was a difficult exhibition for Germans to see. As *Die Zeit* noted: 'It's a terrible thought. Suddenly, when looking into this photographic album of crime – where every wall, every corner, cries "Murder!" – one might see one's own father or grandfather.' In the next few years, the exhibition travelled throughout Germany, sometimes stirring up protests; these protests, in turn, gained international headlines, providing alleged proof of German reluctance to confront the past. The exhibition was forced to close in 1999 after factual errors were identified, including wrongly captioned photographs. Those errors came to seem potentially fatal; they allowed critics to argue that the exhibition was based on a slanderous premise. In reality, the protests were merely the last-ditch resistance of the losing side. Before the Wehrmacht exhibition, Hitler's army could safely be portrayed as innocent; afterwards, no longer. In 2001, a new version of the exhibition opened, stronger and more self-confident than ever. It included additional details about the state of international law in 1939, so that it would no longer be possible to excuse the crimes of the Wehrmacht by referring to the legal situation in force at the time. Mass shootings, the policy of starving whole regions, the murder of civilians under the pretext of describing them as partisans, the barbaric treatment of prisoners of war: all this was in contravention of the Hague Convention, which Hitler's Germany had never unsigned. For the crimes of the past, there could and would be no clean bill of health.

The newest schoolbooks reveal what might be called the Hamburg effect. Photographs and captions are chosen to show that the Wehrmacht was neither innocent nor ignorant. The unusual degree of who-where-when detail in the captions seems deliberately designed to head off sceptical comments ('we acted according to the Geneva Convention', as the elderly architect had told me in Hamburg) that might be heard from Grandad or his friends. Thus, one photograph shows a Jew being shot in the back of the head, falling into a pit full of bodies. The brief caption notes – in what would, without knowledge of the Hamburg dispute, seem a superfluous detail: 'The spectators are mostly soldiers.' Another book names the regiment responsible for an execution in 1941 where, as the precise, dated caption notes, '36 uninvolved civilians were shot and hanged as expiation for the shooting of two SS men'.

This growing openness about the criminal behaviour of German soldiers in the Second World War went hand in hand with more relaxed attitudes about the prospect that German soldiers might in future act not just as medical orderlies, nor as peacekeepers – but might even go into battle, for the first time in half a century.

When Helmut Kohl and the CDU were ousted in 1998 after 16 years at the top, the Social Democrat Gerhard Schröder became Chancellor, with Joschka Fischer, the troublemaking Green, as his foreign minister. Less than six months later, Nato was involved in its first-ever European war, bombing Kosovo and the Serbian capital, Belgrade. Given all that had happened in recent years – including the Social Democrats' constant complaints about 'salami tactics' with regard to much more modest German military involvement less than four years earlier – it seemed impossible to imagine that the new government could contemplate sending ground troops to the Balkans. In reality, it was now that the serious changes began.

Helmut Kohl had in previous years overturned conventional wisdom by arguing that, despite German history, it was now possible for German troops to be sent abroad. But the new Social Democrat government went much further. Nor was it just the Social Democrats who were in favour. Fischer, representing the largely pacifist Greens, insisted that German troops should be able to go into Kosovo if required. Fischer turned Kohl's previous logic around, saying that Germany should become involved not despite but *because* of its history. 'This is the first time in this century that Germany is on the right side,' he declared, with reference to the bloody ethnic cleansing unleashed by Milosevic against Albanians in Kosovo. 'Kosovo is the first war in which the united Europe stands up against the nationalist Europe of the past.'

Many in Fischer's own party passionately loathed what they saw as his militaristic stance. At a party conference in a Bielefeld sports hall in May 1999, an angry protester struck Fischer with a scarlet paint bomb, perforating his eardrum and splattering paint over his head and down his suit. The protesters chanted 'Joschka Goebbels!', but he refused to give way, retorting fiercely: 'No more Auschwitz, no more genocide, no more fascism. All that goes together for me.'

A month later, when German troops arrived in Prizren in western Kosovo, they were stunned by their reception. Thousands hugged and kissed the conscripts, and put flowers in their flak jackets. Crowds chanted: '*Deutsch-land!*' A young Kosovo Albanian described her reaction on seeing the German tanks. 'I fainted right on the street. This was a miracle.' Germans had spent years telling each other that the world would be horrified if they were to set foot in a war zone ever again – especially in an area, like the Balkans, where Germans had committed horrific crimes in the past. Now, it was clear that this assumption was based on a misconception. If the Germans had sought to unleash renewed mayhem and murder, they could undoubtedly have expected a hostile reception. When, however, a lone German officer faced down a group of armed Serbs in Prizren, thus forcing the gunmen into a sullen retreat, even newspapers which had happily German-bashed for years fell over themselves to express their admiration for the courage of Major Harald List of the Bundeswehr.

This German involvement in the Balkans – so unthinkable, just a few years earlier – marked the opening of the floodgates. Less than four years earlier, when the lacklustre Rudolf Scharping was still opposition leader, he argued that the use of German planes in Bosnia to back up the UN mission was inappropriate 'because of the German past'. Now, Scharping was defence minister – and the world had changed beyond recognition.

Scharping dispatched troops not just to Kosovo, but to a clutch of troublespots in the Balkans and elsewhere. When German ground troops formed part of the international force in Macedonia in 2001, that caused more German heartsearching. Within a few months, however, that drama, too, seemed old hat. When British and US troops were withdrawn from Macedonia to go to Afghanistan in autumn 2001, Germans duly took command of the Nato force there.

And still the pace of change accelerated – faster than ever. In the aftermath of 9/11, the world's attention was understandably focused on the criminal catastrophe, on the one hand – the choreographed murder of thousands, seen live on TV – and the international consequences of the war in Afghanistan and President Bush's proclaimed 'war on terror', on the other. In Germany, meanwhile, a separate revolution took place, eclipsed in the international media by more obvious dramas elsewhere. Gerhard Schröder, in a phrase that would within two years seem quite unthinkable, declared his 'unlimited solidarity' with the United States. Above all, he declared his government's willingness to send troops to Afghanistan. Schröder explicitly acknowledged that this was a milestone. This, he implied, was where the *Sonderweg* – 'Germany's separate path – could finally come to its end: 'After long periods of confusion in the nineteenth and twentieth centuries, Germany has at last joined the West. That's what's at stake for us. The argument that we cannot take part because of our history no longer holds true.'

This volte-face – a political handbrake turn, compared with the policies that Schröder's predecessor as SPD (Social Democrats) leader had stood for – was made simpler by the fact that the shift in German public opinion was as dramatic as the politicians' change of heart. Two-thirds now believed it appropriate for Germany to take part in military action abroad – a threefold leap from a decade earlier. Unsurprisingly, the idea that German soldiers should go to fight alongside the Americans in the Hindu Kush did not go down well with many Greens. The three-year-old 'red–green' coalition was in mortal danger as a result of Schröder's commitment of German troops. Everybody agreed that endgame was near. In the words of *Der Spiegel*: 'Marching orders for the Bundeswehr would be the beginning of the end for red–green.' The mass-circulation *Bild* asked: 'Will Schröder's government fall apart over the war?' The assumption was: yes, absolutely.

Schröder offered to send 4000 troops to the region, including 100 elite KSK troops to hunt down members of al Qaeda. Schröder made it clear that, on this issue at least, there could be no Third Way. He called a vote of confidence and thus linked the government's very survival to the issue. It was only the fourth such vote in the history of the Federal Republic – and the first time that such a vote had been linked to a substantive issue. After intense lobbying of reluctant MPs in the final days, hours and minutes, the coalition survived by a handful of votes. Even now, however, the coalition still seemed set to fall apart over this most controversial issue of all. Antje Vollmer, a leading Green and vice-president of the Bundestag, gave a confusing gloss to her vote of confidence by explaining: 'My yes was actually a no.' The cover headline in *Focus* magazine, with reference to the continuing ructions, declared succinctly: 'Green suicide.' *Stern* magazine was sympathetic and brutal in equal measure: 'Thank you, Greens – you were wonderful!'

Unnoticed, however – by most Germans, let alone by the rest of the world, for whom this all sounded like another obscure coalition row – Germany was in the midst of a momentous sea change, the culmination of all the other changes which had taken place in the past few years. Fischer made it clear that he would resign if he failed to receive backing for the decision to send German troops to war. The stakes could hardly have been higher. Over a wet November weekend, the Greens met in the port of Rostock to debate the issue. On the streets outside, the weather was autumnal-dank; inside the cavernous conference hall, the atmosphere was heated. Politically, this was a battle of life and death. Many speakers insisted that the Greens must abandon the government coalition, come what may, so that the party could stay true to its principles. Banners draped around the hall attacked what many saw as an abject parliamentary climbdown in the Bundestag vote the previous week. And then, Fischer came to the rostrum. Tieless in his ministerial three-piece suit, one hand casually in pocket, the other hand slashing through the air with angry emphasis, Fischer argued that the Greens, despite their qualms about military action, were morally *obliged* to vote in favour – Germany, he argued, needed to be on the right side of history. Initially, there were boos. Gradually, however, the jeering gave way to noises of approval. The end of this speech was extraordinary to watch. Fischer received a prolonged standing ovation from delegates in the packed hall, many of whom had half an hour earlier seemed to deeply resent everything that he was arguing for. Two-thirds of the Green delegates finally voted in favour of sending troops to Afghanistan.

It would be argued later that the delegates had acted cynically to save their political skins. In reality, since many Greens remained deeply ambivalent about their participation in the Schröder government, that partly missed the point. The paradox and change of heart at the heated Rostock meeting reflected a change of heart in modern Germany, not just among the Greens. A few years earlier, even the most gung-ho conservative would not have dared to suggest that German ground troops could be sent into action in Afghanistan – because of the Second World War. Now, the party which was more obsessed than any other with the need to confront the past had given its blessing to this extraordinary move.

The story of the near-collapse of the German government was dramatic. If the government had collapsed – in other words, if the Bundestag or Rostock vote had gone the other way – that would have been more dramatic still. In some ways, however, most dramatic of all was the *non*-story – the resolution of the crisis, and the ovation for a Green minister who insisted on sending German troops to a distant war zone. The multiple complexes of the past were now giving way to an acceptance that endless breastbeating and self-accusation – proclaiming Germany's past crimes, as though those and only those must determine German foreign policy for all time – was not, in the end, the only way forward. In 2001, Germany embarked on its own voyage into the unknown, a political space odyssey.

Not for the first time, Germany seemed surprised by its own boldness, as it digested the implications of the changes now under way. 'Germans on all the fronts' was one cover headline a few months later. The decision to send German troops to Kosovo in 1999 had been extraordinary. The decision two years later to send troops to distant Afghanistan was more remarkable still. It represented a dramatic change – confirmation of Germany's new self-confidence. All the to-ing and fro-ing to the constitutional court in the mid-1990s and the anguished cries of 'salami tactics' were now part of history. Germany had moved into a different world.

There was, however, still more to come, in terms of Germany, politics and war. For the moment, a German 'yes' to sending troops to distant countries seemed revolutionary enough. Within barely a year, a German 'no' to a foreign war, in defiance of what had come to be known as the world's hyperpower, would prove – in terms of Germany's growing self-confidence – more remarkable still. When German troops were dispatched to Afghanistan, excited German headlines talked of 'the new alliance' and 'step into the first row'. Soon, however, such taboo-breaking changes of attitude towards German military action would seem almost trivial. In 2002, Berlin showed that it was ready to confront Washington for the first time since 1945.

In 1991, Helmut Kohl was unwilling to send German troops to Iraq in the first Gulf War. But there was no question of his defying America's wishes at that time. Instead, he contributed billions to the war coffers of George Bush senior. As George Bush the Younger began preparations for *his* war on Iraq 11 years later, the diplomatic battlelines had changed. Gerhard Schröder made it clear that Germany was not prepared to sign up for the war on Baghdad on Washington's terms – German foreign policy, he insisted, 'is made in Berlin'. He complained about Washington's failure to consult: 'It just isn't good enough to learn from the American press about a speech which clearly states: "We are going to do it, no matter what the world or our allies think." That is no way to treat others.' Joschka Fischer was equally blunt. At a meeting in Munich, he told the US Defense Secretary, Donald Rumsfeld: 'Excuse me, I am not convinced.' There was no longer any hint of a hand-wringing 'sorry, but'. Instead, Germany for the first time since 1945 publicly told its conqueror, protector and chief ally: 'No.'

At one level, electoral considerations spurred on the German opposition to the Iraq war; 80 per cent of Germans were opposed to a war. A policy that distanced the German government from the Washington hawks was thus politically useful for an embattled Schröder. His public defiance of the proposed American war against Saddam Hussein helped the red–green coalition slip back into power by the margin of just a few thousand votes in September 2002. In this context, however, Schröder's motives are less important than the simple fact that Berlin was willing publicly to defy Washington, whatever the circumstances. No Chancellor of the Bonner Republik would ever have dared to do that – however tempting the electoral gains might have seemed.

For decades, America had been the Federal Republic's unassailable friend. The Marshall Plan helped get the German economy back on its feet after 1945. The airlift and the *Rosinenbomber* secured the independence of West Berlin in 1948–49. In 1963, John F. Kennedy told the enthusiastic Berlin crowds: '*Ich bin ein Berliner.*' (Or, as his phonetic notes, later put on display in the Museum of German History, put it: 'Ish bin ein Bear-leener.') In 1994, President Bill Clinton gave Germans a warm glow of pride when he talked on a visit to Bonn of the 'truly unique relationship' between Germany and the United States. In 2001, after the attack on the Twin Towers, Schröder talked of the 'unlimited solidarity' between the two countries. Now, suddenly, all that changed – and the German mindset changed, too.

Even as he came to power in 1998, Schröder declared that Germany had 'come of age', and intended to pursue its national interests 'without a complex', like other countries. Now, he seemed ready to put those words into practice by snubbing the most powerful country in the world.

German Soldiers Wanted

Saying yes to military missions had enabled Germany to stand comfortably shoulder to shoulder with its American ally. Saying no to an American-led war in 2003 meant something very different. It meant that Germany had entered an era where it reckoned to be entitled to make its own decisions.

In the immediate aftermath of the war, President Bush was still smarting at the German rebuff – compounded by the fact that a leading Social Democrat had compared his policies on Iraq with those of Hitler. Rumsfeld said the relationship with Germany was 'poisoned', and Schröder was cold-shouldered. Gradually, however, it seemed that America still needed allies, just as they still needed America. America wooed the United Nations to become more involved in the complexities of rebuilding Iraq. Many Germans remained unimpressed. *Stern* magazine's cover illustration of George Bush in September 2003 was headlined: 'From Bigmouth to Beggar.' Commenting on US power, Fischer sounded conciliatory and defiant in almost equal measure:

The power of the United States is a totally decisive factor for peace and stability in the world. I don't believe Europe will ever be militarily strong enough to look after its security alone. But a world order in which the national interests of the strongest power is the criterion for military action simply cannot work.

Schröder made clear that Germany had no intention of returning to its old-fashioned diplomatic coyness. Speaking in New York in 2003, 30 years after Germany became a member of the United Nations, Schröder appeared to bid for Germany to take an official seat at the diplomatic top table by becoming a new permanent member of the UN Security Council. It was another sign of how things have changed. The word 'Europe' remains ubiquitous in German diplo-speak. But 'national interests' are allowed to be just that, for the first time. There is no longer the uniquely German pretence that every political and diplomatic decision is on behalf of or at the request of others. Even decisions which could reasonably be portrayed as containing a sprinkling of altruism – the dispatching of troops to northern Afghanistan, for example, in response to repeated requests from Afghan leaders to strengthen the country's security – are described in terms of national interest. Peter Struck, the defence minister, declared, even as German soldiers were being killed in Afghanistan: 'Germany's security is also being defended in the Hindu Kush.' There are now more than 9000 German troops worldwide – from the Balkans to Afghanistan, and from Uganda to

Uzbekistan. In Kabul, a German general took command of Isaf, the 5000-strong international security force, in 2003. Germans are an international fighting force for the first time in six decades. At last, that fact frightens neither the Germans nor the rest of the world.

11

Do Mention the War

The German resistance hardly had any support in the population.
That is why it remained small in numbers and isolated.
(A modern German schoolbook portrays the mindset of the 1940s in a
rather harsher light than earlier textbooks on the same theme)

The historians criticize *Hitler's Willing Executioners* – and the
public finds the book liberating.
(*Die Zeit* records the reception for Daniel Goldhagen's bestseller, which
argues that Germans were inclined to commit genocide even before
Hitler came to power)

'Don't mention the war,' Basil Fawlty, the world's most deranged hotel
manager, tells his colleagues in an insistent not-quite whisper. After all, the
German guests in the restaurant might be offended. Basil himself, meanwhile, obsessed by his desire to avoid the subject, does an involuntary
goosestep past the bemused Germans, finger across his lip to form a Hitler
moustache. Fawlty's famous phrase, first uttered in 1975, has passed into
the English language as a jocular shorthand for everything connected with
German attitudes to the Second World War. John Cleese, creator of the
Fawlty Towers series, emphasizes that he set out to mock the absurdity of
Fawlty's views: 'The point I was trying to make is that people like Basil are
utterly stuck in the past.' Cleese is right: Basil *is* stuck in the past. The
insufferable Basil was not, however, completely wrong at the time when
the German sketch was first broadcast. In the 1970s, many German taboos
were still in place – or, as the defenders of the taboos liked to put it: 'Too
much has already been said on the subject.' They reacted like my fidgety

neighbour when watching *Cabaret* in Berlin in 1973. Liza Minnelli's high-kick songs and 'Life is a cabaret!' were fine – but not a biergarten scene which implied popular support for Hitler. For many older Germans especially, 'don't mention the war' was indeed still the rule.

More surprisingly, Basil Fawlty's logic – in effect: 'They're all in denial, so let's not embarrass them by drawing attention to that fact' – has remained popular long beyond its natural sell-by date. Many who would never admit to any Fawltyesque qualities are nonetheless convinced that Germans dare not speak freely about the past. British and American newspaper editors eagerly clear space for stories which confirm the alleged ubiquitousness of German taboos with reference to the Holocaust. In reality, the subject of the Third Reich has been difficult to avoid in Germany in recent years – in political discourse, in the bestseller lists, and on television.

Especially from the 1990s onwards, the reactions of cinema audiences, too, emphasize the dramatic contrast between the new openness and the old reluctance to confront uncomfortable truths. Steven Spielberg's *Schindler's List* was by far the biggest film of the year in Germany in 1994. Many audiences saw this as a film, above all, about the Holocaust; the cruelty and horror of the Final Solution are vividly represented. And yet, the nightmare of the Holocaust is in a different sense only a brutal backdrop to the extraordinary story told here – how one man was able to save more than 1000 people who would otherwise have been murdered. The ring which the *Schindlerjuden*, as they described themselves, presented to Oskar Schindler in the hours before the Nazi surrender emphasizes his achievement in that context. The ring was from melted-down gold bridgework which a Schindler survivor demanded should be wrenched out of his mouth, explaining: 'Without Oskar, the SS would have the damned stuff anyway.' The ring carries the Talmudic inscription: 'He who saves a single life, saves the world entire.'

For German audiences, this was not just a film about Nazi crimes. Those were self-evident. Nor did Schindler provide a feelgood factor, proof that there *were* good Germans, after all. In the past, that had indeed been the dominant tone. An innocent observer might have concluded that Hitler's Germany was full of thwarted Hans and Sophie Scholls, eager to rise up against the tyrant. Now, by contrast, the fact that such courage was exceptional was itself the talking point. Audiences flocked to see the film. Showings were sold out well in advance. The emotional impact was dramatic. When I watched *Schindler's List* in a packed cinema in Hamburg, nobody moved for several minutes after the film ended. People looked stunned when they finally walked out. I asked one woman what, for her, was the main significance of the film. She gave the same answer that others were giving, up and down the country. 'One asks oneself: why didn't people *do* something?'

One writer criticized Spielberg's alleged historical inaccuracy. He claimed that the clearing of the ghetto 'could not have been so bloody', because (he argued, apparently in all seriousness) such brutality would have been against the rules. The writer, a teenager in the Third Reich, explained his indignation. 'Like almost all Germans who only heard of Auschwitz in 1945, I found it an impertinence to be retrospectively smeared with blood.' Born in 1929, he found it an impertinence to be forced to think about Auschwitz, or to be confronted with brutality in the ghetto. For newer generations, however – not just the young but also the middle-aged, the students of 1968 whose hair was now turning grey – it was the failures of the past which were now centre-screen. *Stern* magazine summed up the film's message for a modern German audience: 'One single man put civil courage before German obedience.'

Zivilcourage was now an important theme in the schoolbooks, too. In earlier decades, schoolchildren were constantly told that their parents in the Third Reich had known nothing of what was happening around them – and that they could have done nothing, if they had known. From the 1990s onwards, by contrast, young Germans have been encouraged to ask not *if* more could have been done, but *what* could have been done to ensure that the Third Reich's murderous plans were blocked. Teachers used Spielberg's film to reinforce the message that, as one textbook put it: 'The excuse that "all resistance is pointless" does not work.' Another book, quoting the 'I was only obeying orders' logic, notes that few Germans resisted Hitler – and goes on to emphasize the constitutionally guaranteed right and duty to resist 'illegal state violence'. In short: modern Germans are encouraged to absorb the disturbing lessons of Milgram's laboratory experiments, as exemplified in brutal reality by the Third Reich, and to take responsibility for the society in which they live. The importance of preventing a repetition of the past, 'today and in the future', is repeatedly referred to.

During these years after German unity, the taboos of previous years were not just carefully unpeeled. They were dramatically exploded. One schoolbook, in a section entitled 'Resistance without a people', is merciless in its conclusions: 'Partisans in the occupied countries were supported by their compatriots. But the German resistance hardly had any support in the population. That is why it remained small in numbers, and isolated.' The new books pay homage, as earlier books did, to Hans and Sophie Scholl, beheaded for their bravery. They no longer make any pretence, however, that the Scholls enjoyed widespread support. Of the 1944 plot against Hitler, too, new books note that 'there was little sympathy for the attempted coup among the population at large'.

In this context it is easier to understand the remarkable reception in Germany for Daniel Goldhagen's *Hitler's Willing Executioners*, published in 1996. Outside Germany, the success of Goldhagen's book was unsurprising. The exploding neo-Nazi violence of the early 1990s, on the one hand, and Germany's growing new political confidence, on the other, were seen as signs that the country wished to turn its back on the past. Goldhagen's argument was thus especially resonant, with its suggestion that Germans 60 years earlier had been eager to commit mass killings of Jews, even before Hitler came to power.

> Antisemitism moved many thousands of 'ordinary' Germans – and would have moved millions more, had they been appropriately positioned – to slaughter Jews. Not economic hardship, not social psychological pressure, not invariable psychological propensities, but ideas about Jews that were pervasive in Germany, and had been for decades, induced ordinary Germans to kill unarmed, defenceless Jewish men, women and children by the thousands, systematically and without pity.

Historians have long agreed that ordinary Germans went along to a remarkable degree with the Nazi crimes. In 1961, Raul Hilberg wrote in *The Destruction of the European Jews* that the perpetrators 'were not different in their moral makeup from the rest of the population'. More recently, Christopher Browning documented in chilling detail in *Ordinary Men*, published in 1992, how a group of unexceptional middle-aged Germans, members of Reserve Police Battalion 101, were transformed into brutal killers. German historians also note that – despite the best efforts of many defendants' lawyers to argue the contrary – there is not a single documented case where refusal to kill civilians resulted in dire consequences for those who remained true to their consciences.

All this was, however, very different from suggesting that in Germany of the 1920s and 1930s there was a pre-existing German desire to commit genocide. which Hitler merely gave the green light to – because Germans, as Goldhagen put it, 'wanted to be genocidal executioners'. Most Holocaust historians treat Goldhagen's thesis with caution, at best. Browning, in a post-Goldhagen edition of *Ordinary Men*, criticizes Goldhagen's 'untenable' arguments, and notes: 'A methodology that can scarcely do other than confirm the hypothesis that it was designed to test is not valid social science.' Yehuda Bauer, introducing a collection of essays on *Probing the Depths of German Anti-Semitism*, endorses the obvious truth that Hitler's Germany was by the 1940s a 'natural recruiting ground' for willing murderers – but describes Goldhagen's main headline-grabbing thesis, of an alleged eliminationist tendency, as 'patent nonsense'.

For German readers, however, these perceived professional failings proved almost irrelevant. Instead, Goldhagen became a bellwether of German readiness to confront the past. The accuracy of his work was, in this context, of secondary importance. Millions of Germans who wished to acknowledge the (undeniable and well-documented) fact that ordinary Germans participated in the Holocaust welcomed his work; his suggestion that Germans were predestined killers was accepted as part of the uncomfortable package. Goldhagen's book was treated as a way of ensuring that Germany came to terms with its past. The book's critics, meanwhile, included (in addition to many professional historians, who wearily pointed to the methodological flaws) those who were reluctant to admit that many ordinary Germans bore responsibility for the crimes that they had witnessed or committed.

In earlier years, it would have been scarcely imaginable for a book which lumped Germans together as would-be murderers to be published in Germany, let alone enjoy success. Even a book documenting the participation of ordinary Germans in the Holocaust would have been controversial. In the last decade of the twentieth century, however, *Hitler's Willing Executioners* was a publishing phenomenon, in Germany as much as it had been in the United States. The first printing was sold out even before it appeared in the shops. A special volume of *Letters to Goldhagen* was published, where German readers lined up (mostly) to praise him, or bewailed the fact that they had been unable to hear Goldhagen in person ('I tried to get a ticket for the discussion at the Munich Philharmonia, but it was sold out.'). Many of the critics in *Letters to Goldhagen* are of an older generation, who unwittingly bolster Goldhagen's own thesis through their revealed attitudes. One correspondent refers to 'your problem – the Jews', and insists: 'We knew that many Jews had emigrated. But no more than that!' With critics like that, Goldhagen hardly needed further praise. His work, with its flagellatory style, appeared to younger Germans as a breath of fresh historical air. *Die Zeit* summed up the ahistorical oddity: 'The historians criticize *Hitler's Willing Executioners* – and the public finds the book liberating.'

The word 'liberating' may sound paradoxical, in the face of such an extraordinary assault on Germany and Germanity – *A Nation of Murderers?*, in the words of one book about the sensational effect of

Goldhagen. And yet, younger Germans could indeed feel liberated by Goldhagen. The acceptance of any and all attacks on the old Germany provided a yardstick for modern Germans to remind themselves that they had indeed confronted the terrible past, thus helping to neutralize its demons. Goldhagen became a player, at just one remove, in Germany's own arguments with itself. The details of his arguments – untenable or otherwise – mattered less to the Germans than his readiness to be tough on Germany. In the words of the leading Hitler historian, Ian Kershaw: 'The more the experienced historians tried to combat the broad sweep of Goldhagen's grand accusation, the less effective – even if accurate – their criticisms appeared to be to a generation ready and prepared to think the worst of their grandfathers.'

In the years to come, Germans would become more distanced from such polemic, and would be eager to see their own history in the round, with a sense of balance that only time would permit. For the moment, however – in the transitional chaos of the 1990s, where nobody had a clear sense of the shape of the newly united Germany – it still seemed as if no amount of criticism of German historical behaviour could ever be enough.

Zimbardo's and Milgram's experiments had already suggested that, in the wrong circumstances, many people are easily persuaded to act brutally and commit murder. The necessary circumstances to demonstrate that banality of evil were merely that an authoritative figure should create a permissive climate. That was sufficient, the Stanford and Yale experiments both demonstrated, for cruelty and killing alike. Neither of those laboratory experiments included the additional ingredients that have been part of the recipes required for real-life mass murder in different parts of the world – including social and economic collapse, well-harnessed propaganda, and pre-existing ethnic tensions or prejudice. In Nazi Germany, the *Völkischer Beobachter* and speeches by Hitler and Goebbels helped create the necessary climate. During the Rwandan genocide in 1994, Radio Mille Collines urged its listeners to 'kill the Tutsi cockroaches'. More than half a million were slaughtered in three months while the West looked the other way; Hutu who refused to kill their Tutsi neighbours were themselves killed. And in Europe, too, we have seen the Zimbardo effect become real in recent years – a miniature but recognizable version of the poisoning that Germany suffered 60 years earlier.

In 1989, the multi-ethnic Yugoslav federation was not a place of mutual hatred, despite the terrible memories of ethnic massacres in the Second World War. Serbs, Croats and Bosnians worked comfortably side by side; mixed marriages were not the exception but the rule. As

Communism collapsed throughout Europe, Serbia's Communist Party leader, Slobodan Milosevic, realized he was electorally doomed unless he found himself a new trump card. He found a trump card: its name was nationalism. With the help of Serb state television, which he ruthlessly purged for his own aims, Milosevic persuaded Serbs of three powerful new Orwellian truths. First, Serbs were surrounded on all sides by terrorists and fascist killers, eager to repeat the crimes of the past – these killers would stop at nothing. Second, Milosevic was the Serbs' great defender ('Nobody will beat you!', he famously declared) against hostile groups in multi-ethnic Yugoslavia who wished Serbs ill. Third, under Milosevic's powerful leadership, Serbia the poor embattled victim – prevented for so long from standing up for itself – would once more achieve the greatness it deserved. It was nonsense – but it was effective. Though Western politicians seemed determined to ignore it, war soon came to seem inevitable, in these circumstances – not least when Milosevic's nationalism helped propel an almost equally nationalist Franjo Tudjman to power in neighbouring Croatia. An article that I wrote after travelling through Yugoslavia in March 1991 carried the headline 'A nation at boiling point'. Yugoslavia, I noted, was 'not so much approaching a precipice, as sliding down it'.

Late one night in a London hotel suite in 1992, I talked to the all-powerful Milosevic, after the conclusion of a conference where governments had let him off the hook for the Bosnian war that he had recently unleashed. Not surprisingly, Milosevic was in cheerful mood as he sipped his whisky. He even talked enthusiastically of recent proposals to prosecute war crimes in Yugoslavia. When I tentatively suggested that he himself might be a candidate for such prosecutions, he seemed astonished at the thought. 'We have a policy for peace,' he assured me. 'I will not allow anything in my policy to be against peace.'

The shameless lies of individual, power-hungry politicians like Milosevic should come as no surprise. During my travels through the Balkans in the Milosevic years, I was constantly unsettled – as Martha Gellhorn and others had been in Germany 50 years earlier – by the extent to which large numbers of ordinary, decent citizens found it equally easy to deny the undeniable. The scale of the murders and massacres – the cold-blooded slaughter of mere thousands, not millions – did not stand comparison with the crimes of the Third Reich. Nonetheless, 1990s Serbia shared one thing in common with Germany of the 1940s: a widespread refusal by law-abiding citizens to acknowledge the reality of the regime under which they lived.

Both Germany and Serbia have shown how, in the wrong circumstances, disease can quickly affect an entire society, transforming the country into a political cancer ward. In the Balkans, the visitor was constantly confronted by the avoidance of simple truths – and not just when people felt pinned into a rhetorical corner. In the Bosnian Serb capital of Pale, in the hills near Sarajevo, a friendly young man asked, unprompted (the mere presence of a foreigner in the town was enough), 'What have Serbs done wrong?' I gave what I thought was a mollifying answer, agreeing that collective demonization is never appropriate. But that was not enough. He repeated insistently: 'But tell me: what crimes have Serbs have committed?' Eventually I settled on the single word 'Srebrenica' – where 7000 men and boys were led off and shot in a well-documented massacre in 1995. One might have expected a defensive response when discussing the worst atrocity in Europe since 1945. But no. It turned out that I, like other foreigners, had failed to understand the true situation. 'There was no massacre,' he told me. In spring 1999, even as Serb forces used lethally brutal methods to expel tens of thousands of Kosovo Albanians from their homes, the abbot of a monastery asked me why Serbs were no longer as welcome as they had been. He answered his own question. It turned out that Serbia was being crucified for the sins of others. 'There was a need for one nation to take all the sins on its back.'

The confidence in Serb innocence sometimes trumped the known facts. In Serbia, unlike the Third Reich, a few independent newspapers and magazines continued to tell the truth even in the darkest days. Such publications lay almost untouched in the newspaper kiosks; they were regarded as unpatriotic because they hold the truth. Serbs who *were* ready to confront the truth – and such people always existed, just as they had in Hitler's Germany – felt isolated except in their immediate circle of friends. As one Belgrade friend put it: 'It's a gap in the head. If you believe Serbs did nothing wrong, that helps you to survive.' The resistance to truth could sometimes be armour-plated. At considerable personal risk, a Serb friend travelled widely in Kosovo in the mid- to late 1990s, documenting repression and violence against the Albanian majority there. After one such trip, she told her parents about some of the crimes that were taking place in the province, invisible in the mainstream Serb media. Her mother informed her that what she had just described could not be true. The logic was simple, and overrode the detailed factual account that she had just heard from her own daughter: 'Serbs would never do that.'

That was a widespread view – the equivalent of the German architect's 'We acted according to the Geneva Convention', which sought to neutralize all the evidence at the Wehrmacht exhibition. In a Belgrade bookshop, shortly before the fall of Milosevic, I came across a book called *Eliminate the Serb Virus*. At first, I thought the title referred to this problem of Serb denial – what Gellhorn might have called the 'loose gene'. The subject interested me, even if I saw the poisoned Balkan environment as the problem, not poisoned genes. I remembered a pre-Milosevic Serbia, after all, when Serbs had genuinely wanted peace, not the Serbia where people cheered those committed slaughter. It soon became clear, however, that I had misunderstood. The title was dripping with sarcasm. *Eliminate the Serb Virus* – subtitled *A Small Anthology of Racism and Chauvinism* – was a collection of critical quotations from foreign politicians and writers. The overall message of the book was that anybody who dared to criticize the Serbs was a malicious liar. It was unsettling and (in the company of politicians like Vaclav Havel) flattering to find that my words, too, were singled out for alleged Serbophobia. The book quoted a profile of Radovan Karadzic: 'In person, he is thoroughly amiable. On a good day, he can even seem sane. And yet the gap between his words and reality is endless. Some politicians may be evasive; Karadzic simply lies.' That assessment was based on several meetings with the Bosnian Serb leader, and on the known facts (some of which I had listed in my original article); the war crimes tribunal in The Hague had, six years on, indicted Karadzic for genocide. For the author of *Eliminate the Serb Virus*, however, facts were irrelevant. Just as Nurembergers told Gellhorn in 1945 that photographs of concentration camps must have been faked – in effect, 'Germans would never do that' – so, too, anybody who sought to criticize Karadzic or any other Serb must, the argument ran, be a liar and a hater of all Serbs.

In October 2000, street protests finally ousted Milosevic after his bloody decade in power. The streets were filled, day after day, with demonstrators who cried '*Gotov je!*' – 'He's finished!'. And, gloriously, he was. On the day before the final victory, I talked to Vojislav Kostunica – constitutional lawyer, driver of a battered old Yugo, and about to be president. Even though Milosevic had not yet surrendered to the crowds, Kostunica was optimistic about Serbia's future. 'The moment we get rid of Milosevic,' he told me, 'the poison will be taken out of the body politic.'

In reality, it was not so easy. Kostunica himself played an important role in paving the way for Serb democracy – but he himself sometimes seemed unwilling to confront the extent of the crimes committed. Despite the work of a small number of courageous Serbs, including politicians and journalists who did everything possible to ensure a confrontation with historic facts, the worm of denial remained alive even after Milosevic was delivered up to the war crimes tribunal in The Hague the following year. It took until 2003 – eight years after the Srebrenica massacre – for Bosnian Serb television to 'discover' that Serbs were responsible for the slaughter.

The experience of Serbia in recent years serves as a reminder of what Germany already showed so vividly, in more extreme circumstances. Once evil gets into the bloodstream, a society can quickly become daangerously sick, especially when the media is tightly harnessed. Pre-Milosevic Serbia was fragile, but sane. Under a boundlessly cynical leader, it lost its equilibrium with frightening speed. Contrary to the comforting myth that later grew up (again, shades of Germany), Milosevic did not always need to rig elections in order to be returned to power. While he was winning wars, millions of Serbs supported him.

If the poisoning takes effect quickly, the cleansing and healing process, by contrast, can last for many years – even when, as in Serbia, the crimes are much smaller than those committed by Germany, and even if the rejection of the tyrant finally comes (as it did in Belgrade but not in Berlin) from within the country itself. That prolonged convalescence can be seen as a reason for pessimism or optimism, depending on whether you prefer to think of your glass as half-full or half-empty. It is depressing that the removal of a dictator does not mean that the society achieves instant 'normality'. Equally, however, the example of Germany has shown that, even if a society is still in dubious political health many years after the dictator has left the stage, that does not mean that a country is poisoned for all time. With luck – and with encouragement in the right direction – it merely means that the process is not yet complete.

In Germany, that process began in earnest more than 20 years after Hitler's death, 40 years after his death, the process was well under way. But it was the 50th anniversary of the end of the Second World War which marked the date when Germany confronted its past more robustly than ever before. President Roman Herzog gave a series of powerful anniversary speeches through the spring of that year. Each of the speeches helped to demonstrate that late twentieth-century Germany really was a different place.

At the former Belsen concentration camp, where stones in the heather bear witness to the 100,000 who died amidst the birch woods, Herzog declared: 'The passage of 50 years since the end of the Nazi regime cannot mean the end of remembering. What we need now is a form of remembrance which will be effective in future.' Herzog insisted: 'Nothing must be repressed or forgotten. We bear responsibility for ensuring that something like this is never repeated.' Not everybody agreed. One elderly lady in the nearby town of Bergen told me, with reference to Herzog's speech – in words that one could hear again and again in previous years – that enough was enough. 'They should leave the matter. Of course, lots of bad things happened – but I find it is a bit overdone.' By now, however, such voices were a defiant minority, not the dominant tone. Herzog's own insistence on the need for nothing to be 'repressed or forgotten' served as an implicit rebuke to those who had launched an initiative to put the German crimes of the past into a sealed box, and to highlight the past suffering of the Germans instead. The indignant tone of the high-profile campaign partly reflected an awareness that this attempt to close the doors to Germany's own criminal history was likely to be doomed.

It was significant, in this context, that Herzog was not a classic soft liberal, but a conservative Bavarian judge. By this time it was clear to all that Germany must shoulder the burdens of the past, if it wished to feel unburdened. As Herzog's successor Johannes Rau noted, pride in the good is only possible if the bad is also acknowledged; controversely, acknowledgement of past crimes makes it possible also to be proud of the best that a country has achieved. In his speech marking the 50th anniversary of VE Day, Herzog emphasized the change in attitude: 'We do not even need to discuss the fact that Germans carried out the Holocaust against innocent people from many nations.' This guilt, said Herzog, was 'even clearer today than it was 50 years ago'. In 1985, Herzog's predecessor, Richard von Weizsäcker, had confronted one taboo by declaring that 1945 should be seen as liberation, not defeat. Now, just 10 years later, Herzog's partial reversal of von Weizsäcker's dictum helped confirm that an even more difficult taboo was ready to be destroyed.

In objective terms, 1945 was indeed a liberation: it paved the way for the creation of a stable German democracy for the first time in history. The word liberation suggests, however, that somebody is eager to be freed; in 1945, this was not the case. Echoing von Weizsäcker, Herzog described 8 May as 'a day on which the door into the future was opened' – in other words, liberation. He also noted, however, in a statement which would in previous years have seemed highly controversial but which now seemed uncontentious: 'Nobody can say that the Germans, in spring 1945, were great enthusiasts of the state of law and of democracy.' In other words, this had also been a defeat – because of the distorted German mindset at the time.

Herzog's words made clear that, for a modern German president, leaving history behind was no longer an option, whatever diehards of the *Historikerstreit* in the previous decade might still be pressing for. The confrontation with politics was, by now, stronger than ever. Nor were such confrontations only in the realm of high politics. For many years, Hitler's victims found it difficult to make their voices heard. Ursula Hochmuth, who attended school in Hamburg before and during the war, had long been eager to share her own experiences with schoolchildren in her native city. Her parents were both sent to concentration camps; her father died there. She wanted German children to grow up with a true understanding of what it meant to live in the Third Reich. For years, schools kept her at arm's length; the Third Reich was considered an inappropriate topic. Gradually, she was allowed to tell her story more freely. More than 50 years after the events that she described, interest was, she said, higher than it had ever been. On the day that I heard her talk, there was a steady stream of interested questions from her teenage audience. A 13-year-old asked the question which, for a later German generation, seems baffling and disturbing – and a reason for constant reflection: 'Hitler must have been crazy. And lots of the old people today *voted* for him. They wanted him to come to power. That's what I can't understand.'

Grandad wasn't a Nazi, a sociological analysis of family discussions about the Third Reich and the Holocaust, caused a national stir on publication in 2002. It revealed the unsettling extent to which children are inclined to blank out the evidence of their grandparents' active or passive complicity, even when that evidence is acknowledged and uncontested. Nonetheless, there can be no doubt that the extent of the overall confrontation with national history – even if not with a grandparent's personal history – is now far greater than in previous years.

Initiatives previously rejected as too uncomfortable have multiplied many times over. In Cologne, I met the artist Gunter Demnig, who found a simple but effective way of commemorating the Holocaust – not with a grand memorial, but by forcing people literally to stop in their tracks. Demnig designed a series of *Stolpersteine* – 'stumbling stones'. The stumbling stones each show the name of a man, woman or child killed by the Nazis, set amongst other cobblestones in the pavement outside the house where the murdered person once lived. The design of each stone is simple. A brass plate nailed to a stone, with an inscription with the basic information in simple lettering: 'Here lived Elsa Abraham née Marx. b. 1899. Deported 1941. Riga. ???' 'Here lived Moritz Rosenthal. b. 1883. Deported 1941. Lodz. Died 28.2.1942.' And so on, in pavements all over Cologne.

When Demnig first proposed the idea, he was repeatedly rebuffed. The city fathers did not wish residents and visitors to be constantly confronted with the crimes and tragedies of the past. His first *Stolpersteine* were illegal. It was not until 1999 that he received the official green light. By the time that we met in 2001, he had already placed more than 1000 stumbling stones in front of houses all around Cologne, with sometimes a dozen or more names outside a single house. One school class raised funds for more than 30 such stones. The concept has in the meantime become popular in Berlin and other German cities.

Demnig's work is one of a number of art-political projects which seek to make people stop and think about what the Holocaust meant in human terms. In Berlin, an equally remarkable project is installed around the Bayerischer Platz in the district of Schöneberg. A series of information signs bolted to lampposts represent the gradual tightening of the noose against Jews from 1933 onwards, culminating, as the artists put it, 'in an insidiously logical way' in the Holocaust. Most of the 80 signs are simple in design: a basic pictogram on one side, with Nazi decrees printed on the other. The signs range from an end to state reimbursement for visits to a Jewish doctor or dentist, to 'Aryan and non-Aryan children are forbidden to play together' or 'Jews are allowed no more cigarettes or cigars'. Finally, a stylized picture of a letter near the post office bears the inscription: '"The time has come, I must leave, and that of course is very difficult . . . " Before the deportation, 16.1.1942.' The Schöneberg memorial is powerful because it is so simple and matter-of-fact. Each sign reminds the passer-by that the essential inhumanity of the Third Reich was visible to all who wished to see – and that greater evils inevitably begin with lesser evils. For Germans today, that is an important message from history – with relevance not just for Germany but also elsewhere.

Civil courage (and its rarity) is a theme that emerges strongly from the story of a unique series of demonstrations that took place in Rosenstrasse, just off Alexanderplatz in central Berlin, in February 1943. The story of Rosenstrasse is now well known, as conspicuous in the new schoolbooks as it was invisible in the old ones. One reason why the protests had been ignored and unmentioned for so many years was, perhaps, that they were so extraordinary. The Rosenstrasse protests represented a moment when Berliners publicly risked their lives by defying the Nazi regime – with remarkable results.

In February 1943, the Nazis began the final clear-out of Jews from Berlin to make the city *judenfrei* – 'free of Jews'. Goebbels noted with satisfaction: 'They were thrown together in one fell swoop last Sunday and will now be shoved off to the east in short order.' Many of those who were arrested were from mixed marriages; they were held at a former Jewish community centre on Rosenstrasse, ready for deportation. So far, so Nazi-simple. There was, however, a hitch. Non-Jewish wives, on learning where their husbands were held, gathered outside the building. Within a day or two, hundreds of them were standing there all day. They began to chant: 'We want our husbands back! Let our husbands go!' One participant described the scene:

> As I arrived, I saw a crowd – at six in the morning already! People flowed back and forth. The street was full. This short little street was black with people. They were like a wave, and they moved like a body, a swaying body.

Guards with machine guns threatened to shoot. Undaunted, the women chanted: 'Murderers!' – and continued their protest, and all within earshot of the Jewish Desk of the Gestapo. For the all-powerful Nazis, it was a catastrophic confrontation – 'a disagreeable scene', as Goebbels noted in his diary. And then came the even more extraordinary conclusion to an already extraordinary week. In the face of a protest by a few hundred women, armed with nothing but their lack of fear, the Nazis backed down. Goebbels ordered the men at Rosenstrasse to be released. Some were even fetched back from Auschwitz. (As one survivor later described, they were obliged to tell the Gestapo about the excellent conditions in Auschwitz. '"How was the food?" "Good!" "Were you beaten?" "No, sir!" "Did you see anyone else being beaten?" "No, sir!" Well, I'm not stupid.')

In one respect, the story, like that of *Schindler's List*, can be seen as heartwarming for those who wish to emphasize that not everybody supported Hitler. But the Rosenstrasse story also undermines the idea, which many had been so eager to propagate, that resistance was always impossible, and therefore not worth considering. In the words of one of the protesting wives: 'If you had to calculate whether you would do any good by protesting, you wouldn't have gone. But we acted from the heart.' It is that element of the story which propels it into the foreground for teaching new generations of Germans. The fact that 'few Germans found the courage to protest against Hitler and the Nazi regime' is directly contrasted with the Rosenstrasse story of defiance. (Some historians now claim that the Gestapo had always planned to release the men. Even if that is true – and the claim is controversial – the wives could not have known. In other words, it does not affect the question of personal courage.) Vaclav Havel's 'power of the powerless' remained largely untested in Nazi Germany. Rosenstrasse is thus presented in twenty-first century Germany as food for thought – for the grandchildren of the generation that almost always obeyed.

It is always heartening to meet those who *did* disobey. Those who displayed astonishing courage appear to find it difficult to understand what all the fuss is about. How, they ask, could one *not* risk one's life, in such circumstances? Frieda Adam, a former seamstress, saved the life of her Jewish friend Erna Puterman by taking her into her apartment under a false identity. On a shelf in her small east Berlin apartment stands a framed saying: 'When a person takes action, more is possible than one thinks.' Frieda has lived – and might have expected to die – by that motto. 'I can't really use the word fear,' she said, when describing the two and a half years Erna spent with her. 'It's a funny thing. We knew that if we were found out, it would mean death. But we refused to think about it.' During most of our conversation, Frieda was calm and cheerful. She only became indignant when she talked of those who said they did not know what was happening to the Jews. 'When they were taken to the Lehrter Station [in central Berlin], people just looked the other way.' Erna contrasted the modern reaction to far-right violence with the lack of reaction 50 or 60 years earlier. 'Today, people do something. Then, they didn't want to do anything. They wore blinkers, like horses.' Frieda agreed: 'If people had gone on to the street, like today, that would have been different.'

There are many examples of Germany's new readiness to confront the past. At the same time, the retrospection is less agonized than before, as demonstrated by one of the most popular films of recent years, Joseph Vilsmaier's *Comedian Harmonists* – the true story of the rise and destruction of an internationally acclaimed *a cappella* group in Germany in the 1920s and early 1930s, released in 1997. As with *Cabaret*, the catchy songs give the film an obvious box-office charm. Scratchy old recordings were digitally dusted off and convincingly mimed; the Comedian Harmonists' most famous musical numbers are sprinkled entertainingly throughout the film, whose designer was also responsible a quarter of a century earlier for the glossy look of *Cabaret*. Like *Cabaret*, the Nazi madness is a mere backdrop to the film – an evil which does not need to be spelt out; in the foreground is the story of the musicians themselves. Three of the six members of the group were Jewish, which inevitably meant that the group had to disband. By 1935, it was unthinkable that Jewish musicians could be part of the most popular group in Germany. (Roman Cycowski, son of a Polish cantor, and a member of the Comedian Harmonists, said later: 'If we hadn't been forced to split up, we'd probably be more famous today than the Beatles.')

The growing thuggery and anti-Semitism in German society, as the Nazis come to power, provide one theme. Oddly, however, *Comedian*

Harmonists is in many respects a feelgood movie – again, like *Cabaret*, which was marketed as 'a divinely decadent experience'. By the end of the twentieth century, German film directors and filmgoers alike no longer felt the need loudly to proclaim their sense of anguish about the past, on the one hand, or to avoid discussing Nazism altogether, on the other. Thus, the Oscar-winning German film *Nowhere in Africa*, released in 2001, tells the story of a Jewish couple who flee with their young daughter from 1930s Germany to live on a farm in Kenya. This is not a film about the Holocaust. It is a film of Europe and Africa, about childhood, and changing and overlapping identities. And yet, the Holocaust is a constant underlying theme even in this 'soft' film with its beautifully photographed landscapes. The girl's grandparents, who stay behind in Germany, are of course murdered. At the end of the film, the husband wants to return to his native country to practise as a lawyer once more. His wife asks: 'Do you think that the Nazis have all vanished? You'll be dealing with the murderers of our parents.' In past years, the inclusion of such remarks would have seemed difficult, even courageous. In modern Germany, by contrast, such observations are uncontroversial, even in a box-office hit. In films like *Nowhere in Africa*, the madness of Germany's criminal past is no longer trumpeted; the lunacy is too self-evident for that.

Until now, many Germans felt obliged to behave like the television comedian Harry Enfield's character Jürgen the German, who constantly corners people in order to tell them how sorry he is for what Germans did during the Third Reich. Thus Jürgen tells an unsuspecting man at the bus stop, apropos of almost nothing:

I feel I must apologize for the conduct of my nation in the war . . .'
   'But you weren't even born then.'
   'As a German, I share in the guilt of my forefathers. The crimes committed during those dark years are a stain on my nation's history. And you must never, ever let me forget this!

In the last few years, the breastbeating Jürgen – a comic exaggeration, but recognizably real – has begun to fade into the background. This is not a matter of the Holocaust being put to one side. Rather, the lessons of the past have begun to be absorbed as an important but uncontroversial part of Germany's legacy. That normality, in turn, makes it possible to address other themes for the first time in decades – themes which until the beginning of the twenty-first century seemed entirely taboo.

12

Neighbours

Horrific suffering, such as the world no longer believed possible in the twentieth century . . .

> (A 1956 school textbook describes the horror of the Second World War. The reference is not to German crimes – which are scarcely mentioned – but to German suffering in 1945.)

If we talk of expulsions, we cannot leave out what came before . . . I can understand the pain over what has been lost. But it must be the pain over what we have done to ourselves, not what others have done to us.

> (Joschka Fischer on proposals for a Centre against Expulsions, possibly to be located in Berlin)

German crimes against its neighbours in the years between 1938 and 1945 were obvious to the world. In Germany, meanwhile, there was often more interest in what the Germans themselves had gone through. That suffering was on a horrific scale. If it were not for what Germans themselves had done to others in the previous few years, one might almost say the suffering was incomparable. Poles, Czechs and Russians drove 15 million Germans out of their homes between 1944 and 1947. They were piled into horse-drawn carts, sometimes with just a few minutes' notice, or crammed into cattle trucks and expelled to a shrunken and ruined Germany. Many who had lost their homes and families were beaten, raped, shot, or froze to death on the roads. Two million civilians died. The scale of the catastrophe, in short, was difficult to overstate.

These serial acts of inhumanity did not, of course, take place in a historical void. Even if we leave to one side the Nazis' meticulously planned programme of mass murder, the German war in the East was criminal in a previously unimaginable sense. It was unrecognizably different from the Nazi occupation of western Europe, which was almost civilized by comparison. The French village of Oradour, destroyed in 1944 together with its inhabitants, is etched in the memory of many in western Europe as if were a high point of Nazi horror – which, in western Europe, it was. In Poland and Russia, by contrast, the nightmare of Oradour was a daily routine. There were far too many such massacres to be individually commemorated. The slaughter of men, women and children and the destruction of their homes was deemed an effective way of keeping support for the partisans in check – as was described in a soldier's letter home to his family: 'The day before yesterday a Wehrmacht car was shot at when it drove through a village. Thank God, they immediately torched the whole village and burnt it to the ground. The inhabitants were shot.' An unnamed Oradour, in short – mentioned with pride by a German soldier to his nearest and dearest, and then instantly forgotten.

Even the earliest stages of the war were brutal, by comparison with previous wars. The invasion of Poland began in 1939 with a million Poles being driven from their homes, often with no notice, to make way for ethnic Germans from further east who were to be fetched 'home to the Reich'. Violence and killing were routine from the start, in this efficient programme of ethnic cleansing. As one German wrote home from Poland: 'The most fertile imagination of horror propaganda is poor by comparison with what an organised gang of murderers and plunderers does there, with permission from the top.' This behaviour would, he argued, become 'the misfortune of the entire German people'. In the years to come, millions were taken for slave labour, or to die in the camps. Sometimes, it was simpler to leave children behind, killing them *in situ*. A witness of one typical incident remembers: 'They took them by their legs and hit them against the corner of the barrack.' A German professor, quoted by Alexandra Richie in *Faust*'s Metropolis, found it interesting to examine the leftovers of Poles who had been burnt in the basement of his institute:

How little remains of a person when all organic matter has been burnt! A glimpse inside the ovens is very thought-provoking . . . At the moment the Poles are very uppity, and consequently our oven has a lot to do. How nice it would be if one could chase the whole society into such ovens. Then there would finally be peace in the East for the German people.

Germany made considerable progress in achieving that goal of 'peace in the East'. Three million Polish gentiles and three million Polish Jews died during five and a half years of German occupation. In the Soviet Union, though numbers are still argued over, perhaps 20 million died – including two million prisoners of war; starvation was used as a weapon of war.

Then, in 1943, the tide of war began to turn. As the German forces retreated, it was the turn of German civilians to suffer at the hands of the vengeful Soviet forces, who reached the border with Germany in August 1944. Hundreds of thousands were raped, often repeatedly; it was considered unusual *not* to have been raped. '*Frau, komm!*' was the endlessly repeated, dreaded phrase. (In 1945, the phrase became part of a children's game in Berlin because the children had witnessed it so often: '*Frau, komm!*', then the girl's clothes came off.) The writer Ilya Ehrenburg believed that the rape of German women should be seen as the Russian soldier's just reward: 'Take them as your lawful prey!' One Russian recorded in his diary the standard pattern: 'Nine, 10, 12 men at a time – they rape them on a collective basis.' Children begged their parents to kill them, so that they would be spared further misery. Chemists handed out poison on demand.

The cruelty of permitted revenge, as the invading forces fought their way through eastern Germany towards Berlin, overlapped with cruelty against civilians as a matter of official policy, to ensure that the ethnic cleansing was complete. German crowds had greeted Hitler enthusiastically ('Führer, we thank you!') when he annexed the Sudetenland in 1938. Now, Czechs forced the Sudeten Germans to wear Third Reich-style armbands ('N' for Nemec, or 'German'). In 1945 and 1946, almost three million Germans lost their homes and possessions under the merciless terms of the Benes decrees, approved by President Edvard Benes in 1945. Benes argued: 'It has become impossible for us to live alongside them, and therefore they must leave the country. We have the moral and political right to demand that.'

Hitler had wanted extra German *Lebensraum* – 'living space' in the East. Now it was Stalin's turn to demand political *Lebensraum*, which he justified by the need to compensate the Soviet Union for its losses, and to protect Russia from renewed attack. After all, he pointed out, 'Poland has served as a corridor for enemies coming to attack Russia.' The Western Allies agreed that Soviet borders should be expanded westwards, once victory against Hitler was achieved. This involved Poland losing a large slice of its territory to the Soviet Union; in return, it would receive a Soviet-style reward, including a substantial chunk of eastern Germany.

The Polish government in exile objected to this arbitrary redistribution of territory, but to no effect. The Germans had no say because they were defeated; the Poles had no bargaining power against the wishes of London, Washington and Moscow. At Potsdam in August 1945, the Allies set the seal on a process that was already well under way. Germans were to be driven out 'in an orderly and humane fashion'.

In reality, Poles, Russians and Czechs alike needed little encouragement to 'treat the Germans the same way they treated us', as one official declaration put it, so that the Germans would 'flee of their own accord'. This was, as Poland's new Communist leaders put it, 'the hour of revenge for the torment and suffering, for the burnt villages and destroyed cities, the churches and schools, for the arrests, camps and shootings, for Auschwitz, Majdanek, Treblinka, for the destruction of the ghetto'. The Germans lost much of their most treasured land, including east Prussia and the industrial heartland of Silesia. The old German city of Breslau became the Polish city of Wroclaw, filled with Poles driven out of areas that now formed part of the Soviet Union. The razed university city of Königsberg, birthplace of the philosopher Immanuel Kant, became the Soviet city of Kaliningrad.

In many German towns and villages, the pattern soon became familiar. Soldiers surrounded houses. The German inhabitants were driven out of their beds at gunpoint, robbed and set on the road. The decrees which ordered Germans to abandon their houses and all their possessions – 'Between 6am and 9am a resettlement of the German population will take place . . . Each German may take a maximum of 20kg baggage . . . Failure to carry out orders will be met with the most severe punishment, including the use of weapons' – were eerily similar in tone and wording to the Nazi decrees that had been plastered across eastern Europe in previous years. The familiar and much-feared cry of 'Raus!' was now used against the Germans themselves. Those who had sown the whirlwind, reaped the (less fierce, but still unimaginably cruel) wind.

At one level, it was understandable that school textbooks after 1945 focused on this suffering. How could children not be taught about what had happened to them and their compatriots in the past few years? Throughout the 1950s, the textbooks talked of the 'indescribable misery of millions of refugees', and 'a catastrophe such as the German people had never experienced in their 2000-year history, so rich in suffering and hardship'. Children were encouraged to explore the extent of Germany's bitter losses, with questions asking: 'What do you know of . . . ?' – followed by a list of lost German territories in the East.

All of this would have seemed normal and appropriate – except that these same books rarely found room for more than a passing reference to crimes committed by the Germans themselves. One schoolbook talks of: 'Horrific suffering, such as the world no longer believed possible in the twentieth century . . . ' It seems easy to guess where a sentence like that must be leading. This was not, however, a reference to Auschwitz or other German crimes. Instead, the complete sentence reads: 'Horrific suffering, such as the world no longer believed possible in the twentieth century, broke over millions of Germans.' The mass murder which Germans themselves had carried out was, as ever, pushed to one side.

After 1945, the new Communist governments of eastern Europe were not eager to tell the truth about the brutal expulsions and murders of German civilians – though they were happy to boast about the end result. As late as 1965, Poland issued postage stamps boasting of 'the liberation of the western territories'. Guidebooks performed verbal gymnastics (or simply told lies) to avoid revealing the uncomfortable fact that Germans had previously lived in cities like Breslau-turned-Wroclaw. Streetnames were changed, and history was reversed or ignored.

It was logical that unelected Communist governments refused to admit the truth. In the eager new parliamentary democracy of the Federal Republic, meanwhile, the reluctance to confront the truth was almost equally striking. Throughout the 1950s and 1960s, the powerful expellees' association helped divert attention from the subject of German crimes against others. Instead, the expellees wanted their land and property back – and were furious when Willy Brandt, 'the traitor', opened a dialogue with Russians and the Poles in 1970 which implied a partial acceptance of the existing borders.

For decades after 1945, the bitterness was still sharply felt, even when it was obliquely expressed. On my shelf is a photographic album of Berlin, which I acquired when I first lived in Berlin as a student in 1973. The format and contents are familiar: architectural monuments, street scenes, Berliners relaxing in cafés. The captions are simple: 'A winter's day, Teufelsberg', 'View over the Hansa quarter', and so on. All very unsurprising. Then on the last page comes the angry twist. A signpost points the way to a clutch of distant towns: 'Königsberg in Prussia 590km', 'Breslau 330km', 'Gleiwitz 478km'. Alone among all the photographs in the book, this final image has no caption. It was intended to be self-explanatory – which, for Germans at that time, it was. In effect: 'Others have seized lands which are rightfully ours. We neither forgive nor forget.' This photograph is the only reference to the Second World War or the effects of the war in the entire 120-page album; even the historical introduction scrupulously avoids the words Hitler, Nazi or Third Reich. The book includes photographs showing the majestic architecture of pre-war Berlin, but nothing from the swastika years, nor the post-war ruins. The reason *why* Germany suffered such robbery of its territory was, in short, not yet hinted at, let alone openly acknowledged.

As West Germans became increasingly ready in the 1970s and 1980s to confront the crimes that Germans had committed, the pendulum swung the other way. In a post-1968 world, the theme of German suffering was pushed to one side. German victimhood was now highlighted only by those who occupied one corner of the political spectrum. In 1985, President von Weizsäcker felt able to talk only in oblique terms of the 'forced journey' that his compatriots had undergone in 1945. Despite the continued lobbying power of the expellees' association, German suffering was gradually airbrushed out of the picture with the same care that German crimes had been avoided in earlier years. Schoolbooks of the 1980s and 1990s devote page after page to German crimes – but no longer find room for a single word about the experiences that millions of Germans had gone through. Grandparents might talk about such things at home; their stories could provide one source of knowledge about the past. In polite public discourse, however, the horror of those years was almost entirely absent.

It was the collapse of Communism, on the one hand, and German unification, on the other, which paved the way for a greater openness all round. The arrival of democracy meant greater honesty in those countries where German civilians were treated so brutally at the end of the war. At the same time, the achievement of German unity meant that Germans felt less need to scratch at old sores. In 1990, at the 11th hour before unification, Helmut Kohl finally confirmed that Germany no longer had any claims on Polish territory, and that history could therefore now be seen as history. The nightmares of 1938–45, on the one hand, and of 1945–47, on the other, would remain a painful scar. The subject of German crimes and German suffering respectively would, however, no longer be open, seeping wounds. The journalist and publisher Marion Dönhoff, who fled her family's estate in east Prussia in January 1945 – and who later played an important role in reconciliation with Poland – described the loss of territory in terms that German society as a whole has gradually come to accept.

Six centuries wiped out. In the first years I couldn't believe it, I didn't want to accept it, I hoped against all reason for a miracle. That is now long ago. What the madman gambled away can never be won back.

The new self-confidence that came with unity sometimes seemed to suggest that history could be overturned. When the borders to the East were opened, Germans became fascinated with their formerly German heritage. Bookshops were piled high with books about the lost beauty of Pomerania and East Prussia, now in northern Poland. New maps were published which marked the old names of once German villages, allowing Germans to visit the place where they were born or where parents or grandparents had been born – often for the first time in 50 years. Even now, some were resistant to the idea that the lost territories should be seen as truly lost. Comments by the head of the expellees' organisation: 'We will not allow our upper Silesia to be permanently taken from us – not by Warsaw, nor by Bonn!' awakened Polish mistrust. Gradually through the next decade, however, the greater openness on both sides allowed the political temperature to fall. Germans returned to their former homeland by the coachload – no longer with a sense of vengeance nor with a determination to turn the clock back, but in an attempt to seek a kind of closure. German travel guides to what is now northern Poland talk matter-of-factly of the deportation and deaths of German civilians in 1945, and describe what came before in equally straightforward terms. The description of German expulsions is preceded by phrases like: 'The entire Polish intelligentsia in the region was driven out, murdered or deported to concentration camps.' When discussing the fact that Poles settled after 1945 in previously German towns like Allenstein/Olsztyn, guides note that the new arrivals were themselves driven out from areas that Poland lost after 1945. In short, the blame game is no longer popular. My photographic album from Berlin, with its reproachful signposts reminding the reader of stolen territories in the East, is a relic from another era. The historical subtext of modern guidebooks is no longer: 'Look what has been stolen from us,' but 'Look how brutally the Third Reich overturned the history of the entire continent.'

Even now, there are still ambiguities. One February day, I visited the little village of Mosina, south-west of Gdansk or Danzig. Ducks and geese wandered across the frozen village pond; in the village stores, the selection of goods was almost as meagre as in Communist times. For the Polish villagers, this is not a place of affluence. But at least it is theirs – or seems to be. Jerzy Gawel and his family have lived in Mosina for more than half a century; they have no other home. Before 1945, however, Mosina was the German town of Mossin – which is where the problems start. In 1999, Gawel, whose father rebuilt the house from ruins after the Second World War, began to receive suavely threatening letters from the man who lived in the house as a child. A west German engineer demanded the return of the house, together with the surrounding property – a small brick shed and a couple of fruit trees. In a letter to the mayor, the engineer repeatedly referred to international law, and the 'painful but necessary' changes in law that Poland must make, including the 'restitution of property to the Germans', if it wished to be considered for membership of the European Union.

All of this might be dismissed as a bad joke – the work of a malicious eccentric – were it an isolated case. Some of the demands for restitution were, however, on pre-printed, bilingual forms, which the families of expellees have been encouraged to submit. Such demands, though they may seem justified at one level, hardly make for an easy approach to history. If Mosina is given back to the Germans, does that mean that Lviv and Vilnius, Polish university cities before 1939, should be snatched from Ukraine and Lithuania respectively?

A mixture of guilt (at Polish treatment of the Germans) and continued resentment (at German treatment of the Poles) creates a deep wariness. Anna Pertek, 12 years old when the Germans arrived in 1939, tells a familiar story about her village, just across the pre-war border from Mossin into Poland: 'They took the village teacher and shot him. He was such a good man. They took him, they took the priest. They murdered them all – and we're supposed to forget it. We should – but it's difficult.' The inhabitants of her village were forced out, minus their possessions, so that her village could become a Pole-free zone – rid of those who Hitler described as 'more like animals than human beings'.

Increasingly, the aggressive demands of Jerzy Gawel's west German engineer are the exception, not the rule. Many Poles are glad for the income that visiting German tourists bring. Others are pleased at the friendships they have struck up with German families who once lived in Mossin. 'We've been to stay with them in Hamburg several times,' one man told me with something akin to pride. 'If we don't write, they ask us: "Have we done something to offend you?"' The picking at sores has sometimes continued, under the guise of sorting things out. Thus, the Bundestag complained in 1998 of the expulsions as a 'great injustice in violation of international law' (which, of course, they were – like so much else at that time), and insisted that Poland must change its laws if it wished to 'help overcome the consequences of war and expulsion'. Poland exploded at what it saw as a deliberate provocation; the Polish parliament, the Sejm, passed an almost unanimous condemnation of the 'dangerous tendencies' of the Bundestag resolution.

At the same time, however, there are many new attempts to make sure that the ugliness of the past – ugly on both sides, even if one side's actions were even uglier than the other – stays in the past. One small but symbolic sign of change is that a statue of the poet Schiller, kept under wraps for half a century, has been re-erected in Polish Wroclaw, in an explicit acknowledgement of Breslau's German past. In a development that would have seemed unthinkable in previous years, Poland launched a prosecution of a Polish camp commander under whose command more than 1000 German civilians, including many women and children, were murdered in 1945 and 1946. Equally remarkable was the presence of Polish president Alexander Kwasniewski as guest of honour at a meeting of German expellees in the pre-war German town of Elbing, now the Polish town of Elblag; Kwasniewski praised the association, and talked of 'a shared legacy'. One of the expellees' leaders became an honorary citizen of his (now Polish) home town.

In the Czech republic, reconciliation has been more difficult. After the Velvet Revolution of 1989, things seemed to start well. One of Vaclav Havel's first acts as president of a democratic Czechoslovakia was to apologize for the brutal expulsion of millions of Germans – a quarter of Czechoslovakia's pre-war population – after 1945. Few of his compatriots were, however, impressed by such sentiments. Because of Germany, the Czechs suffered 60 years of oppression – first German occupation and then Soviet-imposed Communism, a Nazi legacy at just one remove. Now, the Czechs were not inclined to be generous in return. The Germans, in turn, sometimes seemed eager to stoke the fire of mutual resentments. In 1995, the foreign minister, Klaus Kinkel, argued that compensation for the victims of Nazism would be linked to Prague's attitude on the expellees, which caused an explosion of national indignation. A joint Czech-German declaration in 1997 suggested that bygones should now be bygones: both sides regretted their respective crimes, and 'both sides agree that the injustice committed belongs to the past'. In practice, however, frictions have remained strong. In 2001, Gerhard Schröder cancelled a trip to Prague after the Czech prime minister, Milos Zeman, said Sudeten Germans had been 'Hitler's fifth column'. In 2002, Edmund Stoiber, Bavarian prime minister and Schröder's conservative challenger, suggested that the Czechs could not join the EU until the Benes decrees had been repealed. The Czech parliament, in turn – wary that an official repeal would open up a can of worms regarding property and land ownership – voted by 169 votes to none against repeal.

When stickers like 'Sudetenland was and will be German' appear in Czech towns, it is hardly surprising if there is more than a continued frisson. Many Czechs are worried, too, that membership of the European Union will make it easy for wealthy Germans to re-Germanize Czech towns – not with guns this time but with cash. Others are, however, pleased that the prospect of reconciliation now at least seems closer than it was. One inhabitant of Smrzovka – pre-war Morchenstern, with a 90 per cent German population – told an interviewer he was pleased to meet the former owner of his house. 'He touched the parquet floor, remembering how he had laid it decades before. We cried together – and I told him he was welcome back at any time.'

Often, the German economic muscle remains a source of bitterness. Many in eastern Europe, theoretically on the winning side against Nazi Germany in 1945, feel that they lost the war twice or three times over. After the brutality of German occupation and the one-party Communism which resulted from it, they emerged free in 1989 to join a new Europe – only to discover that the country which had launched and lost the war was now the richest and most powerful country in Europe. It is perhaps unsurprising if Poles are disconcerted to find that their bank account is no longer with a Polish bank but, after a change of ownership, with the Deutsche Bank instead; in those circumstances, it is an odd liberation. Even on theoretically Euro-friendly matters, there is still room for friction. When it was suggested that the Poles might need German guards to help guard the new eastern border of the European Union, there was Polish unease. In the words of one diplomat, 'We're just not ready for the idea of Germans patrolling our frontiers.'

At the same time, Germany is eager to be seen as the friend of those it once invaded. Germany has played a key role in supporting the bids of central and eastern European countries to join the European Union, despite French concerns. There are concerns about Germany continuing to be the 'milch cow' of the European Union – subsidizing others and getting nothing back. Senior ministers talk of the German economy having to 'sacrifice itself' to the goal of integration. In political terms, however, attitudes have moved a long way since 1995, when the Against Forgetting initiative – in other words, against forgetting German suffering – was launched. The title of the initiative could hardly have been more misleading. In reality, this was an initiative Against Remembrance. Most obviously, it was against remembering Auschwitz and the Holocaust. Those who supported the Against Forgetting initiative insisted that enough was enough, as regards discussion of German crimes. And, at the same time, the one-sidedness of the initiative made it more difficult for remembrance of German suffering to be real.

Highlighting German suffering at that time would have seemed a surrender to the demands of those who wished to draw a line under history. Only when the shrillness of the 1995 initiative was almost forgotten, and when those who had launched it had gone back into their resentful shells, did the real, substantive change in attitude become possible.

As President Herzog made clear through his outspoken speeches on the 50th anniversary of the end of the war, Germany was unblinkingly prepared to confront the past. In these circumstances, it became possible to address the suffering of Germans, too. As the new twenty-first century dawned, the suffering of Germans became a new dominant theme. In 2001, the two main public television channels each broadcast a series of programmes devoted to the apocalypse of 1945, *The Expellees* and *The Great Flight*, both of which gained large audiences. It seemed that the clock was turning back, to emphasize German victimhood once more at the cost of German crimes. In reality, perceptions were now radically different from the 1950s and 1960s, when German victimhood was such an important theme. Both these TV series were framed in the context of the Third Reich. *The Expellees* had as its subtitle 'Hitler's Last Victims'. Guido Knopp, presenter of *The Great Flight*, made a similar linkage, describing the murderous injustice as the result of 'the criminal war unleashed by Hitler'. Knopp, author of many books and programmes on the crimes of the Third Reich, made clear that this was not a revival of the *Historikerstreit* arguments of the 1980s, with a new relativization of the Holocaust: 'It has nothing to do with relativization or balancing out if we remember those who died on the icy roads of East Prussia in winter 1945 . . . The ability to mourn goes hand in hand with the courage to remember.'

Programmes like these helped open floodgates which had until now remained closed. Politicians regretted that they had been so fixated on the crimes of the perpetrators in their parents' generation that they failed to address the subject of German suffering. Antje Vollmer, a leading Green, said that the avoidance of the subject had been 'no glorious page', and acknowledged: 'We felt that somebody had to pay for the unimaginable German crimes.' Otto Schily, Social Democrat interior minister, said that he and others had 'looked away from the crimes of the expulsions, the millionfold suffering that was done to the expellees'.

In 2003, a new controversy over the proposals for a Centre Against Expulsions served as a reminder that the subject remains sensitive on all sides. In theory, everybody is in favour of such a centre. That is in itself a radical change in attitude. In the years after German unity, the very idea would still have seemed dangerously explosive. Poles and Czechs would have refused to contemplate any project which commemorated their role in the brutal expulsion of millions from their homes. German supporters of such a centre, in turn, would have been eager to insist that the depth of German suffering meant that a final line must be drawn under the discussion of Nazi crimes.

Now, by contrast, all sides agree not just that a centre is appropriate to commemorate the suffering and pain of ethnic cleansing and killing. All sides agree, too – at least in theory – that such a centre should not *only* deal with expulsions suffered by one side. The burning question is thus not whether such a centre should be built, but where. The German expellees' association wants it to be in Berlin. Critics fear that a Berlin location would mean that the new centre, though theoretically dealing with ethnic cleansing in all its forms, could drown in self-pity. Above all, there are fears that a Berlin centre would be perceived as dangerously 'balancing out' the new Holocaust memorial that is now being built. Joschka Fischer, whose ethnically German family left Hungary in 1945, emphasized his wariness of the Berlin plans, saying that the expellees' association, which spearheaded the proposal, 'does not make a good museum curator'. Fischer insisted that crimes against Germans in 1945 can only be seen in context:

> If we talk of expulsions, we cannot leave out what came before . . . I can understand the pain over what has been lost. But it must be the pain over what we have done to ourselves, not what others have done to us.

Günter Grass argued in similar terms:

> I am very much in favour of documenting the terrible barbaric expulsions of the twentieth century. But that is a European, not just a German task. The expellees' associations have certainly changed over the years, but I wouldn't like to leave something like that to them. Whether you like it or not, that would lead to navel-gazing.

Among those arguing for a different location for the new centre were former German foreign minister Hans-Dietrich Genscher; two former Polish foreign ministers, Bronislaw Geremek and Wladyslaw Bartoszewski; and the dissident-turned-editor of the Polish daily *Gazeta Wyborcza*, Adam Michnik. One suggestion for a location was Polish Wroclaw, formerly German Breslau. (18,000 Germans died in the notorious 'death march of the Breslau mothers' in January 1945; hundreds of thousands of Poles came to live in Wroclaw after losing their homes in the East.) Other suggestions have been Görlitz, on the modern Polish-German border, or the Bosnian capital, Sarajevo. At the time of writing, these bitter arguments continue unabated. If one is looking for a crumb of optimism, it is the fact that Germans, Poles and Czechs (Prague is mentioned as another possible location) agree in principle on the proposed creation of such a centre. The centre would emphasize that driving people out of their homes and killing those who do not wish to leave, is always wrong – no matter who does it and why. That change of heart – including, at least theoretically, the attempt to see events in an international context – can perhaps be a step forward for the new century.

13

Squared Circles

> Never, he said, should his generation have kept silent about such
> misery, merely because its own sense of guilt was so overwhelming,
> merely because for years the need to accept responsibility and show
> remorse took precedence, with the result that they abandoned the
> topic to the right wing. This failure, he says, was staggering.
>
> (Günter Grass explains to his own narrator in *Crabwalk* (2002) his regret
> that for many years he acknowledged the suffering of only one side)

The relationship in the 1950s between a sexually innocent teenager and
an uneducated tram conductor twice his age. The death of a mountain
guide in the Swiss Alps in 1914, electroconvulsive therapy in upstate New
York in the 1950s, and an artist with pulmonary emphysema in north-
west England in the 1990s. None of these themes from late twentieth-
century German bestsellers sound as if the authors are eagerly seeking
confrontation with the themes of the Holocaust. In the examples above –
Bernhard Schlink's *The Reader* and W. G. Sebald's stories in *The
Emigrants* – there is little of the obvious anger which marked landmark
works of the 1960s like Peter Weiss's *The Investigation*, based on the
Auschwitz trial, or Rolf Hochhuth's *The Representative*, about turning a
blind eye to Nazi crimes. Hannah Arendt described Hochhuth's play as
'the most controversial literary work of its generation'. Schlink's and
Sebald's works, by contrast, seem at pains to avoid public controversy.
Indeed, if Schlink's work has been controversial, it is because the *lack* of
anger and indignation, which some German critics take to mean that the
work is dangerously soft. In reality, the more nuanced approach may
reflect the fact that the German world itself has changed. The crimes of

the past and the involvement of ordinary Germans with those crimes are now self-evident. Schlink takes that as a starting point and moves on from there.

Schlink's *The Reader* is a story of sexual innocence and experience, and (suddenly and unexpectedly, halfway through the book) a story of the Holocaust and the nature of guilt. As a teenager, the narrator has an affair with an older woman, Hanna. Later, as a law student attending war crimes trials, he finds that Hanna has a secret past as a concentration camp guard. In earlier years, this storyline might have seemed interesting on its own account – the mature lover revealed as a perpetrator of evil. As the narrator acknowledges, 'I was guilty of having loved a criminal.' *The Reader*'s real interest lies, however, in the way we begin to see Hanna's guilt in different ways as the story progresses, through constant changes of the narrative light. For some, this was taken as a worrying indication that Schlink himself (a law professor born in 1944, whose curriculum vitae thus runs in eerie parallel with that of his law-student narrator) seeks to let Germans off the hook of their responsibilities. Certainly, it is easy to feel sympathy for Hanna, despite her involvement in mass murder, once the special mitigating circumstances of her life story have been revealed. Schlink's approach can, however, also be seen differently. For him, the crimes of the past are a given, as is the fact that the Federal Republic in the 1960s was still imbued with the Nazi legacy. The narrator (or perhaps Schlink, from his own experience as a law student) notes that many of the defendants' lawyers were themselves old Nazis, who delivered 'Nazi tirades'. He documents matter-of-factly and in detail, the charges against four defendants, including a death march which selected women for Auschwitz ('it was clear to everyone that the women would be killed in Auschwitz') and the murder of hundreds of women in a church:

First the steeple burned, then the roof; then the blazing rafters collapsed into the nave, and the pews caught fire. The heavy doors could not be budged. The defendants could have unlocked them. They did not, and the women locked in the church burned to death.

As the narrator points out, these are not the worst German crimes. Indeed, he wonders if it is 'inexcusable' to try somebody who was present at Auschwitz while failing to charge them in connection with their conduct at Auschwitz itself. Instead, these are what one might call the common-or-garden German crimes of that time. The killers resort to the time-honoured defence, the familiar mantra of the 1950s and 1960s: on the one hand, ignorance; on the other hand, the impossibility of taking preventive action. The other defendants 'had not thought about the church, had not seen the fire in the church, had not heard the screams from the church'.

When *The Investigation* and *The Representative* were written, the Federal Republic was still reluctant to gaze into the past. Schlink, by contrast, writes at a time when Germany has long since addressed the enormity of events half a century earlier. For author and reader alike, it is self-evident that ordinary Germans perpetrated or turned their eyes away from unspeakable crimes (and then claimed to have seen and known nothing). Schlink then turns an additional spotlight on the narrator's fellow-students (in other words, Schlink's own 1968 generation) and their readiness to sit in judgement on others:

> We all condemned our parents to shame, even if the only charge we could bring was that after 1945 they had tolerated the perpetrators in their midst . . . The more horrible the events about which we read and heard, the more certain we became of our responsibility to enlighten and accuse.

Schlink explores the question of guilt. Hanna has committed terrible crimes. We also realize, however, that Hanna is objectively less guilty than those who get off the charges scot-free. In the courtroom, she confesses to everything except the one fact which might help to reduce her guilt. In a pattern familiar from Milgram's electric-shock experiments, the perpetrator of lesser crimes accepts responsibility for guilt more readily than those who were responsible for greater crimes – but who are brazen in their declarations of their own innocence. Schlink reminds us that an individual's motivations and actions are sometimes more complex than they seem at first glance. This is not a soft-soaping approach – 'tidying away the past', in the words of a German critic. Rather, it is part of a rounded view which allows that responsibility may consist of more than just 'one size fits all'.

Other modern authors make clear that confrontation with the past can take different forms. For W. G. Sebald, questions of memory rule supreme. Sebald lived much of his adult life in Britain (he was a professor at the University of East Anglia until his death in a car crash in 2001). Through his work, he sought constantly to fill the historical silence. In connection with the death of a Bernese mountain guide in 1914, and the discovery of his remains on a glacier 70 years later, Sebald writes in *The Emigrants*:

They are ever returning to us, the dead. At times they come back from the ice more than seven decades later and are found at the edge of the moraine, a few polished bones and a pair of hobnailed boots.

It could almost be an epigraph for the work of Sebald himself. He exhumes and examines the bones of the dead, decades after the catastrophe. His writing, constantly blurring the boundaries between fact and fiction, provides an indirect response to the philosopher Theodor Adorno, who questioned whether it was possible to write poetry after Auschwitz. After 1945, artistic beauty seemed impossible to contemplate in the face of such horror. Half a century later, the passage of time means that Sebald's elusive and allusive writing creates an aesthetic link with Auschwitz which in previous years would have seemed insulting to the memory of the dead. In the words of one literary critic, 'Sebald makes exquisite art out of vile history.'

One of Sebald's characters in *The Emigrants* declares: 'Memory often strikes me as a kind of dumbness. It makes one's head heavy and giddy . . . ' Sebald himself, however, gives a voice to memory. He catalogues the past, pinning facts down with the precision of an obsessed butterfly-collector. In *Austerlitz* – the story of a child of the *Kindertransport*, evacuated from Prague to Wales in 1939, who goes in search of his past – he devotes a single, mesmerizing ten-page sentence to the Nazis' 'crazed administrative zeal' at the nightmarish camp of Theresienstadt. The past is inescapable, even and especially when described in matter-of-fact tones. In *The Emigrants*, the narrator (or Sebald himself, for he makes it impossible for us to disentangle the two), visits the Bavarian town of Bad Kissingen. The uncaptioned, Sebaldian-mundane photographs include one of the locked Jewish cemetery. The narrator receives a set of keys to the cemetery, but they do not fit; he must climb a wall to gain entry. When he leaves the town, he explains: 'I felt increasingly that the mental impoverishment and lack of memory that marked the Germans, and the efficiency with which they had cleaned everything up, were beginning to affect my head and my nerves.'

This lack of memory was indeed a conspicuous feature for many years. After 1945, memory-laundering was a national pastime – as Anna Rosmus, the 'nasty girl' from Passau, discovered more than 30 years after Hitler's defeat. At the same time, the success that Sebald himself has enjoyed serves as another reminder of how much everything else has changed. In modern Germany, remembrance is more important than ever. For the first time, that remembrance includes not just German suffering (as it did after 1945) nor just German crimes (as in the last decades of the twentieth century), but German crimes and suffering, as well. Sebald's *On the Natural History of Destruction*, published in 1999, is devoted to the subject of German suffering and the destruction of German cities in Allied bombing raids. Sebald quotes Hans Magnus Enzensberger on Germany after 1945, where 'insensibility was a condition of success', and suggests that there were good reasons why German authors found it difficult for many years to discuss the morality (or lack of it) of Allied actions against the German population. After all, 'A nation which had murdered and worked to death millions of people in its camps could hardly call on the victorious powers to explain the military and political logic that dictated the destruction of the German cities.'

A previous generation which had emphasized German suffering also downplayed German crimes. Now, the generation which was most eager to address German crimes and amnesia has also begun to look at crimes committed *against* the Germans. Sebald's description of the firestorm unleashed by the Allies in Hamburg in 1943, when tens of thousands of civilians died in a single night, is vivid and stark:

> The glass in the tramcar windows melted; stocks of sugar boiled in the bakery cellars. Those who had fled from their air-raid shelters sank, with grotesque contortions, in the thick bubbles thrown up by the melting asphalt . . . Residential districts with a street length of 200 kilometres in all were utterly destroyed. Horribly disfigured corpses lay everywhere. Bluish little phosphorus flames still flickered around many of them; others had been roasted brown or purple and reduced to a third of their normal size. They lay doubled up in pools of their own melted fat, which had sometimes already congealed.

Sebald insists that this catalogue of horror can only be seen in its broader context. 'We actually provoked the annihilation of the cities in which we once lived. Scarcely anyone can now doubt that Air Marshal Göring would have wiped out London if his technical resources had allowed him to do so.' Sebald quotes Hitler himself – 'We can destroy London completely. What will their firemen be able to do once it's really burning?' – before concluding his *Natural History* with the words:

> This intoxicating vision of destruction coincides with the fact that the real pioneering achievements in bomb warfare – Guernica, Warsaw, Belgrade, Rotterdam – were the work of the Germans. And

when we think of the nights when the fires raged in Cologne and Hamburg and Dresden, we also ought to remember that as early as August 1942, when the vanguard of the Sixth Army had reached the Volga and not a few were dreaming of settling down after the war on an estate in the cherry orchards beside the quiet Don, the city of Stalingrad, then swollen (like Dresden later) by an influx of refugees, was under assault from 1200 bombers, and that during this raid alone, which caused elation among the German troops stationed on the opposite bank, 40,000 people lost their lives.

This final thought is more than just a postscript. The connection underpins the whole work – as does the notion that one terrible set of crimes can never justify another set of crimes. This is what is new about the work of Sebald and others, in the last years of the twentieth century and the first years of the twenty-first. Not an either–or approach to the crimes of the past, but a both–and. Not an attempt to reduce the German crimes by putting them 'in context'; nor a shying away from crimes committed against Germans, because it would be 'inappropriate' to mention German suffering.

The destruction of Dresden in February 1945 provides one example of how attitudes have shifted in recent years. The story of the terrible night of 13–14 February 1945 – when 40,000 died in a single night, in a city packed with refugees – was not entirely unknown, inside or outside Germany.

During the Communist era, the East German authorities used the destruction of Dresden – 'Florence on the Elbe', as it had once been known – for their own propaganda purposes. The rubble of Dresden's most famous landmark, the Frauenkirche, lay in an ugly heap in the city centre as a permanent reminder of the war. The regime liked to contrast the murderous policies of Western imperialist bombers, on the one hand, with the allegedly wise and generous behaviour of the Soviet liberators, on the other. The Communist line was propaganda, but the resentments were real. In 1992, when the Queen Mother unveiled a statue in London of Bomber Harris, the man responsible for the lethal firebombing of Dresden, she failed to refer to the civilian deaths. Dresdeners were furious; when the Queen visited Dresden later that year, eggs were thrown and she was jeered.

Within a few years, however, both sides wished to sound conciliatory. The Duke of Kent announced the gift of a golden cross that would stand on top of the dome of the Frauenkirche, whose reconstruction had just begun. He told Dresdeners that the British gift was 'in remembrance of those who died'. The Germans, for their part, emphasized that 'Dresden was destroyed in a war unleashed by a German government'; an exhibition in the town hall on the occasion of the 50th anniversary of the raids focused on Nazi crimes against civilians in Europe, thus giving a different sense of context. As ever, not everybody was impressed by such politeness. An elderly Dresdener grumbled: 'Reconciliation is all very well. But it can't be that we are ready to be conciliatory, while others continue to blame us for what we have done.' By now, however, such views were a minority. Overall, respect and sorrow for the dead no longer slid into self-pity, as they so often did in Germany in previous years. Instead, the new readiness to confront the crimes of the past helped create the climate for a new openness on the subject of the Allied bombing raids, just as it had done on the subject of lethal expulsions from the East.

Sebald's *On the Natural History of Destruction* was followed in 2002 by *Der Brand* – 'The Fire', a 600-page chronicle of the Allied bombing campaign which went straight into the bestseller lists, and was read by millions more in serialized extracts in *Bild*. In Britain especially, the book came under furious attack. Its author, Jörg Friedrich, was described as 'a revisionist'. Commentators talked of a 'historical travesty', intended to justify Hitler's crimes, and asked: 'With four million unemployed in Germany, is this the fertile ground in which a new National Socialism might take root?' The short answer was: unlikely. The British critics of *The Fire* – many of whom had presumably not read the book, which had not been translated – talked as if Friedrich wanted to deny or lessen German responsibility. The reality was different. Friedrich was well known for his writing about the crimes of the Third Reich. His *Cold Amnesty*, published in 1984, catalogued in remorseless detail the extent to which the West German establishment remained infected by Nazism for decades after the Second World War. Friedrich, born (like both Sebald and Schlink) in 1944, is a member of the generation which was determined to make Germany confront its Nazi past. Now, at the turn of the millennium, he and others look for the first time at the other side of the coin, too. British commentators argued that Friedrich wants, through his book, to underplay the Luftwaffe's unrelenting raids. According to this analysis, the Allied raids were doing 'exactly what the Germans had done to London'. The raids on Britain indeed caused huge casualties, and the Germans would have been happy to cause more, if they had been able to. As it happens, however, there was no equivalence of body count. Approximately 80,000 civilians died in two night raids on Hamburg and Dresden alone – more than in the entire United Kingdom during the

Second World War; 600,000 Germans died from the bombing, ten times more than in the UK.

Above all, however, such a reckoning-up is quite pointless, as both Friedrich and Sebald make clear. For them, as for any sane observer, it is clear that Germany's crimes were infinitely more serious, on any broader reckoning – even if Britain, during the Blitz, got off with 'only' 60,000 dead. Friedrich describes the lethal effects of the much-feared V1 and V2 rockets, responsible for the deaths of 9000 British civilians. There were, he notes, 'no alarm sirens, no ducking away, no prayers when the V2 hit a Woolworths store in the London suburb of Deptford and killed 160 midday shoppers, including the passengers on a bus'. Above all, he emphasizes, as Sebald does, that, if many fewer civilians died from the bombing campaign in Britain than in Germany, that was not for want of the Germans trying:

> Hitler was a frustrated destroyer of cities. He loved to watch the film of the bombardment of Warsaw in September 1939, and fantasized about bringing down the skyscrapers of New York . . . He was a born bombing strategist, but without bombers.

The Fire does not create a new equation, stating: 'British and Americans: war criminals; Germans: innocent victims.' Instead, Friedrich explores the futility of a bombing strategy which kills more than half a million civilians and flattens historic towns and cities, for no obvious military gain. In the twenty-first century, it becomes possible for the first time for a liberal German historian to discuss the inhumanity of the Allies' well-planned mass killing, not instead of but in addition to the Nazis' obvious, varied and endlessly documented and discussed forms of murder. These are forgotten themes. Few, for example, have heard much about the bombing of the historic town of Würzburg, destroyed by 400,000 incendiary bombs dropped between 9.25pm and 9.45pm on the evening of 16 March 1945. Friedrich notes that there were no military targets in the town, 'just spinets and altars'. That night, 5000 of the town's inhabitants – one in 20 – died (in the notorious raid on Coventry, for comparison, 568 died). The British report of the bombing noted with satisfaction that 'the old town has been almost completely destroyed'.

The publication of Sebald's and Friedrich's bestselling accounts both represent breakthroughs, in terms of readiness to speak about German suffering, as did the broadcast of the two major television series about the expellees. It was, however, the grand old man of post-war German literature, Günter Grass, recipient in 1999 of the Nobel Prize for

Literature, whose first work in the new century marked the most remarkable turning point of all. Grass has been an influential literary and political figure for almost half a century. His Danzig trilogy chronicled – through the tin-drummer Oskar Matzerath and a host of other characters – the lunacy of the Third Reich on the one hand, and the difficulties in achieving a new honesty after 1945, on the other.

Over the years, Grass has dealt with many themes of twentieth-century German history. One theme, however, he ignored entirely: German suffering. In 2002, with the publication of Grass's *Crabwalk*, that suddenly changed. *Crabwalk* deals with the tragedy of the sinking of a huge German passenger ship, the *Wilhelm Gustloff*. More than 9000 passengers, fleeing the war at home, died when the *Gustloff* was torpedoed by a Russian submarine in January 1945. This was the largest-ever maritime disaster, with a death toll six times higher than that of the *Titanic*. For many years, the subject was taboo. Germany came to find such subjects embarrassing; only those with pronounced right-wing views highlighted tragedies like that of the *Gustloff*. Grass showed that it need not be that way.

The narrator of *Crabwalk* is a journalist, Paul Pokriefke, who came into the world as the torpedoed ship was going down. Paul's mother Tulla, who first appeared in Grass's *Cat and Mouse*, has long been eager for him to tell the story of that night. Paul, in turn, has been reluctant to do so, for fear of being seen as a defender of the far right ('the brown corner'). Instead, he tells us, he wrote pieces on 'organic vegetables and the effects of acid rain on Germany's forests' and 'breastbeating stuff along the lines of "Auschwitz: Never Again"'. Grass, though a generation older than his narrator, might partly identify with that – he, too, after all, had been able to write 'breastbeating stuff' on Auschwitz. (Grass in 1992: 'Whoever reflects on Germany now must also think of Auschwitz.') In addition, Grass himself – 'this person not to be confused with me', 'my employer' or simply 'the old man'– makes a personal appearance. This Grass figure – the author of a novel called *Dog Years*, which is as definitively Grass-like as one could ask for – tells Paul of his regret that he had never written about the *Wilhelm Gustloff* until now. 'Unfortunately, he said, he hadn't been able to pull it off. A regrettable omission, or, to be quite frank, failure on his part.' Grass confesses his failure – and the failure of those like him – to take any interest in German suffering. Through Paul Pokriefke, Grass explains himself:

> This business has been gnawing at the old boy. Actually, he says, his generation should have been the one. It should have found words

for the hardships endured by the Germans fleeing East Prussia: the westward treks in the depths of winter, people dying in blinding snowstorms, expiring by the side of the road or in holes in the ice when the frozen bay known as the Frisches Haff began to break up under the weight of horse-drawn carts after being hit by bombs . . . Never, he said, should his generation have kept silent about such misery, merely because its own sense of guilt was so overwhelming, merely because for years the need to accept responsibility and show remorse took precedence, with the result that they abandoned the topic to the right wing. This failure, he says, was staggering.

The danger of allowing the topic of German suffering to be abandoned to the far right forms a parallel storyline in *Crabwalk*. Paul's son is an enthusiastic participant in a far-right internet chatroom, where virtual insults end in a real murder. This story of possible far-right resurgence remains important to Grass. Above all, though, he is driven by unease at the 'belated and hesitant' attitudes towards German suffering. The narrator explains the complicated gait which gives the book its title:

> Should I do as I was taught and unpack one life at a time, in order, or do I have to sneak up on time in a crabwalk, seeming to go backward but actually scuttling sideways, and thereby working my way forward fairly rapidly?

It is an apt description of Germany in the new millennium – scuttling sideways, reaching back into history (incomparable crimes committed by the Germans; lesser but still terrible crimes committed against them) and moving forward at the same time. This was a theme whose time had come. *Crabwalk* was Grass' most successful work for many years. It topped the bestseller lists, and stayed there – achieving the near-impossible by knocking four volumes of *Harry Potter* adventures into second, third, fourth and fifth places. Germany is sometimes seen as unchanging. In reality, it is a nation of crabwalkers – moving, more rapidly than Germany itself sometimes seems to notice, towards the future and towards the creation of a Germany that we have not seen before.

In connection with the publication of *Crabwalk*, German commentators often described the subject of German suffering as 'taboo' for German post-war literature and history. That view is only partly accurate: German suffering was in the 1950s a subject of obsessive interest for many Germans. In an important sense, however, the publication of *Crabwalk* did mark the destruction of a crucial taboo. An emphasis on German crimes in the 1930s and 1940s is flawed if it refuses to acknowledge the suffering of 1945, just as German suffering can only be understood in the context of German crimes that came before. The two conjoined themes cannot be disentangled, even if some still seem eager to try.

Books like Grass's *Crabwalk*, Friedrich's *The Fire* and Sebald's *Natural History* seek to look at historical life in the round. Some, meanwhile, take the opportunity of the new opening-up to suggest that the Germans should be allowed to mourn their own victims, not in addition to the victims of the Holocaust but (for all the world as though we were back in the 1950s) *instead*. Thus, Klaus Rainer Röhl (former editor of the left-wing *konkret* magazine, former husband of the journalist-turned-terrorist Ulrike Meinhof) published an indignant little book in 2002 called *Forbidden Mourning: The Forgotten Victims*. Röhl refers briefly to the Holocaust. It soon becomes clear, however, that this is mere lip-service. Röhl's far-left politics have changed; his dogmatism, it seems, has not. The heart of Röhl's argument is that millions of Germans were innocent victims of the Second World War, and that they are not remembered in the same way that the victims of the Holocaust have been. Röhl concludes his diatribe with the words: 'That is bad. Bad, bad, bad.'

Those victims should indeed be remembered. Röhl's argument is weakened, however, by the determination to remove the horrors of 1944–46 from their Hitlerian context. Above all, by the time that his polemic thesis was published in 2002, it had in any case passed its sell-by date. Despite Röhl's assertions to the contrary, German suffering is no longer forbidden, nor are the victims forgotten. On the contrary, the fate of German civilians in 1945 is now widely discussed, in a more measured tone than Röhl himself is inclined to adopt. The circle, in short, is beginning to be squared. The distinguishing mark of the new Germany is not revisionism in the classic sense (in other words, airbrushing unpleasant facts out of the picture), but a new form of revisionism which allows German crimes and suffering both to be understood and acknowledged. The two are not equal; they are, however, both real.

Until now, as the title of Grass's story suggests, the German approach has been a confused scuttle – looking sideways or backwards into the crime-filled past, even while trying to move ahead. From now on, backward glances will no longer necessarily be filled with guilt. Nor will looking forward to the future always seem to be filled with trepidation. Germany is regaining its confidence – and is no longer afraid to say so.

14

Going Slow

There will be wailing and gnashing of teeth.
(Gerhard Schröder, Social Democrat chancellor, predicts the reaction
to his proposed economic reforms, 2003)

There will be wailing and gnashing of teeth.
(Christian Democrat opposition leader Angela Merkel predicts the
reaction to her proposed economic reforms, 2003)

They waited until the system was on the edge of collapse.
(Michael Burda, economics professor, 2003)

Germany has steadily gained new political confidence in recent years. And, at the same time, it has become racked by doubt about its ability to deliver the economic goods. Not a week nor a day passes without another clutch of doom-laden headlines. Every politician and every commentator in the country has suggestions for pulling Germany out of its slough of economic despond. Meanwhile, the problems only seem to multiply.

In the 1970s, the Federal Republic was almost content to be known, in the phrase made famous by Henry Kissinger, as an economic giant and a political dwarf. In the decades since then and especially in the last few years, Germany has become Europe's acknowledged political giant. The economy, meanwhile, remains of very restricted growth. Commentators regularly talk of Germany as the 'tail-light of Europe', bringing up the ignominious rear. Thus, average growth in Ireland between 1999 and 2003 was an impressive seven per cent; in most of the European Union it was between two and three per cent; Germany was the absolute laggard, with average growth of 1.3 per cent.

For many Germans, it has been hard to accept the idea that their economy is no longer indomitable – just as it was for the British from the 1960s onwards to accept that they had lost an empire and needed to find a role, or for the Russians to accept that they are no longer a world superpower (a re-adjustment that is just beginning). In the old *Bundesrepublik*, there was at least one thing of which Germans could be proud of: the ever-strong Deutschmark was the currency champion of the continent, perhaps even the champion of the world.

The Deutschmark, created out of the ruins of post-war Germany, was everything that Germans could be proud of – stability and democracy all in a shiny coin. It was the non-Weimar, non-Hitler currency, internationally respected for its reliability, and locally adored. Even in a country which prides itself on its Europhile credentials, there was widespread unease at the loss of the Deutschmark in 2002, to be replaced by a currency which was, *Bild* complained, 'as soft as Camembert'. The disappearance of the German currency and the creation of the little-loved euro was, however, a mere detail by comparison with the much bigger structural problems that were now facing the country. By the closing years of the twentieth century, those problems were hitting the country hard.

A few decades earlier, things had been so very different. The *Wirtschaftswunder*, the economic miracle of the 1950s, was remarkable by any measure. Growth ran in double figures through much of the decade; real wages increased by leaps and bounds. Towns and cities across Germany – rubble and devastation in 1945 as far as the eye could see – were rebuilt from the ruins with astonishing speed. Much of the architecture of the rebuilt towns and cities was (and remains) admittedly bland. Blandness was, however, what West Germany yearned for above all at this time. The national experiment with not-blandness had ended badly. The economic rebirth made it possible to feel proud of something German again (a pride that was helped along by West Germany's unexpected gift from footballing heaven, victory in the World Cup in Berne in 1954). In such circumstances, it was easier to leave politics and history to one side.

In obvious contrast to what had come before, West Germany became the country that adored consensus, above all. The success of the powerful engineering industry, and the civilized deals struck between trade unions and managers, were the envy of the rest of Europe. Foreign managers were astonished that German unionists seemed so reasonable; foreign unionists were astonished that German managers seemed so reasonable. This co-operation at all levels went alongside and helped lay the foundations for an S-class Mercedes of a welfare state, with levels of support that other Europeans could only dream of. The West German luxury model needed huge amounts of fuel to stay on the road. West Germans in the 1980s were confident, however, that theirs was the leading economy in the world. In those circumstances, why bother to change? The Kissinger model – no controversial politics; it's the economy that counts – suited everybody fine.

Even before the continent turned upside down in 1989, the affluent welfare state was starting to run out of steam. As far back as 1983 – at a time when Germans in east and west agreed that the prospect of unification was fantasy – the then finance minister said that the *Bundesrepublik* should not live beyond its means, and warned of 'an unlimited new accumulation of debt, at the cost of our children's generation'. Nobody took any notice. Then came the fall of the Wall. The huge costs involved in unification and *Aufbau Ost* – 'the rebuilding of the east', dented the country's economic wellbeing. No economy, however powerful, could remain unaffected by the haemorrhaging of hundreds of billions of Deutschmarks' worth of subsidies. In order to achieve even a poor man's version of the 'blooming landscapes' that Helmut Kohl (unwisely) promised in 1990, staggering sums were required. (As Helmut Schmidt pointed out, Kohl never made the 'blood, sweat and tears' speech that might have made the difficulties more bearable. It was a serious misjudgement.) Many years after German unification, vast annual transfers continue – around 75 billion euros, almost four per cent of gross domestic product every year.

The scrapping of the useless eastern currency was hugely expensive, too. After the Wall came down at the end of 1989, East Germans continued to stream west in undiminished numbers in the months to come. The prospect of mere democracy, in other words, was not a sufficient reason to stay at home. West Germany offered an incomparably higher standard of living, and East Germany was drained of its people at an alarming speed. The old saying about what would happen if the communists were to open up the borders – 'Last one out, turn off the lights!' – seemed in danger of becoming literally true. In those circumstances, the creation of a one-for-one exchange rate between the Deutschmark and the worthless East German mark when the two currencies were united in 1990 was justified, in terms of maintaining social and political stability. The generous exchange rate was essential if East Germany was not to be transformed into a ghost country. In national economic terms, however, the cost was painfully high.

Germany's problems through the 1990s were more than mere unity pains – agonizing though those were. Arguably, the difficulties caused by German unity delayed the recognition of how serious the economic problems were, problems which had nothing to do with the absorption of the east. In the last decade of the century, other European countries were also forced to confront new economic realities. From Bangalore to Budapest and from Shanghai to São Paulo, international competitive pressures on western European producers steadily grew. In many countries, an increasingly skilled labour force cost a fraction of what their German equivalents were demanding.

Chancellor Kohl talked repeatedly of the need for an investment-friendly *Standort Deutschland* – 'Location Germany'. This was, however, mere phrasemaking. As one commentator noted later: 'The fall of the Wall was the opportunity for West Germans to catch up with the structural change that was needed . . . But none of that happened.' Instead, a 1990s buzzword of German politics was *Reformstau* – 'reform traffic jam'. The decade passed as the economic equivalent of an August holiday weekend on the *autobahn* – permanent *Stau* , with no relief in sight. The economy drifted, and the headlines grew worse. There was endless complacency, on the one hand (the German economy has always been best; why should we expect that to change?) and fear of what change might bring, on the other (how can we tinker with a system that we have worked so hard to build up?). Most agreed that 'something needs to be done' – but there was a deep reluctance to decide what that might mean, in practical terms.

The reluctance to change has in many respects been understandable. The German standard of living remains high, by comparison with other western European countries – let alone by comparison with countries that have emerged from Communism in the past 15 years. In much of the rest of Europe, obvious poverty and deprivation are commonplace. In west Germany – even an economically stagnant west Germany – things look different. Whether it is a question of municipal swimming pools, regional opera houses or welfare benefits for all, the country has dripped with money – at least until now. (For the purposes of these comparisons, east Germany remains another country.) A German who lived in London for some years noted the difference: 'In Britain, there is much real poverty. In Germany, everybody *complains* so much.'

The German welfare state includes a myriad of different, overlapping benefits that other Europeans can only wonder at. The pride in German standards – which, it is assumed, justifies the high production costs – remains undimmed. At the Bavarian Motor Works factory in Munich, I asked a production-line worker if he was worried about the high costs involved in manufacturing a BMW. He and his colleagues received additional holiday money (13th month), additional Christmas money (14th month) and a special profit-sharing bonus (15th month), not to mention generous health and other benefits. No, he said; the costs were 'appropriate'.

In a sense, he was right. At the heart of the country's success has been the concept of thoroughness – *Gründlichkeit*, which Germans themselves identify as the most obviously German of qualities. Another BMW worker told me he was unimpressed by the chaos that he found under the bonnets of foreign cars. He compared such disorder unfavourably with the scrupulous care with which the layout of a BMW engine is designed. 'It's like looking at a cigarette packet, it's so neat. That makes it visually better – but technically better, too. Things are less likely to go wrong.' For him, the connection was clear. *Gründlichkeit* equals neat design, equals neat performance, equals neat export sales, equals good pay, remarkably generous benefits and long holidays abroad. For many years, the equation seemed to work. Even now, despite high costs, Germany remains one of the biggest exporting nations in the world.

Its self-image as a politically flawed but technically perfect nation is clearly reflected in opinion surveys. In other countries, questions like 'What are you proud of in your country?' tend to elicit similar responses, usually connected with political principles or a democratic constitution. The average German, asked the same question, gives a strictly practical answer about German technology. The phrase *Vorsprung durch Technik* – 'staying ahead through technology' – is more than just a neat advertising slogan. It has long since become part of the German mindset.

After years of doing nothing, a new sense of urgency entered the debate at the tail-end of the twentieth century. After the Social Democrat victory in 1998, there was much excited talk of change – and even a little action. Corporate tax rates were reformed – which, in German terms, was seen as revolutionary. *Business Week* felt able to ask, in a cover-story headline in 2001: 'Germany: Can Europe's top economy lead the Continent to reform?' Within a couple of years, even the question sounded like a cruel joke. The country's long-term assumption of an economic dominance is now challenged at every step. Unemployment stands at more than four million, despite a promise by Schröder when he came to power in 1998 that he would bring it down; there is talk of halving the unemployment levels within the next few years, but few believe it. On the contrary, some reckon that unemployment may rise still further. Social security costs have risen more than twice as fast as growth in gross domestic product during the past decade. Non-wage labour costs are more than 40 per cent of gross income, almost twice as much as in the United Kingdom. Germany is both the largest and the weakest economy in the European Union – so that its laggardly perform-ance has important implications not just for Germany but for its neigh-bours, too. For years, German politicians blamed the economic woes on factors beyond their control. Now, they dare to admit that Germany's weak growth is not just due to the downturn in the world economy, nor just because of the continuing high costs of rebuilding the east, but also because of structural difficulties in Germany itself.

Even now, it is possible to get carried away with the extent of Germany's problems. When Gordon Brown, Britain's chancellor, sought to contrast the perceived achievements of the British economy with the problems facing Germany, Michael Prowse noted in the *Financial Times*:

> It would be foolish to exaggerate either Britain's apparent virtues or Germany's apparent flaws. For those who must use Britain's ineffi-cient railways, its congested roads, its overstretched hospitals and retirement homes and its still-failing inner-city comprehensive schools, and for those who rely on its public-sector pensions, the concept of Britain as a beacon for the rest of Europe is laughable.

Nonetheless, Germans themselves have gradually come to understand that *something* must change. Until recently, the consensus remained unbroken that things could go on (almost) as they were. Thus, when launching an 'alliance for work' in 2002, Schröder was photographed as part of a smiling, hand-holding trio together with the union boss and the head of the employers' organization. All three knew that the cheesy grins would not get them far: for the moment, however, appearances were all. Only now does everyone agree that serious change is urgently needed.

All the main political parties have, in the first years of the twenty-first century, come up with reform programmes which (they claim) will get Germany out of its mess. So far, the practical effects remain limited. A cartoon in *Die Zeit* in 2003 depicted a once-grand and now-crumbling building, labelled 'Consensus Society'. The roof is falling in, and the walls and grand balconies are collapsing. Only a few minor repairs are being attempted; falling porticos are propped up by a man on a step ladder. Meanwhile, those inside the crumbling building toast each other in champagne; empty champagne bottles lie scattered amidst the debris. The paper argued that the post-war generation of political leaders have often seemed too frightened to push for real change:

The youth revolt of their generation created a new intellectual and moral openness, but no economic freedom . . . . It seemed as though it was written into the constitution: corporatism is untouchable, and a handful of elderly gentlemen on management boards decide the fate of Germany Inc.

There is common consent that things cannot go on as they were. Nothing symbolizes that more than the word 'Pisa', which in winter 2001 became a German synonym for national humiliation. Pisa is the Programme for International Student Assessment, a comparative study of a quarter of a million schoolchildren carried out by the Organization for Economic Co-operation and Development, the OECD. Germans and non-Germans alike had grown accustomed to Germany always doing well in such studies. This time, it was different. 'Catastrophic' was one of the more polite words used to describe the results of the Pisa study. Germans found that their country was little better than mediocre. That was not what Germans expected to be. Various culprits were blamed: a surfeit of post-1968 liberal teaching methods, too little attempt to integrate non-German children, too few kindergarten places, and so on. Everybody agreed, however, on one point. Things had to change.

A panoply of corruption scandals has, meanwhile, contributed to the perception of a country that is decaying daily. 'Germany is becoming a banana republic', national headlines declared. Within a year of leaving office, Chancellor Helmut Kohl was named in connection with a party-funding scandal involving cash-stuffed briefcases, from donors who the former chancellor refused to name. Two years later came a series of scandals involving senior Social Democrats. In 2002, even the squeaky-clean Greens (quickly followed by all the other main parties) were embarrassed by a corruption scandal involving the unauthorized use of frequent-flyer points, gained on business and spent on pleasure. Cem Özdemir, a rising star of the Greens, was forced to resign, as was Gregor Gysi of the post-Communist PDS.

By the standards of Italy, France and elsewhere, such corruption scandals might seem tame. When it comes to structural problems, however, Germany's difficulties are up with the worst of them. In the years leading up to the introduction of a single European currency, Germany looked with ill-concealed disdain at the financial discipline of its neighbours, suggesting that they might be unable to match the demanding standards required for a country to enter the euro-zone. Now that the euro exists, Germany cheerfully and repeatedly breaks the rules.

The proposals for reform have often seemed timid by comparison with the scale of the problems. In the words of Oswald Metzger, former budget spokesman for the Greens (not usually thought of as a party that speaks for big business): 'Both government and opposition encouraged the belief that, one or two problems aside, Germany would somehow get over the economic slowdown.' Or, as economics professor Michael Burda put it: 'They waited until the system was on the edge of collapse.'

Peter Hartz, personnel director of Volkswagen, was appointed to chair a government commission which made a number of recommendations for change in labour-market policy in 2002 and 2003. The commission proposed, for example, that Germany's generous unemployment benefit – up to a remarkable two-thirds of previous salary – should be paid for only a year, instead of almost three. For some, that was a cutback too far; the proposals were duly diluted, allowing for full benefits for 18 months, and 50 per cent of wages indefinitely thereafter. At the same time, the commissions multiplied. The Rürup commission, chaired by economics professor Bert Rürup, proposed a series of reforms to the system of health insurance and pensions. Germany's health-care system remains one of the world's most expensive; health-insurance contributions represent around 14 per cent of gross wages. The problem of pension payments – a ticking timebomb, as people live longer – is now, at last, recognized as a crisis issue for the first time. Rürup argued that the retirement age should be raised from 65 to 67. The Christian Democrats created a Herzog Commission, meanwhile, chaired by former President Roman Herzog, which came up with yet another set of plans for how to save the country.

Schröder's package of proposed reforms, 'Agenda 2010', implies a visionary quality, gazing ahead towards a bright new future. Few believe, however, that Agenda 2010 – whose proposals include greater flexibility and easier bookkeeping procedures for the *Mittelstand*, the small and medium-sized companies which provide about three-quarters of all German jobs – will survive the process of political consensus unscathed. The proposed reforms are in any case only visionary in a German context, where even small changes can seem to represent a radical revolution. Nor is there any sign that any other politician on the horizon has a more coherent vision than Schröder himself. Angela Merkel, the Christian Democrat leader; Edmund Stoiber, leader of the CSU (the Christian Democrats' Bavarian sister party) and failed challenger in 2002; and Roland Koch, state premier in Hesse and another of Schröder's possible challengers in 2006, all make confident statements about the need for wide-ranging reforms – and at the same time eagerly block reforms proposed by the other side.

All insist that *their* proposed reforms involve more taboo-crunching than reforms proposed by the other side. With reference to a much-flagged speech in spring 2003, Schröder predicted that pain of the reforms would provoke 'wailing and gnashing of teeth'. Angela Merkel, the opposition leader, apparently visited the same soundbite consultant as the chancellor himself. Later that year she, too, announced that her economic proposals would cause 'wailing and gnashing of teeth'. Stoiber and Koch, her conservative rivals, were not to be outdone. Each came up with separate sets of proposals which would get Germany back on an even keel. The one consensus, in short, is that *something* needs to be done. Little else is agreed.

Until the late 1990s, the consensus was that nothing needed to be done. Germany's economic pre-eminence remained unquestioned. When the creation of a single currency was finally agreed at a summit in the Dutch town of Maastricht in 1991, one key intention was that this would bind Germany into Europe for all time. In this, modern Germany was following Thomas Mann, who declared in 1945: 'We do not want a German Europe, but a European Germany.' Mann's *bon mot* became almost an official mantra in the newly unified Germany.

At that time, even though there was a widespread fear of Germany off the political leash, the country's economic strength was still taken for granted. As late as 1997, Germany insisted on the imposition of tough conditions in the European Union's pact on stability and growth, in order that less financially responsible countries would be kept in line. Within a few years, Germany was itself failing to meet the targets that it had been so determined to set. The budget deficit has repeatedly crashed through the specified three per cent limit; in 2003, it was the highest in Germany's post-war history. Germany has suffered the indignity of being reprimanded by the European Commission for breaking the rules which Germany itself was so eager to create. The sagging corpulence of Germany, with a GDP a third larger than that of Britain or France, threatens to drag others down with it. Germany has signed up for membership of the reformers' gym. But it remains constantly unclear whether it is ready to move from good intentions towards reality.

Everybody agrees that there has never been so much talk of the need for reform. Schröder refers to 'talks without taboos'. Certainly, this is a defining moment for the future of the German economy. A political friend in Berlin (a Christian Democrat) compares the economic crisis of 2003 with the country's political crisis 25 years earlier in 1968. 'Then, as now, it was *Umbruchzeit*, a time of historic upheaval. Thank God the confrontation happened then. At that time, we were running on to the rocks – now we are running aground on a sandbank.' The ponderous German supertanker may yet swing its massive bulk round, allowing the country to steer a course into the future. Perhaps, in retrospect, that is how the period that we are now living through will be remembered. A popular German saying declares: 'Those who have been pronounced dead live longer.' Thus it might yet prove with the German economy, whose obituary has been written endless times in the last few years.

At the time of writing, that still seems an over-rosy prospect, at least for the next few years. There were signs that things were getting serious at the end of 2003. Schröder threatened to resign unless he gained a parliamentary majority for his reform package. Six renegade Social Democrats, whose threat to rebel threatened the government's working majority, were eventually persuaded to back down – after Schröder had watered down some of his proposals. Even then, the situation was still so finely balanced that Schröder was obliged to ask President Jacques Chirac to speak on Germany's behalf at an EU meeting in Brussels, allowing the chancellor himself to hurry back to Berlin for the crucial vote.

One problem is that all the different parties pull in different directions, even as they pronounced the same magic word, '*Reformen!*'. No country is better than Germany at blocking political change when there is disagreement in the country. As in so many other contexts, this ability to block change was determined by the desire to find a contrast with what came before. One reason why Hitler was able to amass unlimited power for himself was the weakness of the constitution. In the new *Bundesrepublik*, by contrast, it would be impossible for one man – even a leader with considerable popular support – to force political changes through against the wishes of the opposition parties.

In modern Germany, consensus has dictatorial power. Many laws can only be passed if they have the support not just of the Bundestag, but also of the Bundesrat, the federal council made up of representatives from the governments of the 16 *Länder* or regional states. The government of the day is frequently in the minority in the Bundesrat. This means that governments are unable to implement legislation unless the opposition, too, can be cajoled or browbeaten into giving its approval. In these circumstances, it is perhaps unsurprising that progress on contentious issues is painfully slow. The government's negotiating position is made even shakier by the fact that, by 2004 – at just the time it was trying to push its economic reforms through – the Social Democrats' own ratings were disastrously low. In a sense, the only good news was the fact that the economic situation was so bad. One official argued, with almost Marxian logic (the worse the situation, the better the chances of a revolution): 'If we had 2.5 per cent growth this year, the reforms would have been put off yet again.'

In 1948, when the constitution of the new Federal Republic was agreed, it was understandable that the idea of too much German democracy sounded like an oxymoron. For decades after the agreement of the Basic Law, the emphasis on consensus in German politics served its purpose well. Increasingly, however, many Germans have begun to worry about 'the blocked republic' and 'the dusty constitution'. Modern Germans yearn for the greater flexibility that other European democracies already enjoy – a flexibility which allows the government of the day to make clear decisions on important issues without being blocked at every turn. In late 2003, yet another commission was created – this time not to reform the economy, but to 'modernize the federal structure', and to get rid of what *The Economist* has described as the 'near-constipation' of the system.

Even the Bundesrat is not the final arbiter on what may or may not happen next. German politicians regularly send their most sensitive decisions up to the country's highest court, the constitutional court in Karlsruhe, like nervous schoolchildren needing to have their essays marked. The constitutional court, created as a bulwark of modern German democracy, is treated by millions of Germans with almost religious awe. Criticism of the constitutional court is akin to an old-fashioned royalist daring to criticize the Queen: such things happen, but they smack of sacrilege. The red-robed and red-capped judges of Karlsruhe are Germany's modern equivalents of the oracle at Delphi. They provide careful answers to all difficult questions – including and especially those which clearly have no single 'correct' answer. Thus, for example, the court was asked whether it was appropriate or inappropriate for Germany to send troops abroad. Answer: Appropriate, if you are sure the troops are needed. Or: is the Maastricht treaty, which paved the way for the single European currency, legal? Answer: If it matters to the government very much, yes. Or, a Karlsruhe brainteaser which in 2003 received an answer which was as authoritative as it was opaque: is it appropriate, in modern German society, for a Muslim teacher to wear a headscarf in the classroom? Karlsruhe's endlessly dissected answer amounted, in effect, to: 'What an interesting and important question. We hope you will think about it hard.'

Germany's political and economic identity are in the midst of enormous change. Beyond that, the political geography – and thus, Germany's role in Europe – is shifting. The enlargement of the European Union to include a clutch of former Soviet-bloc countries in central and eastern Europe means that Germany is now at the heart of the newly expanded EU, leaving Bonn and Paris far to the west. It is a change of historic importance, affecting the very philosophy at the heart of the Union.

The Franco-German axis played an important role in past decades. Like everything else, it was explicitly connected with the experience of the Third Reich – a way of neutralizing the past, and of ensuring that bloody history did not repeat itself. Adenauer made clear that he saw this relationship as a way of preventing a revival of nationalism – and thus a way of preventing Germans from hurting others. When Adenauer first visited General de Gaulle at home in Colombey-les-Deux-Eglises, he was driven past one war cemetery after another, full of Frenchmen killed by Germans. The chancellor reflected that Germans could not be welcome in France; the fact that de Gaulle received him warmly was seen, in that context, as a generous gift. The feeling of German gratitude remained undimmed for many years. In the 1980s, the conservative Helmut Kohl and the socialist President François Mitterrand formed a close friend-ship. Physically, Kohl was the giant, towering over his friend when the two held hands – as, for example, at the military cemetery at Verdun. Politically, however, Mitterrand called the shots. Germany remained grateful that it was allowed to sup at the European democrats' top table. It took Kohl's twenty-first century successor to create a relationship where Germany is no longer afraid to assert itself as an equal partner. France has not always been impressed by this change. For the French, the old first-among-equals relationship was a comfortable fit. In Germany, however, pleasing their western neighbours is no longer the only factor that needs to be considered.

For most of the past century, German power and democracy have been seen as natural opposites. A politically strong Germany has been undemocratic; a democratic Germany has been politically weak, by force of circumstance (in Weimar) or by choice (in the *Bonner Republik*). Only now do Germans themselves begin to see democracy and power as potentially reconcilable – even in Germany. In its relations with the rest of central and eastern Europe, Germany must tread a delicate path. Germany looks east to Warsaw and Prague (Berlin is just an hour's drive from the Polish border), just as it previously looked west from Bonn to Paris. Joschka Fischer, echoing the deeply pro-European Helmut Kohl, insists that Germany would never dream of taking action out of line with the rest of Europe. In a speech at the Humboldt University in Berlin in 2000, Fischer talked of the need for a strong federal Europe and called for a new European constitution – a dream that, with much confusion and argument, began to come true four years later. At the same time, Fischer insisted that Germany has now come to terms with its identity. The debate about Germans' troubled relationship with the nation-state, he declared, 'can in my opinion now be ended'.

If one is looking for evidence of the renewed strength of the nation-state, one need perhaps only look at the fierce arguments that erupted between Germany and Poland in December 2003, when European governments tried to choose an appropriate voting system for the new European Union. Through the 1990s, Germany had strongly supported Poland in its bid for membership of the EU. Now, however, Berlin was indignant at Poland's refusal to allow a voting deal agreed at Nice three years earlier to be overturned – a deal which was highly favourable to Poland and much less favourable to Germany. The two countries eventually walked out of the negotiations, causing the ignominious collapse of a key summit and a crisis for the European Union itself. In theory, Germany wants to be politically generous to the Poles, not least for historical reasons. Increasingly, however, good intentions are liable to crumble – as in any other country – when they come into conflict with the national interest.

Modern Germany sees itself as a morally driven country. That view is not entirely fictional. But nor is it the whole truth. As the historian Thomas Speckmann points out:

> The land of *Dichter und Denker* – of 'poets and thinkers', feels morally superior to the Americans in particular. Books which compare the image of a peaceful Germany with that of a war-loving America dominate the bestseller lists [in 2003]. Does this division of roles correspond to reality? It is appropriate to harbour some doubts.

German criticism of repressive regimes tends to be muted, at best, where important commercial interests are at stake. Where morality and money come into conflict, lucrative contracts usually win the day.

Fischer's suggestion that there might be an end to the German debate about national identity still seems implausible. The continued agonizing about Germany and Germanity in every German newspaper certainly tells a different story. It is, however, interesting that a left-leaning (and, above all, non-nationalist) foreign minister can make such a suggestion aloud. The remark would have been unthinkable a few years earlier. The old political bashfulness has given way to a new self-confidence – and endless self-interrogation about whether that confidence is appropriate or justified. Even as economic confidence collapses, meanwhile, questions are asked about whether the former economic confidence can ever be restored. Both politically and economically, this is a story of unfinished business.

15

Crumbling Taboos

The previous generation, if I remember rightly, demonstrated all day long. That's probably why we found it stupid from the start.

(Florian Illies, in *Generation Golf* (2000))

I myself had difficulty in establishing a perfect logical connection between the Holocaust and the Second World War, on the one hand, and the resulting shame at the fact that Bayern Munich dominated European football, on the other.

(Florian Illies, in *Instructions on Being Innocent* (2001))

In the summer of 2001, a poster with a startling message appeared near the Brandenburg Gate in Berlin. 'The Holocaust never happened', it declared; the background photograph was an idyllic scene of mountains and lakes. The slogan, encased in inverted commas, drew the attention of the crowds, as it was meant to. The smaller print revealed the punchline: 'There are still people who believe that. There could be more of them in 20 years. So give a donation for the murdered Jews of Europe.' A telephone number, address and bank details followed for a proposed new Holocaust memorial to be built on that site. The poster's heart was clearly in the right place. But that was not sufficient. In drawing attention to itself, the poster was too successful for its own good. Its publishers were threatened with prosecution for denial of the Holocaust, and the poster was withdrawn. In due course, thought-provoking slogans which seek to confront the dishonesty of the past may be permitted. The Holocaust poster made clear, however: 60 years is still regarded as too soon.

Taboos have been part of the Federal Republic's identity from the start. First came the most blatant taboos: Germans had seen no evil, heard no evil, done no evil. Then, once those taboos were conquered, they were replaced by their opposite: seen too much evil, done too much evil – and therefore we mustn't talk about what our own country went through. And finally, still in force to this day, a myriad of taboos covers, for example, visual echoes of the Third Reich. The bans can affect almost anything – from placards at a pacifist demonstration to the graphic design of serious history books. These taboos reflect the worry that Germany might somehow revert to the madness of the past – or (to make life more Germanly complicated) the fear that *others* might suspect Germany of reverting to its past, even if German law-makers themselves see such a prospect as unreal.

One obvious taboo affects a basic source for any student studying the genesis and development of Nazism. In bookshops in London and New York, it is easy to find copies of *Mein Kampf*. As the English-language edition notes: 'It remains necessary reading for those who seek to understand the Holocaust, for students of totalitarian psychology, and for those who care to safeguard democracy.' Try asking for Hitler's work in Munich or Berlin, however, and the bookstore assistant will react with a jaw-dropping look of disbelief. In the land of its birth, *Mein Kampf* is forbidden. As one commentator argued (in connection with the prosecution of a bookseller who sold *Mein Kampf* several decades after the end of the war): 'The scars are still too fresh, the bacillus too lively, the danger of infection too acute.' Few German politicians believe that being permitted to buy a copy of *Mein Kampf* in the twenty-first century would dramatically strengthen neo-Nazi support in Germany. Many factors – economic, social and political – could increase the dangers of the far right; it is difficult to argue that the availability of *Mein Kampf* in bookshops is high on that list. In a range of contexts, however, the bacillus is treated as if it were still too lively, and as if Hitler's mesmerizing power to impress the crowds were still real.

Thus, history books about the Third Reich may not have a swastika on the cover, lest they breach §86a of the criminal code, on anti-constitutional symbols; many books about the Hitler era translated from other languages into German are likely to need a new cover design. At an anti-war protest in 2002, police confiscated a portrait of a German soldier; the swastika on the soldier's helmet was illegal. Police were only faintly embarrassed when it turned out that the photograph was of Gerhard Schröder's father, killed in the Second World War. The implication of the existing legislation (never fully spelt out, but an obvious subtext) is that the sight of the swastika might inspire Germans to re-found the Third Reich or commit another genocide – once a nation of willing execution-ers, always a nation of willing executioners. Few German politicians on left, right or centre would subscribe to that analysis. And yet, the legisla-tion remains in place.

One day, it will be permitted for the German public to show a swastika in public in a neutral context, as elsewhere in Europe. The mere act of printing a swastika (as opposed to following Nazi ideology) will seem no more dangerous in Germany than it does elsewhere. For some, that moment of relaxation will no doubt be seen as more evidence that modern Germany wants to sweep the past under the table. In reality, that moment will be a welcome sign that normality is approaching at last. Already the picture is changing. A reformed alcoholic dare not risk even a single drink for fear of a dangerous relapse. Nearly 60 years after Hitler's death, Germany is beginning to accept that a political relapse is no longer an active, ever-present threat. The fact that a grandfather succumbed to lethal alcoholism does not mean that his grandson should be banned from looking at a wine label. Taboos are crumbling constantly. When I saw *The Producers* on Broadway in summer 2001 – Mel Brooks' hugely successful, magnificently bad-taste musical comedy, with a goosestepping 'Springtime for Hitler' as its best-known number – it was obvious that here, at least, was a German taboo that could not soon be broken. Raucous laughter at a Hitler musical was fine in New York or London, but unthinkable for German audiences. Less than three years later, negotia-tions for a Berlin opening were well under way. A German audience was flown to New York in spring 2004 to ensure, in Brooks' words, that the show was not 'too unspeakably rude' for the Germans to stomach.

In past decades, a key buzzword in connection with the attitudes to German history has been the unwieldy *Vergangenheitsbewältigung* – 'dealing with the past', 'coming to terms with the past', or even (since the etymology of the word contains a hint of force) 'wrestling down the past'. *Vergangenheitsbewältigung* was absent in the 1950s and 1960s. In the 1970s and especially 1980s, *Vergangenheitsbewältigung* was every-where. Now, a new and almost equally untranslatable word has come to represent the new Germany. *Unbefangenheit* has become a favourite self-description – a state of being unencumbered, uninhibited or simply unbothered.

Until recently, German liberals used the word with distaste as if it were a dirty word. *Unbefangenheit*, like Kohl's much-mocked 'grace of being born late', was taken to mean that Germany did not feel burdened by its history, even when it *should* feel burdened. Now the word no longer has automatically negative connotations. Instead, it has come to suggest the opposite of 'angst-ridden'. It suggests a nation that is beginning to feel relaxed. 'The new unbotheredness' describes a country that begins to be at ease with itself at last. The huge success in 2003 of Sönke Wortmann's film *The Miracle of Berne* can be seen as reflecting that *Unbefangenheit* at only one remove. The main theme of *The Miracle of Berne* is Germany's World Cup victory in 1954 – an unexpected victory that allowed Germans to feel proud of something for the first time in many years. As one of the film's advertising lines declares: 'Every country needs a legend.' The feelgood factor underlines the sense of liberation that Wortmann and other film-makers feel through this *Unbefangenheit* – addressing such themes without feeling that they are occupying the far-right *braune Ecke* – 'brown corner', by doing so.

Wortmann makes it clear that only the changes that have taken place in Germany in recent years enabled him to make such a relaxed movie about national achievement and pride. 'Ten years ago, I wouldn't have made the film,' he told me. 'Things are changing in a positive way. The Germans are not so *verkrampft* – so "uptight".' In another notable example of the new relaxedness, German television followed the example of the BBC's successful *Great Britons* series with a German equivalent. Millions of Germans voted in November 2003 to choose the greatest-ever Germans, in a series entitled *Unsere Besten* – 'Our Best'. Konrad Adenauer, who ushered in an era of German democracy, topped the poll. Others in the top ten included Willy Brandt, Albert Einstein, Karl Marx, Hans and Sophie Scholl, and Martin Luther – all of them representatives, in their different ways, of independent German thought. The rebellious Luther ('Here I stand, I can do no other') is also the hero of a German-made film of the same name, with the title role played by Joseph Fiennes. The simple, previously unthinkable message: Germans can be heroes, too. *Der Spiegel* even dared to ask: 'Is Germany, six decades after Hitler, suddenly a country just like any other?' The answer, of course, was no – hence the need to ask the provocative question. Nonetheless, change is undeniably on the way.

As ever, the change of generational guard has helped paved the way for the *Unbefangenheit* of today. One huge German bestseller in recent years has been *Generation Golf*, by Florian Illies, published in 2000. *Generation Golf* (the reference is not to the game, but to the car that became the badge of a new generation) partly addresses discomfort about German identity, an endlessly familiar theme. New, however, is the teasing tone. Illies, born in 1971, draws a line between his own generation and that of his parents – the angry generation of 1968: 'The previous generation, if I remember rightly, demonstrated all day long. That's probably why we found it stupid from the start.' Illies notes that his generation – in effect, the crabwalk children – no longer feel stressed by their German identity as their parents so often did. Illies' 2001 follow-up to *Generation Golf* was *Instructions on Being Innocent*, another best-seller, which analyses different forms of guilt. Much of the book is apolitical; indeed, that is one of its selling points. The chapters describe guilt about the failure to recycle (a key reason for guilt in any German household, where there are always at least four different-coloured categories of rubbish); guilt about wearing or failing to wear expensive designer clothes; guilt about buying or failing to buy a cheap rose for a lover in a restaurant – and so on, 20 little chapters of social observation. In addition, however, Illies mocks specifically German forms of guilt, including 'our constant desire to scatter ashes over our heads'. In previous years, that phrase alone would have been a reason to rebuke the author for alleged revisionism. Now, the mockery is uncontroversial. Illies' verbal sallies complement the new opening-up by the older, self-critical generation in the last few years on bombs and refugees. He encourages Germany to loosen up for a change. Germany, in turn, seems eager to do so.

Illies describes the tangled thickets of identity, starting from one basic premise: 'Anybody who is born German learns at an early age that that is a problem.' Thus, he and his classmates are told that they must change their chosen name for a school magazine because the comically bureaucratic title has Nazi overtones. In reality, the name dates back not to 1933 but to 1803. But that, Illies decides, is too complicated to explain:

We just swallowed it, because we saw for the first time those eyes that Germans make, when the worry-wrinkles stretch almost over the retina because of anxiousness that someone might forget how undeniably dreadful were the things that happened in the Third Reich.

Elsewhere, Illies describes how a small-talk conversation with an Italian taxi driver went wrong – with Illies in the role of a full-blown, breastbeating Jürgen the German. The taxi driver talks enthusiastically about a recent victory by Bayern Munich. Illies responds by belittling this and other German sporting victories. Eventually the taxi driver, who thought it was a basic form of courtesy 'to pay compliments to people about nice things from their country', becomes irritated. Illies finds that he has boxed himself into a very German corner:

I couldn't explain to him that with us Germans things aren't that simple – partly because I myself had difficulty in establishing a perfect logical connection between the Holocaust and the Second World War, on the one hand, and the resulting shame at the fact that Bayern Munich dominated European football, on the other.

Each chapter in *Instructions on Being Innocent* concludes with a curative exercise. In the chapter dealing with German footballing success, the prescribed exercise for getting rid of one's guilt is to enter an Italian restaurant dressed in German army uniform, and 'sing all three verses of the *Deutschlandlied*'. Here, Illies shockingly hacks at one of the ultimate German taboos. Each country has its own national anthem, and Germany is no exception. In 1922, the Social Democratic government declared *Deutschland, Deutschland, über alles* – a song in praise of the German unity with music by Haydn – to be Germany's official anthem. The *Deutschlandlied* would, in the words of President Friedrich Ebert, 'accompany us on our hard path towards a better future'. After 1933, the Nazis banned the third verse, whose references to 'unity and justice and freedom' were regarded as offensively tolerant. After 1945, in turn, the Allies banned the anthem altogether. A German anthem was a bad anthem. In 1951, the third verse of the anthem was permitted once more. The first and second verses, meanwhile, remained out of bounds. (In 1990, the constitutional court in Karlsruhe, final arbiter on arcane points of German self-doubt, was asked to rule as to whether singing the *Deutschland, Deutschland, über alles* verse should still be regarded as a criminal offence. The response, a classic piece of Karlsruhe fudge, could be summed up as: 'Probably.') One day, a German parliament may lift the *über alles* ban. For the moment, however, such a taboo-breaching move is difficult to contemplate. The likelihood, in other words, of Florian Illies following his own prescription and singing the anthem's first verse in public, look slim. Moronic skinheads sing *Deutschland, Deutschland, über alles*; respectable Germans do not. Even in the twenty-first century, some taboos – in this case, the words of a nineteenth-century poet, approved by democrats but made offensive by Hitler – seem unbreachable.

One way of tracking the strange course of modern German taboos is by looking at the biography of the man polls regularly show to be the most popular politician in the country. His history embodies the contradictions of modern Germany – not least because he has changed so much while staying recognizably the same. Joschka Fischer, German foreign minister from 1998, is the best-known figure in a party whose national support has rarely run into double figures. For, although few

Germans may be ready to vote Green, millions have made clear their sympathy for Fischer himself.

This book is intended as an account of how German society has changed and continues to change; it is not primarily about the country's political leaders. A compare-and-contrast exercise between Chancellor Gerhard Schröder, the Social Democrat from Hanover in the north, and Edmund Stoiber, the Bavarian conservative who came within a whisker of defeating him in 2002, would give only limited insights into the nature of modern German society (beyond the obvious truth that voters everywhere are impressed by a politician who gives the impression of confidence and competence). If Angela Merkel, the Christian Democrat leader, replaces Schröder in 2006, that will mark an important shift in two respects. She will be Germany's first woman leader and – crucially – the first east German politician who is accepted as a German political leader first, Ossi second. That could prove important in the historical search for German unity. It is Joschka Fischer's biography, however, which reflects most vividly many of the dramatic changes that have taken place in the Federal Republic in past decades. Fischer's success can be seen as the story, at just one remove, of the changes that have taken place in the wider Germany.

The twists and turns of Fischer's life story have caused him embarrassment, above all in connection with his time as a Frankfurt streetfighter in and after 1968. He has been described as a cynic who will do anything to achieve or stay in power. That is only partly true: Fischer, the ambitious pragmatist, can also be seen as a conviction politician par excellence. His core values – including, above all, the need to confront Germany's Nazi past – have allowed him to survive almost unscathed, despite political knocks which would normally have proved terminally damaging to a respectable politician's career.

In 2001, photographs were published which showed that the German foreign minister had been involved in more than mere scuffles three decades earlier. A helmeted Fischer was seen beating up a policeman on the edges of a Frankfurt demonstration in 1973. 'Yes, I was militant,' the foreign minister commented laconically. That drama was followed in short order by a subpoena for Fischer to testify in the trial of a former terrorist and friend, Hans-Joachim Klein. Klein was involved in the attack on an oil summit in Vienna in 1975. Three people were killed; Klein escaped. Klein publicly denounced terrorism shortly afterwards, but remained in hiding until his arrest in 1998. In court, Fischer, the foreign minister, walked across the courtroom to shake the hand of his friend, the former terrorist.

Damaging stories about Fischer's past continued to multiply. In court, he angrily rejected suggestions that members of the terrorist Red Army Faction had stayed at his Revolutionary Struggle squat in Frankfurt. Then, after his on-oath denials, it turned out that at least one RAF member *had* spent a few days there (and written about it in her auto-biography). Whereupon the state prosecutor wanted to put Fischer on trial for perjury. All in all, a messy business. In a country where *Ordnung* (order, order everywhere) is still treasured, such evidence of *Unordnung* on a grand scale should, on the face of it, have spelt Fischer's political doom. In reality, the storm passed with remarkable speed. Fischer, the ex-revolutionary radical, was soon as popular as he had ever been. Partly, voters accepted that he had turned his back on his violent past. As importantly, however, they found a partial continuity. Fischer seemed almost unrepentant when confronted with his radicalism of 30 years earlier: 'That's my biography. Without my biography I would be a different person today – and I wouldn't find that good.' The voters' readiness to forgive Fischer his past suggested that not just the foreign minister but German society itself had moved on. The Sixty-eighters' once controversial thesis – that Germany in the 1960s needed to heal itself – had in the intervening years come to seem self-evident.

It was clear that Fischer had changed his views – even before he was forced, in the embarrassing glare of publicity, to apologize to the policeman by the name of Marx whom he had beaten up three decades earlier. But that change has been smaller than might sometimes appear. When Fischer played a key role in ensuring German support for the war against the Taliban in Afghanistan, some of his new admirers in the United States approvingly talked of him as a 'neo-conservative'. In reality, Fischer's radicalism in opposing the establishment in 1968 and after can be seen as related to the radicalism which persuaded him to speak out in favour of military action three decades later. The slaughter in 1995 of thousands of Muslims at the Bosnian town of Srebrenica, and the world's failure to protect them, was a defining moment in shaping Fischer's views on military intervention, just as the selection of Jewish passengers had been a defining moment for him in making a final break with the men and women of violence at the time of the Entebbe hijack in 1976. As a young man, he was motivated, like others of his generation, by the perception that Germany had failed to confront the legacy of Auschwitz. Some 30 years later, he was influenced by the perception that the lessons of Auschwitz had been insufficiently understood. At the end of the twentieth century, some argued that the world's favourite post-Holocaust phrase 'Never again!' was used so narrowly that it had been drained of all meaning. David Rieff, the author of *Slaughterhouse Bosnia*, acidly noted, 'Never again!' had come to mean: 'Never again shall Germans kill Jews in the 1940s.' Fischer was acutely aware of the Western failure to confront tyrannical regimes. That partly affected his support for military action in the Balkans and Afghanistan. One of his colleagues sums up Fischer's philosophy: 'Auschwitz is the single red thread that goes through his political biography.'

Fischer is not a man plagued by self-doubt. When I first met him in his environment minister's office in the state of Hesse (his bicycle was propped against the wall; the minister was wearing jeans) Fischer did not hide his confidence that it was his view that would eventually prevail. With reference to continuing Green battles between the radical *Fundis* and the pragmatic *Realos*, he airily proclaimed that all his defeats eventually turned into victories. 'I never won [battles against the *Fundis*]. And yet, today they're all *Realos*.' Within a few years, when we met again, the uniform had changed. The foreign minister was dressed in a dapper dark three-piece suit ('it's a uniform'). Our conversation took place beneath a huge portrait by Andy Warhol of Willy Brandt, Social Democrat and moral visionary. Fischer, the streetfighter, had never voted for Brandt; he and his friends in the 'extra-parliamentary opposition' thought voting was bourgeois. Now, though, Fischer seeks to follow in the footsteps of the man who helped Germany take a crucial step towards normality, with the famous *Kniefall* in Warsaw which encouraged his compatriots to confront the German past. Merely thinking about the past, however, is not enough in the end. At some point, Germany must be able to move into a more normal future. That is where Fischer, the radical, can play a role, by forming a bridge between the angry past and the potentially more tranquil twenty-first century.

Sometimes, the new century has not felt tranquil at all. Neo-Nazis planned what would have been a devastating attack on a ceremony in Munich in November 2003. A huge bomb was planned to be detonated during the laying of the foundation stone for a new complex of Jewish buildings, including a synagogue, museum and school. The ceremony was on the occasion of the anniversary of *Kristallnacht* – the night of Nazi anarchy in 1938, when dozens were killed and hundreds of synagogues were burnt down. Guests at the ceremony included President Johannes Rau, interior minister Otto Schily and Paul Spiegel, head of the Central Council of Jews. If that attack had been successful, the destabilizing consequences would have been incalculable. Even without such spectacular assassination attempts, xenophobic skinhead violence remains widespread. In the years immediately after German unification, such violence multiplied tenfold. After a lethal peak in 1992 and 1993, the number of attacks dwindled in the years that followed – but there was an upsurge of far-right violence in 2000, including a bomb attack at Düsseldorf station and the trampling to death by three young skinheads of Alberto Adriano, a Mozambican who had lived in east Germany for 20 years.

In electoral terms, meanwhile, the far right has made little progress, in sharp contrast to the situation elsewhere in Europe. In Italy, Gianfranco Fini, who described Mussolini as the greatest statesman of the century, became Silvio Berlusconi's deputy prime minister in 2001. Jean-Marie Le Pen, leader of France's National Front, who described the Nazi gas chambers as 'a detail of history', forced Lionel Jospin, socialist challenger to President Chirac, into third place in 2002. In the Netherlands, the party of the (later assassinated) anti-immigrant Pim Fortuyn gained more than a third of the vote in local elections in Rotterdam. In Britain, Nick Griffin, leader of the British National Party, gained a 16 per cent share of the vote in his Oldham constituency in 2001, pushing the Liberal Democrats into fourth place. In Switzerland, the People's Party – criticized by the UN refugee agency in Geneva for its 'nakedly anti-asylum' propaganda – gained the largest share of the vote in parliamentary elections in 2003.

In Hitler's native Austria, the populist right has enjoyed some spectacular successes in recent years. Jörg Haider's far-right Freedom Party gained more than one in four votes in the elections of 1999, forcing the governing party into third place. The victories of the charismatic Haider – who famously told a gathering of Waffen-SS veterans that they had fought for 'order, justice and decency' – gained international headlines. Those cries of dismay were, however, *sotto voce* by comparison with what we would hear if a nationalist party in Germany were to achieve a fraction of Haider's success. Until now, Germany's far-right parties have failed to gain a single seat in the Bundestag. There seems to be no immediate likelihood that that will change. There was a string of headlines when the far-right German People's Union, the DVU, gained 13 per cent of the vote in regional elections in the east German state of Saxony-Anhalt in 1998. In federal elections a few months later, the party's share of the vote in the state fell back to three per cent; it later collapsed altogether.

The contrasting pattern of electoral politics is all the more interesting, given that the two countries have much in common, culturally and historically. If one seeks features which distinguish Germany and Austria from each other, and might help to explain this contrast, the question of

Vergangenheitsbewältigung, dealing with the past, inevitably looms large. Germany is constantly looking backwards, seeking to understand what went wrong. In Austria, by contrast, there has been (as there was in West Germany in the 1950s and 1960s and in East Germany until the Wall came down) an eagerness for the country to wash its hands, treating the events of the Third Reich as if they affected Austria only at one remove.

The *Anschluss*, Hitler's annexation of Austria in 1938, is portrayed as if it were a brutal act of political rape, instead of the reality – vast crowds who thronged in excitement to greet their compatriot the Führer. Millions of Austrians were as enthusiastic about the thousand-year Reich as the Germans themselves. After 1945, many Austrians liked to see themselves as victims, not perpetrators (for their own reasons, the Allies played along with this distorted view). In the tart judgement of Wolf Biermann, East Germany's most popular chansonnier (banned from returning home after a concert tour to the West in 1976 because he told too many uncomfortable truths): 'Austria and East Germany were linked by a common piece of hypocrisy: both pretended to have been forcibly occupied by Hitler's Germany in the Second World War.'

During the filming of *The Sound of Music* in Salzburg in 1965, the city fathers forbade swastika flags to be hung for a scene to be filmed on the Residenzplatz. After all – the argument ran – Salzburgers never supported the Nazis. Only when the producers said that they would in that case use contemporary newsreel footage instead did the authorities partly back down. That ostrich-like behaviour continued. When Kurt Waldheim stood for election as Austrian president in 1986, it was revealed that he had served with a unit in the Balkans which deported tens of thousands of Jews to their deaths. Waldheim said that he 'could not remember' what he had seen or done at that time. A worldwide storm erupted – which only strengthened Waldheim's hand when his supporters implied that accusations against him were part of an international (i.e. Jewish) plot. Pro-Waldheim election posters declared: 'We Austrians will elect who we want.' And so they did: Waldheim was duly elected for a six-year term.

Even after the Waldheim affair and the more recent successes of Haider, the international perception of Austria remains softer than that of Germany. However much Germany changes, the shadow of Hitler is always present. Austria, by contrast, remains the country of Strauss waltzes, *Sachertorte* and the von Trapp family; the once-adored Führer is nowhere to be seen. It is an odd asymmetry, which Germans occasionally comment on aloud. Over coffee and cake, before the beginning of a formal interview in his offices in Bonn, Helmut Kohl mused aloud on the differences between Germany and Austria. I no longer remember how the subject arose. But I was struck by the Chancellor's half-wistful observation about the lop-sided view which allowed Austria to adopt the good guys, leaving the bad guys as a German responsibility: 'Of course, Hitler was German – and Beethoven was Austrian. That's how it is.' On another occasion, Kohl explained to Pascale Hugues, author of *Le bonheur allemand*, why being German is always different:

> When a French person comes out of the airport in Israel, he simply speaks French. When a German comes out of the airport in Israel and gets into a taxi, it is possible that the driver's family was murdered in Auschwitz. That's the difference. No point spelling it out for you. You have to live with it – like with the weather.

As in other European countries, some German politicians have success-fully exploited popular resentments for their own political benefit. Racism and xenophobia have, however, not (yet) proved a German electoral goldmine. Thus, the Christian Democrats' racist slogan of *Kinder statt Inder* – 'children, not Indians', in North Rhine-Westphalia in 2000 left the party worse off than if it had never ventured down the xenophobic road. When the Free Democratic Party seemed willing to dabble in anti-Semitism, it experienced electoral humiliation as a result – a humiliation which was finally mixed with tragedy. The FDP have long been eager to find any way of ensuring that they do not sink below the five per cent mark which allows them seats in parliament. Ahead of elections in 2002, the FDP declared its eagerness to raise its share of the vote to a remarkable 18 per cent. 'Project 18' became the new buzzword. The former economics minister, Jürgen Möllemann, was especially eager to achieve this ambi-tious goal. He publicly blamed Michel Friedman, TV chat show host and vice-president of the Central Council of Jews, for anti-Semitism, and then distributed millions of election leaflets which, as one commentator put it, 'played with the anti-Semitic taboo'. Möllemann clearly expected this new strategy to pay electoral dividends. The 'Haiderization' of the FDP, as it soon came to be called, was, however, rather less successful than the original Austrian model had been. Instead of rising to 18 per cent, the FDP's support slumped to seven per cent. Möllemann and his alleged anti-Semitism were blamed for the debacle, and his colleagues forced him into the political wilderness. Meanwhile, investigations began against him for alleged corruption. Nine months after the elections, Möllemann, a keen and experienced parachutist, apparently committed suicide during a parachute jump, when he plunged 1000 metres to the ground.

As with the confused attitudes towards German-born Turks and other non-ethnic Germans – the Germans' own version of Tebbit's 'cricket test' – many Germans still find it difficult to perceive Jews as fully German and fully Jewish. Their 'otherness' is a constant theme, despite and because of the past. Germany is not alone in having seen many attacks on synagogues and Jewish cemeteries in recent years; such attacks have been common throughout Europe. Nonetheless, the concept of 'differentness' undoubtedly makes such attacks easier. In 2003, Michel Friedman, host of the television programme '*Caution! Friedman*', was questioned, in connection with the break-up of a smuggling ring, about visits to Ukrainian prostitutes and the alleged use of cocaine. So far, so almost normal, in the world of showbiz scandals. Germany divided, however, not just into the pro- and anti-camps that are traditional on such occasions, when the spotlight is turned on private lives. Much of the debate revolved, bizarrely, around Friedman's Jewishness. Friedman's defenders believed he was being targeted because of his Jewishness; his critics believed that he was being let off lightly for the same reason. *Die Zeit* summarized the absurdity: 'Before we can even establish whether Friedman has fallen victim to his habit or to justice, he has fallen victim to the national passion for navel-gazing.'

There has been no shortage of such navel-gazing. There was a storm of protest when the writer Martin Walser warned in a lecture in 1998 of the danger of 'instrumentalizing Auschwitz'; accusations against him famously included the suggestion that he was an 'intellectual arsonist'. Then, four years later, the *Frankfurter Allgemeine Zeitung* publicly and contemptuously rejected Walser's latest novel, *Death of a Critic,* for serialization. The paper – which had strongly supported Walser in the debate about 'instrumentalizing Auschwitz' – based its rejection on the alleged anti-Semitism in the book. (The storyline deals with the apparent murder of a Jewish critic, André Ehrl-König – easily recognizable for German readers as Marcel Reich-Ranicki, a well-known critic and television personality.) Critics were divided: some believed that the book is indeed anti-Semitic; others thought it to be merely unpleasant. Whatever the conclusion, the huge controversy served to emphasize that the subject of anti-Semitism is as sensitive as ever – including more navel-gazing.

German politicians still sometimes seem so eager to prove their normality that they end up proving the opposite. Thus, the Christian Democrat Martin Hohmann suggested in 2003 that the Jews had acted 'like a race of perpetrators' in the Russian revolution, and that their actions could be compared to those of the Nazis. His remarks, with echoes of the *Historikerstreit* of the 1980s, caused a storm – but maybe not enough of a storm. The head of Germany's special forces, Reinhard Günzel, praised Hohmann in a letter for his 'excellent speech, of a courage, truth and clarity which one seldom hears or reads in our country'. Günzel was duly sacked. Commenting on the controversy, *Focus* magazine noted the permanent German difficulty: 'The dilemma of the nation is the tightrope walk between the right to innocence and the duty to remembrance, together with the responsibility to prevent such crimes in the future.' The historian Arnulf Baring points to the absurdity of the concept of collective guilt. 'The concept of a "nation of perpetrators" suggests we are particularly prone to murder, as if all Germans run around with revolvers in their pockets and knives in their mouths.' But, he notes, that is no reason for Germans to shuffle off responsibility for the past. 'All Germans bear responsibility for the crimes of Nazism. The memory will stick with us, as long as there are Germans in the world.'

Despite occasional dramas like that involving Hohmann and Günzel, there is plenty of evidence that a newly normal Germany can finally begin to be perceived not just in terms of its murderous history but also as a democratic and tolerant country judged by the standards of the present day. In 2002, more Jews from the former Soviet Union emigrated to Germany than to Israel or the United States. In the past few years alone, 60 synagogues have been built or restored. Anti-Semitic attacks continue. But when the Israeli president, Moshe Katzav, was asked if he was worried by anti-Semitic attacks in Europe, the answer was perhaps not quite what the German interviewer was expecting: 'Yes – above all, in France.'

For obvious reasons, the German government is eager to be on good terms with Israel. In recent years, however, Germany has begun to assert itself, too. Berlin blocked arms exports to Israel because of violence against civilians by the Israeli armed forces in 2002. In a development that would have been unthinkable in previous years, it drew up a set of peace proposals for the Middle East, including a proposed withdrawal of Israeli forces from the occupied territories, and the question of the right of return of Palestinian refugees. Germany's criticisms were often tentative by comparison with other European countries. As Joschka Fischer pointed out, 'Whenever Israel is discussed in Germany, the fundamental debate about German identity is never far behind. Can we criticize Israel? The very question raises suspicion.' Nonetheless, even the fact that Germany now feels entitled to express an opinion on the region is a sign of how radically things have changed. Year by year and month by month, the taboos are crumbling.

16

In Search of Normality

Now we are over the worst. The first 10 years of freedom were very eventful. Many farewells and new friends. The next 10 will be more tranquil. We are the first Wessis from east Germany, and we can no longer be identified by our language, looks and behaviour. Our adjustment has gone well. We wish we could say the same of our parents and families.

(Jana Hensel in Children of the Zone (2002))

'There are difficult fatherlands. One of them is Germany,' said Gustav Heinemann, on becoming president of West Germany in 1969. At the beginning of a new century, Heinemann's words are, perhaps, finally becoming obsolete – not through an attempt to forget the past, but with an insistence on the importance of memory. Ernst Nolte, in the *Historikerstreit* of the 1980s, complained of the 'past that will not pass'. Nolte failed to realize that the simplest way of allowing the past to pass is not by pushing it away but by continuing to remember.

It is now, six decades after the events that it commemorates, that a huge Memorial to the Murdered Jews of Europe is being built in the heart of Berlin, a few minutes' walk from the chancellery offices and the Reichstag. The memorial – whose fundraising poster was banned in 2001, because it dared use the language of Holocaust deniers – is built on what was until 1989 the death strip, close to Hitler's bunker. The memorial consists of thousands of blank standing stones of different heights, creating what the architect, Peter Eisenman, has called a 'waving cornfield' – a maze of remembrance, with an accompanying exhibition underground.

The Holocaust memorial can be seen as a 'mere' symbol – the central wreath-laying drop-off point, as critics have described it. There have been fears, too, that damage to the monument by vandals would send the wrong message to the world. It was therefore protected with anti-graffiti coating – which in turn triggered another classic bad-news story, where all the German complexes emerged once more. It turned out that Degussa, manufacturers of the special anti-graffiti paint, was related to a company which once produced Zyklon B, used in the gas chambers at Auschwitz and elsewhere; amidst much embarrassment, the contract was called into question. This memorial does not, however, stand in isolation. It reflects a broader German readiness to look back without flinching – and thus to look forward at the same time.

Die Zeit argued that a Berlin memorial should be allowed to reflect the fact that Germany itself has changed.

> The memorial will lie above Joseph Goebbels' sealed bunker and close to dominant Nazi architecture. Anyone who here in the centre of Berlin commemorates the millions who were murdered knows where he is. The hope that one could use measures of political hygiene to build a monument of morally sterilized German post-war history underestimates the intelligence of all those who have recognized that Germany, together with its firms, is no longer identical to the state whose Jewish victims the memorial remembers.

In the end that view prevailed, and the contract was allowed to go ahead.

Just a couple of miles from the Holocaust memorial is Daniel Libeskind's Jewish Museum, a jagged masterpiece. (Libeskind is also responsible for the project chosen to fill the gaping hole at Ground Zero, a design noted for its 'Memory Foundations'.) The museum building, including its 'memory void', was completed in 1999; two years later, the historical exhibition was ready. With poignant timing, the museum officially opened its doors to the public on the evening of 11 September 2001, just hours after two planes smashed into the World Trade Centre in New York. For Libeskind, the irregular design is symbolic on a number of levels. Most obviously, it is reminiscent of a crushed Star of David. In addition, Libeskind talks of the spiky pattern he achieved by plotting 'an irrational matrix' linking the addresses where Jewish and non-Jewish writers and artists lived in pre-1933 Berlin. Libeskind makes a link between the Jewishness and Germanness of the old Berlin, thus emphasizing that the programme of extermination was not just an unspeakable crime against others, but also a historic loss for Germany itself. Libeskind believes that the greater openness in Germany in recent years has made it easier for his project, 'a representation of past vitality and future hope', to be realized. 'It had a lot to do with this vortex of incredible change,' he told me shortly before the building's completion. 'Earlier, it wouldn't have been built.'

The Jewish Museum is not the only site where social and political change, on the one hand, and art and architecture, on the other, are intertwined. At the Reichstag, the entanglement of the artistic and the political was already on display in 1995, with Christo's wrapping of the Reichstag. The Bulgarian New Yorker shrouded Germany's old and new parliament in 100,000 square metres of silvery polypropylene, weighing 60 tonnes and tied up with bright blue ropes. Christo had waited more than 20 years for this moment – his first sketch of a Wrapped Reichstag (part of whose facade officially lay in the Soviet sector, though on the Western side of the wall) dates from 1972. In the intervening years, he was officially rebuffed three times; the outcome of the parliamentary vote in 1994 which finally gave the project the go-ahead was unclear till the last moment. (My first inkling of the way that the vote had gone – 292 in favour, 223, including Chancellor Kohl, against – was when I saw Christo, his wife Jeanne-Claude and their advisers hugging each other with excitement in the spectators' gallery before the result was announced. When I approached them to ask the news, an adviser urgently whispered that they should deny everything. 'We know nothing,' he declared implausibly.) Freimut Duve, who spoke in favour of the project, put the issue in an explicitly German context. Christo's artistic project would, he said, be a 'gentle signal to the wounds of our history'. By the time the wrapping took place, rejecters were in the minority. Huge crowds gathered and gazed at the building from morning until late at night; thousands queued through the night in hope of getting the artist's signature on a special Reichstag edition of *Der Tagesspiegel*, a Berlin daily. The country's biggest-selling newspaper, *Bild*, begged (in vain) for a wrap extension.

The wrapping was originally conceived as an artistic event. By the time it became real, the timing – five years after unity, and three years ahead of the government's much delayed move to Berlin – meant it was intensely political, too. The wrapping and unwrapping of the Reichstag marked the political curtain-up for the new Berlin and the *Berliner Republik*. Once Christo had packed his bags, Norman Foster refurbished and rebuilt the Reichstag from the inside – preserving the shell of the building while transforming it for the twenty-first century, in preparation for the building's use as a parliament for the first time since the Reichstag fire of 1933; the old cupola was replaced by a glass dome. The choice of a foreign architect to reshape the national parliament was a clear signal of openness to the world. In addition, Foster's design emphasizes transparency and light, with hundreds of mirrors beneath the dome reflecting daylight into the chamber. High above the debating chamber, visitors to the parliament climb a spiral walkway which looks down on to the debating chamber and out to the city below. Here, as ever, memory is an explicit theme. Graffiti scrawled by Russian soldiers in the ruined Reichstag in 1945 and uncovered during the building works have been left exposed as a permanent reminder of history. MPs walk past the graffiti every day.

These overlapping forms of memory in the German capital – the chequered history of the Reichstag, a commemoration of once-flourishing Jewish German life, and, separately, of the Holocaust itself – are widely accepted in Germany today, in a way that they never were before. Margarethe von Trotta's film *Rosenstrasse*, about the successful defiance of a few hundred ordinary women in the darkest years of the Third Reich, was released in 2003. In earlier years, few would have wanted to hear its unsettling message. (I first heard the story of Rosenstrasse from von Trotta in 1995, when she told me of the new film that she hoped to make; at that time, this astonishing story was still scarcely known.) In twenty-first century Germany, it is widely accepted that, despite the terror, Germans might have done more to resist if only they had cared more or shown more *Zivilcourage*. That acknowledgement of the historical crimes of omission and commission has, in turn, paved the way for the new forms of remembrance which Germany is gingerly feeling its way towards now.

Germany has several overlapping histories of violence in the past 70 years, the threads of which are perhaps being tied up for the first time. Most obviously, there is the story of Hitler and his helpers, which continues even now to be re-explored especially in the context of personal responsibility. There is the story of German suffering – the lethal bombing raids which killed more than half a million civilians, and the millions of expellees who died in 1945 and after. This story was told in earlier decades as if it were a contextless tragedy; then it was left to one side for many years; now it is being re-told, this time within the context of the German crimes which preceded it. There is the lethal and threatened violence of the Communist regime – against East German protesters in 1953, against those who tried to flee across the minefields, walls and barbed wire, and against the *Andersdenkende* – the 'different-thinkers' who dared to speak up for truth. And finally there is the

Bundesrepublik's own slice of historical violence, which Germany is only now beginning to come to terms with – the murder spree in the 1970s by those who said they wanted to make Germany a better place.

A quarter of a century after the German Autumn of 1977, there are new attempts to discuss what the Baader-Meinhof gang means for modern Germany. For many radicals, the series of murders in 1977 was a final breaking-point; Joschka Fischer was only one of many, in that respect. One of Germany's most senior cultural ambassadors today confides that his only reason for not becoming involved in RAF violence in the 1970s was because 'I was too cowardly'. For him, too, 1977 was the point at which it became clear that another path was needed.

Even after the suicides of the main actors behind bars in the high-security jail at Stammheim in October 1977, the RAF did not immediately vanish. The last two assassinations were not until more than a decade later: Alfred Herrhausen of the Deutsche Bank was killed in 1989 and Detlev Rohwedder, head of the Treuhand organization responsible for selling off East German businesses, in 1991. Already by the time that the Wall came down, however, popular support for violent solutions had largely dried up. In 1989, it would have been impossible to suggest – as the interior minister had 12 years earlier – that every capitalist has 'a terrorist in his own intimate circle'. Eventually, in the 1990s the RAF officially conceded defeat. Now, in the first years of the new century, there has been a spate of films and debate about the Baader era, trying to get an overall perspective on this other Meinhof violence.

For some, the RAF and its logo – a Kalashnikov and a five-pointed star – have become little more than a fashion accessory, a splash of 1970s retro style. 'Prada Meinhof' jackets and T-shirts are on sale in Berlin boutiques. Posed RAF-style photographs are published in fashionable magazines. *Max* magazine feels able to ask: 'Is terror cool?' In serious discussion, meanwhile, those who seek a new understanding of the violence of the 1970s, see things less generously than the liberals of an earlier generation. Von Trotta's 1981 film *The German Sisters* (originally *Die bleierne Zeit* – 'The Leaden Age') seems almost reluctant to condemn the RAF outright as brutal murderers, as does Fassbinder's *Third Generation*. The widely praised *Black Box Germany*, released in 2002, is very different in tone. The film tells two stories in parallel: we hear from the widow and friends of the banker Herrhausen, assassinated by the RAF, and from the family and friends of Wolfgang Grams, an idealist-turned-terrorist gunned down by the police. There is no attempt to justify the RAF – merely a reminder of the senselessness and human consequences of such violence.

The theme remains sensitive, even now. For some, 'understanding' the origins of the RAF comes too close to forgiveness. Plans for a partly government-funded exhibition on the RAF in Berlin in spring 2004 stirred up such controversy that the exhibition was put on hold. The organizers insisted that they wanted to confront the 'RAF is cool' mentality. They found themselves accused, however, of seeking to paint the movement in soft pastel tones. Critics said it was too early for such a show, and the interior minister, Otto Schily, expressed 'considerable misgivings'. (Nobody could deny that Schily knows the issues well. As defence lawyer for members of the RAF, he insisted after Ulrike Meinhof's death in 1976 that the terrorist's name was 'synonymous, beyond all power of defamation, with high moral claims, one might say with high moral austerity'.)

Despite the contradictions over the RAF legacy, one change is clear. Where avoidance was once the rule in post-war German society, confrontation with history now dominates. In this respect, the gap between international perception and domestic reality is wide. The problem is partly the casual assumption that all Germans are umbilically linked to Hitler. Germans who spend time in British schools (an increasingly fashionable option for the well-off) learn that some of their classmates regard '*Heil Hitler!*' and the Nazi salute as an entertaining way to greet a German teenager. Nor do such attitudes end at the school gate. German adults who come to work in Britain – for example, as nurses or doctors in the National Health Service – find that they are liable to be treated as if they, and all Germans, are Nazis at one remove. (Sometimes, this is 'a joke'; if the Germans do not laugh, this is presumably because they have no sense of humour.) There is a widespread, Fawlty-like belief that Germany is determined not to address the past. Any attempt to counter such assumptions seems in danger of protesting too much. Most therefore remain silent – irritably or resignedly, according to type. Even the once-prickly German embassy in London is quieter than it was about perceived stereotyping, for fear of being labelled paranoid.

Generalizations by nationality need not automatically be dismissed as absurd. Popular Euro-jokes about heaven and hell (in heaven, the cooks are French, the bankers are Swiss, the mechanics are German . . . ; in hell, the cooks are English, the bankers are Italian . . . – and so on) work partly because they seem at least vaguely connected with a familiar reality. Stereotypes about (say) expansive Russian hospitality versus British emotional reserve may be clichés, and it is easy to find examples which disprove the stereotype. But, as anybody who knows the two countries can confirm, the clichés are not wholly invented. Equally, anybody claiming that German society has no affinity for *Ordnung* – 'orderliness' or 'good order' – either does not know Germany, or is reluctant to acknowledge a self-evident truth. For many Germans themselves, the words *deutsch* and *Ordnung* have long been seen as a matching pair. A German television comedy series, subtitled '*Ordnung muss sein*' ('There must be order') unhesitatingly describes its main character as quintessentially German, *urdeutsch*.

It is difficult to quarrel with such stereotypes if you have been glared at for crossing a pedestrian crossing on a red light (including on a deserted side-street, in the middle of the night); if you have watched the caretaker of your apartment block rummaging through dustbins, eager to rebuke any miscreant who recycled rubbish in the wrong bin by mistake; or (most startling of all) if you have been ordered out of an otherwise empty hotel jacuzzi because you and a mixed group of mostly German colleagues failed to notice or observe the house rules demanding nudity in the jacuzzi at all times. Those *Ordnung*-filled episodes happen to stick in the memory. Almost any German, and anyone who has lived in Germany, could come up with an almost infinite list of similar examples. *Der Spiegel* describes the recycling regulations that German troops must implement in Afghanistan:

> The rubbish is neatly separated – and only comes together again on the rubbish tip outside the camp. Officials ensure that the regulations are enforced and Afghan anarchy remains outside . . . Fire-extinguishing materials containing CFCs are disposed of environmentally; only the system of paying a deposit on returnable aluminium cans has not yet reached central Asia.

The problems in terms of understanding modern Germany begin not with describing the (real) enthusiasm for *Ordnung* itself, but with the widespread implication that love of order, on the one hand, is somehow linked to a secret yearning for goosestepping and jackboots, on the other. Germany, after all, is not alone in its love of *Ordnung*. One of the most successful Swiss films ever made, *The Swiss-Makers*, is a comedy revolving around the story of those trying to gain the coveted Swiss passport. It has as its main theme the national obsession with *Ordnung*. Policemen spy on would-be Swiss passport-holders, including a Yugoslav ballet dancer and an Italian cake-maker, to find out if they have a sufficient love of *Ordnung* to make the grade. As a theme, it is uncontroversial. Few go on to argue that the Swiss love of order makes them politically suspect. On the contrary, Switzerland (mocked by Orson Welles in *The Third Man* for producing no conflicts, only the cuckoo clock) has become a shorthand for peaceful democracy. This image was only partially dented by revelations in recent years about how Swiss banks profited from the Holocaust or by the 2003 election in which a xenophobic party topped the poll (a victory which was buried, in most newspapers, deep on the inside pages).

Only in commentaries on Germany is there an assumption that *Ordnung* and a lack of democracy are umbilically linked because of what orderliness and obedience led to 70 years ago. Sometimes, the love of order does indeed seem to shade into something less savoury, in Germany as elsewhere. Ronald Schill – proud to be known as 'Judge Merciless', because of the severity of the sentences he handed down – made a name for himself with his Law and Order Party which gained a fifth of the vote in the city-state of Hamburg in 2001. He achieved the success with his tough anti-immigrant policy, helped by the fact that a number of September 11 hijackers (including Mohammed Atta, pilot of the lead suicide plane) had lived in Hamburg. Schill became home affairs senator in Hamburg, and there were widespread fears that his xenophobic populism could prove a vote-winner elsewhere.

In the end, however, the Schill phenomenon proved shortlived. Support for his party nosedived. In 2003, he was forced to resign – and revealed, in passing, another aspect of voter tolerance in modern Germany. The Christian Democrat mayor, Ole von Beust, said Schill had sought to blackmail him over an alleged gay relationship with another senator. Von Beust outed himself in response to the apparent blackmail, while continuing to insist that his sexuality was not a political issue, saying: 'Normality does not need any political discussion.' Von Beust's voters agreed; his popularity rose sharply. (The mayor of Berlin, Klaus Wowereit, had already paved the way by declaring at the beginning of his 2001 election campaign: 'I'm gay, and that's fine.')

One sign of an emerging new normality is that, 15 years after the Wall came down, Germany is on its way to becoming a single country at last. The mutual resentments and mistrust of the 1990s still exist. Many middle-aged and elderly Germans will no doubt remain Ossis or Wessis till their dying day – grumbling about arrogant westerners, the *Besserwessis*, on the one hand, or whingeing easterners, the *Jammerossis*, on the other. For younger Germans, however, the divide is less sharp or even non-existent. A 25-year-old east Berliner puts it in simple terms: 'My mother always wants to know if my boyfriend is from east or west. For her, it makes a big difference. For me and my friends, it doesn't.'

That gradual blurring of borders is reflected in German reading habits, too. In the 1990s, east Germans were interested in buying books about the pains of German unity; west Germans were not. West German interest in east German matters usually began and ended with yet another Stasi scandal – a subject which, in turn, tended to weary easterners who had lived in the shadow of the Stasi for longer than they cared to remember. Now, in the twenty-first century, those separate reading habits have begun to merge. One huge bestseller on both sides of the German-German divide in recent years has been Jana Hensel's *Zonenkinder* – 'Children of the Zone'. *Zonenkinder*, published in 2002, is an account of East German and united German life as experienced by Hensel's generation – young teenagers when the wall came down, and now young adults in the united Germany. After the ubiquitous German pessimism of the previous decade (the few brief weeks and months of excitement after November 1989 excluded), the tone is almost startlingly upbeat. *Zonenkinder* partly sees the old and now vanished country through the rose-tinted spectacles of childhood memories – 'the nice warm we-feeling', as Hensel puts it. Her tone is wistful for her remembered childhood:

A time which seems long past, a time in which the clocks ran differently, winter smelt differently, and hair ribbons were tied differently. It is difficult for us to remember this fairytale time because we wanted to forget it for such a long time . . . Just as our entire country wished it, nothing is left of our childhood, and all of a sudden, now that we are adult and it seems almost too late, I notice all the lost memories.

For Hensel, the malign absurdity of the East German state is merely a backdrop to stories of the earnest eagerness of childhood – where she felt it her duty to take the rubbish out and to work towards the victory of Communism: 'Everyone should be able to rely on me . . . I needed to stand up, if necessary with a weapon in my hand, and help to prevent the imperialist danger from spreading.' Hensel addresses the prickly what-if questions which the 1968 generation in West Germany seemed ready to answer so categorically, with reference to *their* parents. She is reluctant to judge her parents' generation, forced to make uncomfortable choices about how far they would obey and collaborate with the Communist regime which looked set to rule their lives until the end of time – a generation which now felt discarded. Instead, she obliquely refers to Kohl's famous phrase about 'the blessing of late birth' after 1945, and applies it to her own experience of a post-Communist country in the last decade of the century:

I never stopped thinking about the generation conflict, which made everybody in the West think of 1968. But with us, the situation was a bit different . . . Our parents were in any case on the bottom, in the midst of a depression that affected an entire generation, and we – who by good fortune and only because of our late birth avoided a GDR fate – did not wish to trample those who were already on the ground . . . How could we credibly declare that we would not have let ourselves be wooed by the Stasi, that we would not have become party members, but would have distributed leaflets, published underground magazines and applied to emigrate? Our GDR was at an end before we had to answer such questions.

Such musings struck a chord on both sides of the old border – the now invisible border which until then had remained so strong in east and west German heads alike. Hensel compares her experience with that of east Germans just a few years older.

> For us it is normal to fall in love with west Germans, while the mid-thirtysomethings mostly remain amongst themselves . . . We reached puberty and came of age in the geographical space that came after. We did not grow up in the GDR or in the Federal Republic. We are children of the zone – in which everything had to be built from scratch, where no stone remained unturned and hardly a single goal has yet been reached.

In looking to the future, Hensel sums up the difference between her generation and that of her parents – hers is a new, integrated generation, that was born to a generation of the dispossessed. In the years after German unity, 'They cursed their west German bosses, we cuddled up in the lecture halls with Friedrich from Lübeck and Julia from Ingolstadt.' She concludes her account on a half-wistful, half-optimistic note. Generational differences, as ever in this story of modern Germany, play a key role:

> Now we are over the worst. The first 10 years of freedom were very eventful. Many farewells and new friends. The next 10 will be more tranquil. We are the first Wessis from east Germany, and we can no longer be identified by our language, looks and behaviour. Our adjustment has gone well. We wish we could say the same of our parents and families.

Zonenkinder is not the only literary success which seeks to bridge the gap between the Communist past and the new, united Germany. *My Free German Youth*, by Claudia Rusch (born in 1971 – she describes her generation as 'the last real Ossis, and the first new Wessis'), became a bestseller in 2003. Where *Zonenkinder* revels in its lack of politics, Rusch's childhood is steeped in politics. Her family life was an oasis of independent thought, surrounded by the Stasi; Robert Havemann, a leading dissident, was a close family friend. Even as a 10-year-old schoolchild, she gets into trouble in class for the swords-into-ploughshares pacifist symbol which her mother has sewn on to her sleeve and which the East German authorities perceived as a challenge to the regime. Rusch's book is partly a tale of the terrible absurdity of the country in which she grew up. In addition, however – and it took most west Germans a decade before they began to understand this aspect of the east German story – part of her still clings to an East German identity, despite all the good reasons for leaving the oppressive memories of East Germany behind. 'I want my apartment to smell of [the East German] Intershop. That much liberty I must be allowed.' Rusch first felt loyalty to an East German identity during the period when the country was vanishing before her eyes in summer 1990. 'Three months before it was all dissolved for ever, we took on the identity which we had so rejected. *We* were also the GDR. Not just informers and careerists, but our families and friends lived here, too.'

Most dramatically of all, Germans have discovered a new kind of unity in the cinema. One of the biggest cinematic hits in Germany in recent years has been *Good Bye, Lenin!*, which took the country by storm in 2003. In east and west, millions flocked to see the film, which allows, above all, for the possibility that the old East Germany was, as Rusch put it, 'not just informers and careerists', but also a country where ordinary people lived ordinary lives. *Good Bye, Lenin!* is an updated version of Rip van Winkle and a story of lost illusions. Christiane, doggedly loyal to the German Democratic Republic, suffers a heart attack and falls into a coma on the day of the first big anti-government protest in East Berlin on 7 October 1989 (she collapses on her way to the official anniversary celebrations, after glimpsing through the car window the beating of her son Alex; because of the demonstrations, the police do not call an ambulance until it is dangerously late). When she wakes from her coma eight months later, the Wall is long gone and a united Germany is about to be born.

The doctor insists that any shocks might cause a relapse. The knowledge that the GDR has collapsed and is about to vanish for ever could be lethal. Her children are thus forced to construct an alternative world –

where the Communists are still in power, where their 79-square-metre apartment is re-furnished (out goes the Ikea furniture; in comes the East German furniture that has been gathering dust in the basement). When Christiane asks to watch television in her bedroom, Alex and an engineer friend are obliged to record East German-style TV newscasts which desperately attempt to explain away some of the things that Christiane has spotted from her bedroom window. She learns, for example, that the East German government has generously permitted all West Germans to flee the materialistic oppression of their country, together with their cars – hence the large number of Volkswagens and BMWs on the street. The Coca-Cola hoarding on a nearby apartment block also requires an elaborate explanation.

The west German director and co-writer of *Good Bye, Lenin!*, Wolfgang Becker, was also the creator of *Motzki*, the comedy series about a vile-tempered Wessi which caused such a storm when shown in 1993. *Motzki* caused indignation by addressing the self-evident truth that all was not sweetness and light within the German-German family. *Good Bye, Lenin!*, 10 years later, implicitly shows the way forward to a new accommodation between west and east, through simple shared enjoyment of the same film. The gentlemen from the Stasi make an early appearance in *Good Bye, Lenin!* The film also hints at an additional truth, however, which west Germans had often seemed reluctant to confront: that life in East Germany was sometimes just that – a life. Depicting East Germany as a country that consisted only of Stasi oppressors and victims reduces 16 million East Germans to mere ciphers at a stroke. Christiane's fondness for (East German, and therefore no longer available) Spreewald gherkins is not glamorous, but life is not always glamorous. Her love of Spreewald gherkins is, in any case, affected by the power of belief, which trumps objective reality. When she eats gherkins out of the jar that Alex brings home, she finds them Spreewald-delicious; she has no way of knowing that Alex has decanted newly bought west German gherkins into an old jar rescued from the rubbish.

For a small number of dissidents, political memories may take precedence over events in their private lives. *Good Bye, Lenin!* reminds us, however, that for millions the personal exists alongside and is entwined with the political. (Alex notes that 1978 was the year when East Germany put an astronaut into space, an event that deeply impressed him: 'The GDR was at world level, and my family went down the plughole.') Falling in and out of love, sickness and health, grief and celebration – all these exist in repressive regimes, not just in multi-party democracies.

Good Bye, Lenin! tells a story of destroyed and recreated illusions, and a world which was made up of more than just one shade of grey. Less inspiring was the slew of nostalgic television programmes which – apparently encouraged by the success of *Good Bye, Lenin!* – suddenly started popping up everywhere in late 2003 like the proverbial mushrooms after rain. There was the *Ossi-Show* (with East German skater Katarina Witt as a co-presenter), the *Ostalgie Show*, the *Ultimate Ost-Show*, and more. Thirteen years after East Germany had come to an end, East Germanness was suddenly impossible to avoid. Some of these programmes avoided talking about totalitarianism altogether (East Germany was treated as one big joke from the old days – funny clothes, funny music, funny cars). Others interwove horror stories from the past ('my time in a Stalinist camp') with tales of gherkins, blue shirts from the Free German Youth, East German equivalent of the Scouts, and favourite songs. It is possible that this rash of television shows will mark the beginning of a depressing new trend – totalitarianism as one big amiable joke. Equally, however, it is possible that this extraordinary outburst of *Ostalgie*, watched by millions in east and west, will merely prove to be one last burst of kitschy fireworks before Germany moves on towards real unity at last.

Certainly, the signs that unity may be on the way continue to multiply. The jokebooks which in the mid-1990s flatly proclaimed that *Five Years are Enough!* carry a slightly different message in the twenty-first century. Titles like *Mama, What is a Wessi?* and *Papa, What is an Ossi?* serve as a reminder that the division need not be eternal; it is eroded by the change of generations. In party politics, too, there have been clear changes in the past few years. In the decade after unification, support for the post-Communist PDS, the party of the unloved east, rose steadily. In elections around the turn of the millennium, one in four of east German voters chose PDS; in east Berlin in 2001, the figure was almost one in two. By 2002, however, that success had fallen back sharply. The east German journalist Christoph Dieckmann analysed the change:

> People were often indignant that the heirs of Erich [Honecker] presented themselves as the party of the east. They were able to do that because none of the west-dominated parties treated east-history as German of equal value. The PDS functioned as the wetnurse of east German rebirth. Now the children can walk, and the nurse is dry.

That pattern seemed a likely possibility from the start. Just a few years after German unity, Lothar Bisky, leader of the post-Communist PDS, explained his party's success in the east in a psychologically divided country: 'We all speak German – but we don't understand each other.' I asked him if, when Germans on both sides of the border finally began to speak the same language, the PDS would therefore no longer have a role to play. Bisky seemed unfazed. 'Perhaps,' he replied. For the moment, the PDS is in some ways stronger than it has ever been. Almost uncontroversially, it is part of the ruling coalition not just in east German *Länder* but also in the Berlin city parliament – thus making decisions about the lives of westerners, not just easterners. It seems likely, however, that it will have to reinvent itself a second time if it is to remain strong – this time as a party with real policies for the first time. In a more normal Germany, where communication between the new west and east German generations is easier than before, the time for a party of lost identity – a role which the PDS so successfully made its own – may finally be coming to an end.

Gregor Gysi of the PDS makes clear that he would like the party to be absorbed in the federal body politic, in a way that has not yet happened. Ahead of the 2002 elections, he admitted that a coalition with the Social Democrats still looked unlikely. But, he added: 'Things could look very different in 2006.' Even the former Social Democrat chancellor Helmut Schmidt now predicts that the PDS could be part of a federal government by the end of the decade. Only an ultra-bold or crazed analyst would have dared to predict such a future for the party in 1990, when East Germany was flushed away; at that time, it seemed that the PDS, the 'party of barbed wire', would in due course become extinct. That may yet happen. But Germany today is still changing its shape. It looks set to continue to do so in the years to come.

17

And Now

Zwei Seelen wohnen, ach! in meiner Brust.
(Two souls, alas!, dwell in my breast.)

(Goethe, *Faust*)

Memory is important for understanding and absorbing the dark lessons of history – thus making it possible to move on. Another kind of memory deserves encouragement, too: the memory of miracles achieved. The line where the Berlin Wall ran through the city until 1989 is now forgotten by many Berliners. The scar is invisible. Only the tourist postcards survive. Berliners take it for granted that they can drive without stopping from Alexanderplatz in the east to the Kurfürstendamm in the west. Potsdamer Platz, previously a death strip, is the site of grand skyscrapers designed by Richard Rogers, Renzo Piano and other star names. In much of once-shabby east Berlin, only the fact that the paint is fresher and the restoration more recent tells you that you are on the eastern side of the old border. Some of the liveliest districts are in the east. Across the rest of east Germany, meanwhile, a new generation takes democracy for granted.

That is understandable. The Berlin Wall is history: some of the newest generation of German voters were scarcely born when the Wall came down. And yet, despite the passage of time, it is worth reflecting on how remarkable the changes have been. Like physical health, political health is conspicuous above all by its absence. East Germany lived through six decades of dictatorship before 1989. Now, political and economic freedoms that seemed unthinkable have become too obvious to mention.

Along with the reasons for celebration, there are plenty of reasons for pessimism about the present and future alike. It is difficult to be complacent when racist attacks remain common. In the future, it is possible that a German Pim Haider or Gianfranco le Pen could, with the usual tempting mix of charisma and xenophobia, gain a large slice of the populist vote. After all, such politicians have emerged across the rest of Europe. Why not in Germany, too? Such a nationalist party, in line with similar parties elsewhere, might demand an end to all immigration; the restoration to Germany of some or all of the territory lost after 1945; compensation for the two million who died when they were brutally driven out of their homes at that time; exclusion of Poland and the Czech republic from the European Union unless they allow Germans to regain their lost property; and, finally, an end to all the talk on every German television channel about Auschwitz and the Third Reich.

All of this is theoretically possible. Unlike, say, Holocaust denial, none of those demands would be illegal, so a politician might scoop up a generous share of the vote with such energizing populist slogans without being locked up in jail. Some of those demands have already been heard from individual politicians in past years. And yet, at the risk of these lines being quoted as an example of supreme naïveté in just a few years' time, it must be said: seen from the perspective of today, it does not look likely that a far-right populist politician can achieve large-scale nationwide success in modern Germany.

Despite the skinhead violence, today's Germany is very different from any Germany that we have seen before. Not necessarily predictable – but locked into its own democracy, perhaps more than other countries in the region. For a far-right party to gain a 20 or 30 per cent share of the German vote, as equivalent parties have done elsewhere in Europe, would be a truly extraordinary change.

Even now, Germany seems to feel uncomfortable with its newly powerful role. In addition, to complicate matters, it feels uncomfortable with its discomfort, asking: 'Why should we be treated differently from others?' When Germans talk endlessly about their responsibility for the past, other nations cry: 'Enough!' When Germany seems eager to shake off the past, neighbours become wary. The attitude is both contradictory and logical. If Germans are appalled by their country's past, that means they do not need to say so; from younger generations especially, that would be unnecessary breastbeating. But if they do *not* distance themselves from the past, that may indicate that they are not appalled.

Only the change of generations can help make the paradox softer, the circle less vicious. Those who (perhaps) committed or turned a blind eye to outrages in the middle of the last century are now grandparents. Those who grew up in the 1950s and 1960s in a tainted Germany, which failed to confront its own history, are in late middle age; they went through the anger barrier against their parents' now elderly generation many years ago. The children of that middle-aged generation – and now their children's children – grow up in a different world. In the east, where confrontation with the past began only 15 years ago, the pattern remains unsettled. Even there, however, a new normality is gradually taking shape. Nobody knows the final shape of the new Germany, just as nobody guessed in the late 1920s what lay just around the corner for Germany and the rest of Europe. But it is fair to say that a repetition of history, even a partial repetition of history, is the least likely option of all. The changes that have taken place over the past 60 years, both gradual and sudden, have seen to that. Modern Germany understands that history matters. That is one reason why history no longer matters as urgently as it did before.

As with Faust, two souls still dwell in the German breast. The country remains suspended between self-confidence and self-doubt. 'Emancipation' is an official twenty-first-century buzzword. Fischer, the old revolutionary, emphasizes that Germany is one of the most liberal societies in Europe, with values 'deeply rooted in all levels of the population'. He explicitly renounces the fears about his country that he himself harboured before 1990:

> This mistrust, which defined my generation for many years – and me personally, until reunification – has dissipated. We must remain alert, for example, against anti-Semitism and the discrimination of minorities. But I am not worried about the essence of our country. To all those who think that there could be historical revisionism, with fatal consequences, I say: I no longer share that fear.

And yet, that confidence remains hedged about with ifs and buts. Fischer himself says that Germany must tread carefully before criticizing Israel. Schröder, even while proclaiming the need for *Emanzipation*, insists: 'We cannot emerge from our past so easily. Perhaps we should not even wish to.' The German conundrum remains. Germany cannot leave the past behind; but it cannot remain chained to the past for ever. Looking back into the past makes it possible for the country to move into a less complex-ridden future – but only if that is the *result* of looking back, not the aim. If any politician expresses the determination that Germany should be an easy fatherland, he or she makes it, on the contrary, a more complicated place for Germany and its neighbours alike.

The philosopher John Stuart Mill wrote: 'Those only are happy who have their minds fixed on some object other than their own happiness . . . Aiming thus at something else, they find happiness by the way.' Replace the words 'happy' and 'happiness' with 'normal' and 'normality', and Mill's words could be a succinct description of the paradox facing Germany and the Germans today. Germans who are obsessed with normality fail to achieve it. Aiming at something else, Germany may perhaps find normality by the way.

The changing generations in the past 60 years have already brought about enormous change. The Federal Republic today is very different from the self-pitying republic of the 1950s, the unresolved conflicts of the 1960s, the murderous violence of the 1970s, or the tangled transition of a united Germany in the 1990s. In the decades to come, it will change again. It is unclear what shape the new normality will take. But one thing seems clear: Germany is not about to relapse into the past. History will not repeat itself, as tragedy or as farce. Instead, the country can perhaps begin to move into a normal, dull future at last.

BIBLIOGRAPHY

Some of the following books I have quoted directly; all have contained useful material or provided food for thought.

John Ardagh, *Germany and the Germans* (London 1995)
Hannah Arendt, *Eichmann in Jerusalem: A Report on the Banality of Evil* (New York 1963)
Neal Ascherson, *The Struggles for Poland* (London 1987)
Stefan Aust, *Der Baader Meinhof Complex* (Hamburg 1997)

David Bankier (ed.), *Probing the Depths of German Anti-Semitism* (Jerusalem 2000)
Antony Beevor, *Berlin: The Downfall 1945* (London 2002)
Jillian Becker, *Hitler's Children: The Story of the Baader-Meinhof Terrorist Gang* (London 1977)
Dieter Bossmann (ed.), *Was ich über Hitler gehört habe: Folgen eines Tabus* (Frankfurt am Main 1977)
Willy Brandt, *My Life in Politics* (London 1992)
Christopher Browning, *Ordinary Men: Reserve Police Battalion 101 and the Final Solution in Poland* (New York 1992/1998)

Christo and Jeanne-Claude, *Wrapped Reichstag: The Project Book* (Berlin 1995)
Gordon Craig, *Germany 1866–1945* (Oxford 1981)
Gordon Craig, *The Germans* (New York 1982)

Marion Gräfin Dönhoff, *Namen die keiner mehr nennt. Ostpreußen –
Menschen und Geschichte* (Munich 1964/2003)

Amos Elon, *The Pity of It All: A Portrait of Jews in Germany 1743–1933*
(London 2003)

Norman G. Finkelstein and Ruth Bettina Birn, *A Nation on Trial: The
Goldhagen Thesis and Historical Truth* (New York 1998)
Joschka Fischer, *Mein langer Lauf zu mir selbst* (Cologne 1999)
Thomas Flemming, *The Berlin Wall: Division of a City* (Berlin 2000)
Jörg Friedrich, *Die kalte Amnestie* (Frankfurt an Main 1984)
Jörg Friedrich, *Der Brand* (Munich 2002)
Mary Fulbrook, *History of Germany 1918-2000* (Oxford 2002)

Timothy Garton Ash, *In Europe's Name* (London 1993)
Timothy Garton Ash, *The File* (London 1997)
Martha Gellhorn, *The View from the Ground* (London 1989)
Martha Gellhorn, *The Face of War* (London 1993)
Anthony Glees, *Reinventing Germany* (Oxford 1996)
Daniel Jonah Goldhagen, *Hitler's Willing Executioners* (London 1996)
Daniel Jonah Goldhagen (ed.), *Briefe an Goldhagen* (Berlin 1997)
Mel Gordon, *Voluptuous Panic: The Erotic World of Weimar Berlin*
(Venice, California, 2000)
Günter Grass, *The Tin Drum* (London 1962)
Günter Grass, *Crabwalk* (London 2003)

Sebastian Haffner, *Defying Hitler* (London 2002)
Markus Heckhausen (ed.), *Das Buch vom Ampelmännchen* (Berlin 1997)
Johannes Heil and Rainer Erb (ed.), *Geschichtswissenschaft und
Öffentlichkeit: Der Streit um Daniel J. Goldhagen* (Frankfurt 1998)
Tom Heneghan, *Unchained Eagle: Germany after the Wall* (London
2000)
Jana Hensel, *Zonenkinder* (Hamburg 2002)
Tobias Hollitzer, *Wir leben jedenfalls von Montag zu Montag: Zur
Auflösung der Staatssicherheit in Leipzig* (Berlin 2000)
Pascale Hugues, *Le bonheur allemand* (Paris 1998)

Florian Illies, *Generation Golf* (Berlin 2000)
Florian Illies, *Anleitung zum Unschuldigsein* (Berlin 2001)
Christopher Isherwood, *Goodbye to Berlin* (London 1939)

Frederick Kempe, *Father/Land: A Search for the New Germany* (London 1999)

Thomas Keneally, *Schindler's Ark* (London 1982)

Ian Kershaw, *The Hitler Myth* (Oxford 1987)

Ian Kershaw, *The Nazi Dictatorship* (London 2000)

Olaf Georg Klein, *Ihr könnt uns einfach nicht verstehen!* (Frankfurt 2001)

Scarlett Kleint, *Verliebt, verlobt, verheiratet . . . : Liebesgeschichten zwischen Ost und West* (Berlin 1993)

Victor Klemperer, *I Shall Bear Witness: Diaries 1933-1941* (London 1999)

Victor Klemperer, *To the Bitter End: Diaries 1942-1945* (London 1999)

Guido Knopp, *Der Aufstand 17. Juni 1953* (Hamburg 2003)

Guido Knopp, *Die grosse Flucht* (Munich 2002)

Sibylle Krause-Burger, *Joschka Fischer: Der Marsch durch die Illusionen* (Stuttgart 1999)

Ekkehard Kuhn, *Der Tag der Entscheidung: Leipzig 9. Oktober 1989* (Frankfurt 1992)

Hermann Kurzke, *Thomas Mann* (Princeton 2002)

John le Carré, *A Small Town in Germany* (London 1968)

Susanne Leinemann, *Aufgewacht. Mauer weg* (Munich 2002)

Anne McElvoy, *The Saddled Cow: East Germany's Life and Legacy* (London 1992)

David Marsh, *The Germans: Rich, Bothered and Divided* (London 1989)

Peter Märthesheimer and Ivo Frenzel (ed.), *Im Kreuzfeuer: Der Fernsehfilm 'Holocaust'. Eine Nation ist betroffen* (Frankfurt am Main 1979)

Mark Mazower, *Dark Continent: Europe's Twentieth Century* (London 2000)

Peter Merseburger, *Willy Brandt: Visionär und Realist* (Stuttgart 2002)

Stanley Milgram, *Obedience to Authority* (London 1974)

Jan-Werner Müller, *Another Country: German Intellectuals, Unification and National Identity* (New Haven 2000)

George Orwell, *The Observer Years* (London 2003)

Cem Özdemir, *Ich bin Inländer* (Munich 1997)

Hella Pick, *Und welche Rolle spielt Österreich?* (Vienna 1999)

Zoran Petrovic Pirocanac, *Izbrisati srpski virus* (Belgrade 1999)

Ernst Reinhard Piper (ed.), *Historikerstreit* (Munich 1987)

Alexandra Richie, *Faust's Metropolis: A History of Berlin* (London 1998)

Ernst Röhl, *Fünf Jahre sind genug!* (Berlin 1995)

Klaus Rainer Röhl, *Verbotene Trauer: Die vergessenen Opfer* (Munich 2002)

Joseph Roth, *What I Saw: Reports from Berlin 1920-33* (London 2003)

Angus Roxburgh, *Preachers of Hate: The Rise of the Far Right* (London 2002)

Claudia Rusch, *Meine freie deutsche Jugend* (Frankfurt 2003)

Bernhard Schlink, *The Reader* (London 1997)

Peter Schneider, *The Wall Jumper* (New York 1983)

W.G. Sebald, *The Emigrants* (London 1996)

W.G. Sebald, *On the Natural History of Destruction* (London 2003)

Gitta Sereny, *The German Trauma: Experiences and Reflections 1938-2001* (London 2000)

J.P. Stern, *Hitler: The Führer and his People* (London 1975)

Wladyslaw Szpilman, *The Pianist* (London 1999)

Nathan Stoltzfus, *Resistance of the Heart: Intermarriage and the Rosenstrasse Protest in Nazi Germany* (New Brunswick 2001)

Kurt Tucholsky (ed. Harry Zohn), *Germany? Germany!* (Manchester 1990)

Mathias Wedel, Thomas Wieczorek, *Papa, was ist ein Ossi? Mama, was ist ein Wessi?* (Berlin 2002)

Peter Weiss, *Die Ermittlung* (Frankfurt 1965)

Harald Welzer (and others), *'Opa war kein Nazi': Nationalsozialismus und Holocaust im Familiengedächtnis* (Frankfurt 2002)

Heide-Ulrike Wendt, *Immer nur das eine (und andere Grenzfälle)* (Berlin 1996)

Charles Williams, *Adenauer: The Father of the New Germany* (New York 2000)

Thilo Wydra, *Rosenstrasse* (Berlin 2003)

Feridun Zaimoglu, *Kopf und Kragen: Kanak-Kultur-Kompendium* (Hamburg 2001)

INDEX